The Romanesque Wooden Doors of Auvergne

The publication of this monograph
has been aided by a grant from the
Samuel H. Kress Foundation

WALTER CAHN

The Romanesque Wooden Doors of Auvergne

PUBLISHED BY

NEW YORK UNIVERSITY PRESS

for the College Art Association of America

NEW YORK 1974

Monographs on Archaeology and Fine Arts
sponsored by
THE ARCHAEOLOGICAL INSTITUTE OF AMERICA
and
THE COLLEGE ART ASSOCIATION OF AMERICA
XXX
Editor:
Lucy Freeman Sandler

Library of Congress Catalog Card Number: 74-15391
ISBN: 0-8147-1357-2

Contents

Introduction

IN 1926, THE FIRST VOLUME in a series intended to form a comprehensive corpus of early medieval bronze doors under the editorship of Richard Hamann appeared in print. Through this collection, specialists and the general reader alike have gained such reliable and attractively illustrated publications as Adolph Goldschmidt's study of the doors of Novgorod and Gniezno, Albert Boeckler's work on the doors of San Zeno in Verona, and the same author's studies of the doors of Bonanus of Pisa and Barisanus of Trani. Hamann's own monograph on the wooden doors of St. Mary on the Capitol in Cologne preceded these outside the series. In more recent times, important studies have been devoted to the doors of Bernward of Hildesheim, the doors of the cathedral of Gurk in Carinthia, and the doors of Byzantine origin in Italy. The present undertaking is designed as a modest contribution in the same direction. It focuses on the only medieval historiated doors to have survived from the territory now comprised within modern France. The group consists of the doors within the open porch preceding the western entrance of Le Puy cathedral and three other sets of valves in monasteries within the same region: Saint-Gilles at Chamalières-sur-Loire, Saint-Pierre at Blesle, and Sainte-Croix at Lavoûte-Chilhac. The doors of Le Puy cathedral have long been the object of considerable fascination and figure in the major handbooks, while those of the churches nearby are not entirely unknown. However, their interest seemed to me to justify a more detailed examination in the light of present-day art historical criteria.

Thanks to the industry of nineteenth-century local historians and earlier writers, the relatively limited number of documents bearing on the history of Le Puy and of the Velay in the medieval period have been published with a commendable degree of fullness. I have drawn on these and on a few additional sources wherever appropriate, though it must be conceded that this body of evidence offers few firm dates or salient facts regarding the monuments which will concern us. The Romanesque architecture of Velay was first dealt with in a comprehensive manner in N. Thiollier's *L'architecture religieuse à l'époque romane dans l'ancien diocèse du Puy* (Le Puy, 1900), a work published over seventy years ago and still in many respects unsurpassed. Le Puy cathedral, by far the most considerable building in the region, occupies a central place in this study, and it is the author's great merit to have removed the history of its construction from the realm of pious legend and trained on it the cold light of archaeological scrutiny. The wooden doors, like those of Chamalières, to which Thiollier first drew attention, are briefly but accurately described by him in this volume. Since Blesle lies outside the diocese of Le Puy, it did not come within the orbit of his interest at the same time. But a few years following the appearance of his book, Thiollier added these doors to the series in a separate study.

In his *L'art roman au Puy et les influences islamiques* (Paris, 1934), A. Fikry devoted a chapter to the wooden doors of the cathedral and to the other works in the group. This has remained the only collective treatment accorded to these monuments to date. Fikry brought much greater authority and precision to bear on the definition of the role of Islamic art in the formal vocabulary employed in the cathedral, its dependencies and Auvergnat Romanesque generally, than earlier writers who initially raised this issue. The famous pseudo-Cufic borders of the cathedral Infancy doors call attention to this problem in a particularly striking way, even if, following the studies of Longpérier, Christie, and Spittle, it now looms as a less singular phenomenon than to an earlier generation of scholars. Fikry's view that the interlace borders which frame the Passion doors of the cathedral as well as the single valve at Lavoûte-Chilhac could similarly be traced to an Islamic source is certainly much less tenable. However, no matter how this question is envisaged, there can be little doubt that a study of the doors limited to their connection with Islamic art is bound to leave untouched much that is central to the understanding of these monuments.

In one important respect, the present study will also be found seriously deficient. The reader should expect the analysis of style and iconography to repose on a secure foundation established by a close examination of the doors carried out with appropriate equipment and methods. The restoration of the Puy doors supervised in Paris by M. François Enaud for the Monuments Historiques in 1960 offered the opportunity to compile a detailed archaeological dossier on the work, but the data collected at that time has been misplaced or lost, following the death of M. R. Hémery, who carried out the work.[1] Neither have the three other doors ever received such attention. As a measure of protection, all three were removed from their setting within the threshold and long ago set with clamps against walls within the church.

As a result, the backs are now hidden from view. In the case of the Puy doors, the gap in our knowledge which might be filled by an appropriate technical procedure concerns chiefly such matters as the reconstitution of the original polychromy where only traces now remain, its chemical constitution, and the identification of additional details of composition within the now more or less bare silhouetted forms. But for the related group in neighboring monasteries, Blesle especially, which has suffered most from neglect, there is a good possibility that careful scrutiny under adequate conditions would lead to the recovery or clarification even of substantial traces of the design now obscure to the naked eye. It is my hope that these pages may bring about such an exhaustive analysis.

This study benefited from the assistance of M. Reymond, the architect of the Monuments Historiques in Le Puy, and of his able collaborator, M. Albert Audiard, who granted me the fullest possible access to the cathedral. I am also grateful for aid received to the following persons: M. A. Faux, sacristan of Le Puy Cathedral; Abbé Martin, Curé of Lavoûte-Chilhac; Professor Herschel Levit; Dr. Susanna Jutte, Visiting Lecturer in Wood Anatomy at the Yale Forestry School; and Mr. E. Jajko, Near East Bibliographer of the Sterling Library at Yale University. The text figures illustrating the construction of the doors have been adapted from drawings originally made for the Centre de Recherche des Monuments Historiques, Paris, which kindly authorized their use in the present publication. My wife Annabelle Simon Cahn, finally, gave selflessly of her time and knowledge toward the completion of my work.

1. Undated letter of M. Enaud received by the writer early in the year 1971.

Abbreviations

Annales Soc. Puy	*Annales de la Société d'Agriculture, Sciences, Arts et Commerce du Puy*
Bull. arch.	*Bulletin archéologique du Comité des travaux historiques et scientifiques*
Bull. hist.	*Bulletin historique de la Société académique du Puy et de la Haute-Loire*
Bull. mon.	*Bulletin monumental*
Cahiers arch.	*Cahiers archéologiques*
Congrès arch.	*Congrès archéologique de France*
Fikry, *Art roman du Puy*	A. Fikry, *L'art roman du Puy et les influences islamiques,* Paris, 1934
Götz, *Bildprogramme*	U. Götz, *Die Bildprogramme der Kirchentüren des 11. und 12. Jahrhunderts,* Diss. Tübingen, 1971.
Gounot, *Collections lapidaires*	R. Gounot, *Collections lapidaires du Musée Crozatier du Puy-en Velay,* Le Puy, 1957
Mém. et Procès-Verbaux	*Mémoires et Procès-Verbaux de la Société agricole et scientifique de la Haute-Loire*
Tablettes hist.	*Tablettes historiques de la Haute-Loire et du Velay*
Thiollier, *Architecture religieuse*	N. Thiollier, *L'architecture religieuse à l'époque romane dans l'ancien diocèse du Puy,* Le Puy, 1900

List of Illustrations

I The Setting

THE WESTERN ENTRANCE of Le Puy cathedral looks over the straight and steeply rising Rue des Tables leading from the lower town. From a promontory at the upper end of the street, a grand stairway of some sixty steps takes the visitor directly within its vast open porch (Fig. 1). Before the restorations of the nineteenth century, these stairs were far less imposing in scale and hemmed in on both sides by constructions of various kinds. Much of the space along the north was occupied by buildings belonging to the Hôtel-Dieu, and the rest with a multitude of shops and stalls filled with household goods and articles of devotion. Some of these shops took shelter under the vaults of the porch. The plan of the site made by the architect Aymon Mallay prior to the restoration shows several of these; one of them (marked D), belonging to a certain Borie, took one of the piers along the southern flank of the central aisle for support and partly masked the wooden door at the entrance of the chapel on the south side (Fig. 2).[1] According to a late eighteenth-century witness, the porch further served for the exhibition of two beams on which were suspended "des débris de chariots, de chaînes, de boucliers, de lances, de cuirasses et autres trophées qu'on disait signaler deux victoires complètes remportées sous les murs de la ville du Puy contre les Sarrazins." [2] Beyond the first two bays of the porch, the path forward becomes a single passage framed laterally by the twin chapels of St. Martin and St. Giles. The Romanesque wooden doors which shall concern us close the western entrances of these chapels. At a point corresponding to the demarcation of the third and fourth bays, the entrance portal of the church proper is reached. It is framed by two porphyry columns, possibly of antique origin, but bearing capitals of twelfth-century workmanship. In the sources, this entrance is designated as *Porte dorée,* a qualification which does not now have any visible justification. However, before the remodeling of the access way from the portal into the nave carried out between 1778 and 1781 by Bishop de Galard, a more imposing set of doors could be seen at this point. References to these doors are unfortunately all too cursory. To Bochart de Sarron, whose panegyrical history of the church appeared in 1693, they appeared to be "couverte(s) de lames de cuivre," [3] while a description of the cathedral made in 1776 by the Abbé de Mortesage mentions "deux battans de bronze ciselés." [4] According to the specifications drawn up for the alterations of the late eighteenth century, the doors were to be opened and fastened to the lateral walls along the stairs "afin que les escaliers soient plus à découvert." [5] In fact, they must have been removed altogether and replaced by the open forged iron grill in place at the present time. Whatever their actual mode of workmanship, the original doors were no doubt different and more sumptuous than those still found in the doorways along the eastern perimeter of the church, the *Porche du For* and the *Porte St. Jean,* which have metal ornaments and lion masks attached to a leather surface stretched over a wooden core. Bochart and other writers no doubt intended the term *Porte dorée* to convey this fact, even if it had much wider and more symbolic connotations.

From the portal, a flight of nineteen steps led straight upward into the nave of the church. In inclement season this orifice had to be screened with matting in order to shield worshipers from unpleasant gusts of wind. This inconvenience motivated the eighteenth-century remodeling, when the present bifurcation was introduced: one arm of the stairway gives access to the south aisle; the other to the gallery of the cloister along the northern side of the edifice.

The western entrance of the cathedral was in an overwhelming sense a public right of way.[6] Newly elected bishops made a solemn entry through the *Porte dorée,* and the processional book of 1763 preserved in the Bibliothèque Municipale in Le Puy contains instructions for the Palm Sunday procession with a station at the foot of the stairs (Rue des Tables) and a second *ante portam auream.*[7] These were, of course, occasions for the reenactment of the Lord's entry into Jerusalem, in which the west portal played the role of city gate to a symbolic heavenly city, and as such, exceptional. In their ordinary dominical perambulations, the canons usually proceeded from the cloister to their stalls in the choir by way of the baptistery and the tower, entering the church through the *Porche du For* on the eastern face of the south transept arm. In Bochart de Sarron's time, visiting dignitaries, both secular and ecclesiastical, seem to have been received at the *Porte St. Jean* on the opposite side of the sanctuary.[8] In the great festive processions or in times of stress when the miraculous image of the Virgin was removed from the sanctuary and borne aloft through the narrow streets of the town, the throng of marchers acceded to the cathedral by means of the same eastern route, entering the church through the *Porche du For* and making a wide half-circle around the high altar before departing through the *Porte St. Jean.* Both of these entrances had wooden doors of a more conventional type, one covered with leather, the other with cloth and decorated with forged iron fittings and animal masks.[9]

Pilgrims were no doubt the largest social group drawn to the western entrance. The central doorway brought them face to face with the statue of the Virgin, which normally stood behind the altar. This arrangement of the pattern of circulation must strike anyone as having been the product of careful calculation. The origin of the Le Puy pilgrimage is shrouded in the mist of time. It must have been a thriving institution by the tenth century, since in 933, the monastery of St. Peter in the town was founded expressly for the purpose of assisting pilgrims and providing those who died on their journey with a proper burial.[10] In 1046, the monks of the abbey of Savigny-en-Lyonnais were given possession of the little church of Bussy (now Bussy-Albieux, near Boën, Loire), which straddled the *via podiensis,* and, along with it, the right to collect donations from pilgrims on their way to Le Puy, Saint-Gilles, Rome, and Jerusalem.[11] Some ninety years later, the *Codex Calixtinus* makes the cathedral the focal point of one of the four recommended routes leading through France to Compostela.[12] In the later Middle Ages, the spiritual incentives which were attached to the journey had crystallized around the institution of the *Jubilé* or *Grand pardon* celebrated "par observée consuétude" in those years when the feast of the Annunciation coincided with Good Friday.[13] On these occasions, the city was crowded with visitors attracted by the promise of massive indulgences. In contrast to the imposing processions which still fill many pages of the chronicle of Etienne Médicis, we are bound to know little about their more informal wanderings. But the location of commercial interests intended to cater to their needs and of the Hospice Notre Dame along the street leading to the west façade indicates that this was the ordinary approach to the cathedral, preferred when the capitular solemnities did not prescribe an itinerary focused on the eastern entrances. As early as 1210, Bishop Bertrand de Chalançon gave to the Hospice, itself narrowly dependent on the cathedral, a monopoly on the sale of pilgrim's badges, and this concession was repeatedly confirmed by his successors.[14] The Hospitalers maintained a permanent stall (*tabula signaculorum)* within the porch for this purpose and saw to it that illicit competitors who repeatedly set themselves up nearby were sternly dealt with.

The attribution of distinctive functions to each of the three major entrances of the cathedral makes understandable, different tastes and changes over a lengthy period of building notwithstanding, their extremely varied designs. By the standards of the time, only the *Porte St. Jean* with its tympanum of the Ascension, now sadly mutilated, represents a fairly orthodox scheme of portal decoration, comparable in the region, for example, to the north door of the church of Saint-Julien at Brioude.[15] In the *Porche du For,* the decorative emphasis is on the architectural canopy preceding the entrance. In the place of a specific thematic entity confined within the boundaries of a single relief, the portal is remarkable first and foremost for its extraordinary structural and ornamental exuberance, which adds an unexpected coloristic touch to the stark masses of the edifice (Fig. 3). In the west, the architectural setting is once again comparatively sober, but attention is made to focus on the doors rather than on their masonry framework (Figs. 5 and 6). While there is only a single entrance, the importance given to the doors of the two lateral chapels effectively simulates the appearance of a façade design with three portals. As we shall see, there is good reason for surmising that the wooden doors were initially devised for a façade that was not yet hidden by the two western bays constituting the porch of the cathedral. By themselves, neither the size of the chapels nor the nature of the cult attached to them could seem to justify such a lavish display of carving and painting.

The lateral chapels are nearly identical groin-vaulted rooms occupying the space beneath the aisles in the third bay of the nave. An arched recess opened in the eastern wall shelters a stone altar (Fig. 4). On each of the lateral walls of this niche, there are small cubicles for storing the utensils of the cult.[16] Both rooms were decorated with fresco paintings, of which substantial traces remain. The open lunettes above the doorways constitute the only source of natural light (Figs. 5 and 6). Before the addition of the two western bays, this was probably no more than barely adequate for its purpose. Following the new construction, the chapels were plunged in virtual darkness, and required illumination by candlelight, which, over a period of time, has left heavy deposits of soot on the walls. Both chapels have small secondary entrances situated at the western end of the inner lateral walls. Their use made it possible to avoid the necessity of repeatedly opening and closing the heavy wooden doors of the principal portals (Fig. 2).

What remains of the frescoes indicates that the decoration of the two rooms is not of the same date. The painting in the chapel of St. Giles on the north side is the more archaic in appearance; the profile of the arch sheltering the altar niche is round rather than pointed, as in the south chapel. The Lord appears in a mandorla between Alpha and Omega at the center of the soffit. A pair of standing figures, probably the evangelists, are seen on each side. The scene is framed by a pleated border. These frescoes are now being brought back into view, following the recent removal of the heating plant of the cathedral installed in the chapel during the nineteenth century. Their existence does not seem to have been recorded in any of the histories of the church, and detailed study is only now under way. On first impression, they were executed by a painter not otherwise represented in the varied fresco decoration of the cathedral, whose art is perhaps closest stylistically in the region to the frescoes from Vieille-Brioude, now in the University of Rochester Memorial Art Gallery.[17]

More of the decorative scheme of the St. Martin chapel is visible (Fig. 4). The Lamb of God in a roundel flanked by angels is represented in the space between the vaults and the soffit arch above the altar. Christ in Majesty in a mandorla surrounded by the symbols of the evangelists is seen at the apex of the soffit. The panels below show a group of six standing apostles on each side. On the eastern end wall, the Virgin and Child seated in a mandorla flanked by a pair of angels occupy the uppermost space. The area below is horizontally subdivided into two bands of unequal width. Immediately beneath the Virgin enthroned, nothing distinct is now to be perceived. The stripe below shows a narrative sequence within an architectural setting of round and mitered arches. There are indistinct traces of additional painting in the dado zone below as well as in the lateral spaces below the cornice molding marking the springing of the vaults. Deschamps and Thibout date this ensemble in the period of the reign of St. Louis and rightly place its execution after the much better known Transfiguration and other paintings in the open passage which separates the two chapels leading to the *Porte dorée.* The vestibule and the St. Martin chapel frescoes both predate the completion of the first two bays and the new façade of the cathedral.[18]

The approach to the chapels in the west was entirely reconstructed in the nineteenth century and is rendered with some imprecision on Mallay's plan made prior to restoration. The western entrances of the chapels are preceded by seven steps corresponding to the difference in the pavement levels between the second and third bays. The first bay lies even lower, and a barrier now safeguards the visitor against the sheer drop. From the west, the chapels were accessible from the central stairway only. The lateral axis in the second bay leads through an arch on the south side to a path known as the Rue des Pèlerins, which threads its way along the flank of the mountain and led originally to a hostel reserved for pilgrims.[19] On the north side, a passage leads toward the Hôtel-Dieu. In 1299, a private house belonging to a certain Durand Chevallier stood between the hospital and the chapel of St. Giles.[20]

Each of the doorways is framed by an arch supported by colonnettes bearing capitals (Figs. 5 and 6). A pair of colonnettes was also lodged in the recesses of the arch in the interior. These are shown on Mallay's plan, but are preserved only in the St. Giles chapel. The tympanum zone is defined by a round arch of a flat and unadorned profile, bonded to a lintel slab of like simplicity. Forced to compensate for the absence of fenestration in the chapels, the architect adopted a portal design with an opening in the tympanum zone, a type of design which is common in northern Italy and occasionally encountered also in Provence, as, for example, at Saint-Gilles and in the Chapelle des Pénitents at Peyrolles (Gard).[21] The substructure of the second bay abuts the portals off axis, leaving the inner jambs with their colonnettes exposed but masking those on the outer side both north and south. The discrepancy was caused by a shift in the first two bays to a narrower plan, pushing the axes of the lateral bays inward toward the center. Here, as at nave level, the masonry of the first two bays joins the fabric of the main body of the structure but is not integral with it. This indicates that the porch and the story above it were not part of the initial scheme. It also contributed, abetted by the steep incline and possibly inadequate foundations, to the grave difficulties which were repeatedly to beset the western mass of the building. Already in the early fourteenth century, the vaults in the porch had to be remade, and a huge buttress was erected against the façade to counteract the downward thrust of the western bays (Fig. 1).[22] In spite of these and later measures, total reconstruction eventually proved necessary.

The chapels do not occupy a large place in the recorded history of the cathedral. In the early decades of the nineteenth century, their original function seems to have been almost entirely forgotten. That on the north side, which adjoins the Hospice, was then described by Mallay as a funerary chapel, and its southern pendant, where baptisms were said to have taken place, as a chapel dedicated to St. John. An older nomenclature, however, is found in an eighteenth-century customary of the cathedral.[23] Here the chapels are cited with dedications respectively to St. Giles and St. Martin. The first document to mention the chapel of St. Giles, so far as I have been able to determine, is a charter recording the sale of land to the Knights Templar of Le Puy written in local dialect in 1204. Concluding this transaction, the seller, a certain Itier Saulnier, swore an oath on the Gospels "en la Graza devant Saint Giri," or, as is to be understood, on the steps in front of the chapel.[24] The chapel also figures in several later sources. One of these indicates that in the early sixteenth century, the incumbent owed his nomination to the administrator of the nearby Hôtel-Dieu.[25] Another, antedating the fifteenth century, lists sums due to the *ostiarius* of the monastery of St. Peter for the provision of eucharistic wafers.[26] If these sums can be taken as roughly indicative of the chapel's relative importance, it stood fairly high in the esteem of the faithful among the special altars in the cathedral, though it was outranked by several oratories in the town, among them the chapel of Saint-Clair and Saint-Michel d'Aiguilhe. A fifteenth-century manuscript and two printed missals of the sixteenth century, on which a reconstruction of the local liturgical calendar in the Middle Ages must rest, record two commemorations for St. Martin, the major feast day on November 11 and the *Translatio S. Martini* on July 4.[27] The commemoration on November 11 was a major church holiday *(fête chomée)* until the decree of Urban VIII in 1644, which sharply reduced the number of such feasts. St. Giles is represented on the calendar of the cathedral by a single commemoration on September 1. This feast was established in 1096 when Count Raymond of Saint-Gilles donated three villages to the cathedral on condition that the memory of the saint be celebrated once every year in the church as well as in all of its dependencies.[28] At this time, Raymond had become the most powerful secular prince in the south of France. His valiant deeds in the wars against the Moors and his loyalty to the church made him a natural candidate for a leading role in the crusading schemes of Urban II. The pope seems to have conferred with Raymond at Saint-Gilles a few days after his meeting with Bishop Adhemar of Monteil in Le Puy on August 15, 1095, when the papal convocation of the Council of Clermont was promulgated.[29] On the basis of the testimony of William of Malmesbury, Adhemar, who had entertained relations with the Count of Toulouse over a period of several years, is assumed to have persuaded him to join the projected expedition to the Holy Land. This he effectively did through the voice of his ambassadors on the final days of the Council three months later, becoming, in the words of Baudri of Dol, the Aaron of Adhemar's Moses.[30]

Before his departure for the Holy Land, from which he had vowed never to return, Raymond accomplished a series of pious gestures. At La Chaise-Dieu, he obtained the cup of St. Robert as a talisman as well as other relics which he was to carry in the expedition. He also sought to repair the slights which he and his family had inflicted on the abbey of Saint-Gilles. Raymond had inherited the abbey as part of his father's domains in Provence. But the title Saint-Gilles which he attached to his name cannot be solely a reference to his possessions and suggests a particular devotion to the saint. He seems in any case to have been unusually insistent in his public expressions of contrition toward St. Giles and his shrine. In 1090, probably under the influence of the reform movement, he abandoned all of his privileges in the abbey, which he declares his ancestors to have usurped. This vow was renewed before the altar of St. Giles in the abbey church on September 1, 1094, and reiterated on July 6, 1096, only a few months before the journey to Le Puy and the donations to the cathedral establishing the cult of the saint there. Shortly thereafter, in the autumn of the same year, he departed on the journey to the east, but not before stopping again at Saint-Gilles to renew his earlier pledges.

The canons of the cathedral, who under the terms of Raymond's donation, were also provided with funds for an annual banquet on St. Giles's day, carried out his wishes by dedicating a chapel to the saint and assigning one of their number to its service. There is no evidence that they went much further to institute a special cult, and no relics of St. Martin or Giles were claimed. Indeed, the chapels remained entirely outside the pattern of liturgical *stationes* within and without the church. In the town, one of the gates was known as the Porte Saint-Gilles and the street leading to it bore the same name. Writing in the middle of the sixteenth century, Etienne Médicis explained that this was because "de ceste porte on yst de ledicte ville du Puy aller à l'antique ville de Saint-Gilles la-bas en Languedoc." [31] Likely, the patronage of the two chapels was in large part designed to capitalize on the reputation of two other major pilgrimage shrines in France, substituting for them symbolically for visitors of limited time and means.

NOTES

1. The substantial dossier which concerns these restorations, now divided between the Archives Départementales de la Haute-Loire, the Archives Nationales, and the Archives des Monuments Historiques, documents at length Mallay's efforts to clear away these stalls from the porch. A letter of November 21, 1839, to the Préfet of the Haute-Loire by the Ministre des Cultes, who then had charge of ecclesiastical monuments in the country, stresses that "la nécessité de faire disparaître ces ignobles constructions pour dégager le perron et pour assurer la conservation de l'une des belles portes sculptées qui se trouvent placées à cette hauteur avait déja été signalée à mon prédécesseur . . . lors de la visite qu'il fit des édifices diocésains du Puy en 1837." But nearly a decade later, the unwanted construction was still in place, since in a letter to the Ministry dated September 13, 1848, and written to accompany the plan illustrated in our Figure 2, Mallay urges that "La baraque des sieurs Borie, marquée D, ne gêne pas la circulation; mais elle cache la porte sculptée de la chapelle St. Jean [*sic*], et de plus, le niveau des escaliers étant changé, elle serait élevée de près d'un mètre au dessous du palier. Il est donc impossible de laisser subsister une pareille construction, aussi choquante qu'incommode" (Arch. Dept. No. 3. V. 20).
2. A. Jacotin, "Mémoire de Duranson sur le Département de la Haute-Loire," *Mém. et Procès-Verbaux,* XII, 1902-3, 95.
3. Th. Bochart de Sarron, *Histoire de l'église angélique de Notre-Dame du Puy,* Le Puy, 1693, 49. The doorway is termed *Porte Dorée* in all of the early sources.
4. As quoted in Faujas de Saint-Fond, *Recherches sur les volcans éteints du Vivarais et du Velay,* Grenoble-Paris, 1778, 415. Faujas himself states (417) that "la porte a deux battans en bronze, grossièrement ciselés," a description which appears also in J. A. M. Arnaud, *Histoire du Velay,* Le Puy, 1816, II, 398. The door is seen in a very sketchy manner on the drawing made to accompany the report on the condition of the church made by Jean de Clapier, who bore the title of Directeur des Travaux Publics de la Province du Languedoc, in 1737. (See A. Lascombe, "Rapport de Jean de Clapiès," *Mém. et Procès-Verbaux,* VI, 1888-90,

193-200.) As rendered here, however, it is made to appear as a conventional eighteenth-century paneled wooden door.

5. Arch. Dept. G. 162, No. 5, entitled "Devis des réparations qu'on prétend faire à l'église cathédrale du Puy." The document was published by Thiollier, *Architecture religieuse,* Pièces Justificatives, IX, 183f. See also A. Jacotin, "Réparations à la cathédrale en 1778," *Annuaire de la Haute-Loire,* 1877, 69-80. In 1785, a few short years after the alteration, recollection of the older door had seemingly become somewhat remote, as is indicated by an account of the ceremonies accompanying the *Jubilé* celebrated in that year: "On ne pourra entrer dans l'église cathédrale pour gagner le jubilé qu'en montant par les degrés et entrant par la porte qu'on appelle *dorée* et qui est fermée aujourd'hui par un grillage de fer" (J. Payrard, "Mémoire sur le Jubilé de Notre-Dame du Puy," *Tablettes hist.,* III, 1872-73m 436).
6. The most detailed source on these customs is the sixteenth-century chronicle of Etienne Médicis, a cloth merchant of Le Puy. It has been brilliantly edited by A. Chassaing, *Le Livre du Podio, ou chronique d'Etienne Médicis, bourgeois du Puy,* Le Puy, 1869-74. A number of accounts of the usages governing the festive processions in and around the cathedral exist. Among these is the *Relation du Jubilé de Notre-Dame du Puy en 1701* by Pierre Rome (ed. A. Lascombe, Le Puy, 1876). On the Rue des Tables constituting the western approach to the monument, see A. Aymard, "Fouilles au Puy et recherches historiques sur cette ville," *Annales Soc. Puy,* XXVII, 1864-65, 405ff.
7. Le Puy, Bibliothèque Municipale, Fond Cortial, Ms. 170, entitled *Processionale ad usum ecclesiae cathedralis Beatae Mariae Aniciensis,* fols. 105ff. Another text of this kind, said to be not earlier than the eighteenth century, has been published by Payrard, "Ancien cérémonial de l'église angélique du Puy," *Tablettes hist.,* VIII, 1877-78, 377ff.
8. *Histoire de l'église angélique,* 49f.
9. See Thiollier, *Architecture religieuse,* 66f., and Appendix II, p. 160 above.
10. The foundation charter is recorded in a seventeenth-century copy (Arch. Dept. H. 5. 150). It is commented on by U. Chevalier, *Cartulaire de l'abbaye de Saint-Chaffre du Monastier,* Paris, 1884, 60. A brief history of the pilgrimage is given by P.-R. Gaussin, "La ville du Puy en Velay et les pèlerinages," *Revue de Géographie de Lyon,* XXVI, 1951, 241-71.
11. M. Valla, "Chemins du Puy et de Saint-Jacques. La 'Via podiensis' en Forez," *Bulletin de la Diana,* XXXVIII, 1964, No. 6, 176-95.
12. *Le guide du pèlerin de Saint-Jacques de Compostelle,* ed. J. Vieillard, Mâcon, 1963, 3, 49.
13. A. Boudon-Lashermes, *Le Grand Pardon de Notre-Dame et de l'église du Puy de 992 à 1921,* Le Puy, 1921.
14. Arch. Dept. Série B, 1.B.1. R. Jouanne, P. Fournier, and E. Delcambre, *Inventaire sommaire des archives départementales antérieures à 1790,* Le Puy I, 1931, 6. See also A. Jacotin, *Preuves de la maison de Polignac,* Le Puy, I, 1898, No. 93, 147, for the edition of this document. Proceedings against persons accused of violating the monopoly of the Hôtel-Dieu on the sale of pilgrims's badges cover several pages of the above-mentioned catalogue of archives.
15. Thiollier, *Architecture religieuse,* 44. The most detailed treatment of the portal is found in R. Hamann's *Die Abteikirche von Saint-Gilles und ihre künstlerische Nachfolge,* Berlin, 1955, 339, who rightly, in my opinion, doubts the traditional identification of the subject as a Last Supper. For the Brioude sculpture, see P. Deschamps, "Tympan de stuc à Brioude," *Bulletin de la Société Nationale des Antiquaires de France,* 1924, 206-13, and L. Bréhier, "Le portail nord de St. Julien de Brioude et son ancien décor en stuc," *Almanach de Brioude,* 1933, XIV, 104-11.
16. Mallay mentions these chapels in a report to the Ministère des Cultes dated November 23, 1849: "Elles ont conservées leurs portes sculptées, leurs autels cubiques en pierre et des peintures murales." (Arch. Nat. F19 7824). He proposed to engage the painter A. Dauvergne to restore the paintings, but this plan does not seem to have been carried out. The paintings are also briefly cited by P. Merimée. *Notes d'un voyage en Auvergne,* first published in 1838, and newly edited by P.-M. Auzas in *Notes de Voyage,* Paris, 1971, 559.
17. The University of Rochester Memorial Art Gallery. *Handbook,* Rochester, 1961, 45. The origin of these frescoes was discovered by Miss Isabel Herdle, who kindly communicated to me the substance of her findings. Other elements from this important and as yet little known ensemble are in the Abegg Collection, Riggisberg, Switzerland.
18. P. Deschamps and M. Thibout, *La peinture murale en France au début de l'époque gothique,* Paris, 1963, 114. A publication of the frescoes in the two chapels is announced by F. Enaud, "Peintures murales découvertes dans une dépendance de la cathédrale du Puy-en-Velay (Haute-Loire). Prob-

lèmes d'interprétation," *Les monuments historiques de la France,* 1968, No. 4, 34.

19. Known in 1331 as *domus de la Rocheta.* See A. Jacotin, "Nomenclature historique et étymologique des rues du Puy," *Bull. Hist.,* VIII, 1923, 19.
20. Arch. Dept., Fond de l'Hôtel-Dieu, I.B. 305, No. 2. Jouanne, Fournier and Delcambre, *Inventaire sommaire,* 61.
21. I refer to the doorway in the sixth bay on the south side of the nave at Saint-Gilles (Hamann, *Abteikirche,* 67, fig. 103). For the chapel at Peyrolles, see B. Bailly, *Les chapelles rurales en Provence,* Avignon, 1969, 129-30.
22. Thiollier, *Architecture religieuse,* 30-31. Clapier's drawing shows two buttresses but it does not seem that a second support was ever built.
23. Payrard, *Ancien cérémonial-coutumier,* 382: "Extra ecclesiam sunt aliae capellae ipsi ecclesiae annexae, scilicet ab introitu portae deauratae: 1. sunt capellae seu ecclesiae parochialis hospitalis: 2. superius ascendendo, a parte dextra, est capella sancti Martini et a parte sinistra est capella sancti Aegidii."
24. A Chassaing, *Cartulaire des Templiers du Puy-en-Velay,* Paris, 1882, No. IV, 4.
25. Arch. Dept., Fonds de l'Hôtel-Dieu, Série H, I.C.6, No. 7. Jouanne, Fournier, and Delcambre, *Inventaire sommaire,* 66.
26. The document, entitled *De officio Hostiarii Sancti Petri de Monasterio Anicii,* appears to be lost, but it was transcribed by Médicis, *Chroniques,* II, 166f. Chassaing believes it to date in the fourteenth century or at any rate earlier than the fifteenth.
27. Le Puy, Bibl. Mun. Ms. 4 (V. Leroquais, *Les sacramentaires et missels manuscrits des bibliothéques publiques de France,* Paris, 1924, III, 91). The printed missals, dated 1511 and 1543 respectively, were used as evidence by A. Chassaing, "Calendrier de l'église du Puy-en-Velay au moyen âge," *Annales Soc. Puy.,* XXXIII, 1876-77, 265-93.
28. The charter of Raymond's donation was published by De Vic and Vaissete, *Histoire générale du Languedoc,* Toulouse, 1872-79, V, 747. A detailed commentary is found in J. H. and L. L. Hill, *Raymond IV, Count of Toulouse,* Syracuse, 1962, 38. J. Bousquet, "La donation de Ségur par Raymond de Saint-Gilles, Comte de Toulouse à l'église du Puy-en-Velay (1096)," *Annales du Midi,* I, 1962, 65-67, proposes that one of the three villages is not Ségrier, as generally assumed, but the castle of Ségur-en-Levezou (Aveyron).
29. The events immediately preceding the Council and Adhemar's role in the launching of the Crusade are still debated by historians. L. Bréhier, "Un évêque du Puy à la première croisade, Adémar de Monteil," *Bull. hist.,* VIII, 1923, 221-48, and A. Fliche, "Urbain II et la première croisade," *Revue d'histoire de l'église de France,* 1927, 289ff., see him as a key figure, while the Hills in their recent study of Raymond of Saint-Gilles (see note 28 above) and in an earlier essay "Contemporary Accounts and the Later Reputation of Adhemar, Bishop of Puy," *Medievalia et Humanistica,* IX, 1955, 30-38, take a much more guarded view of his involvement. The debate is continued by J. A. Brundage, "Adhemar of Puy. The Bishop and his Critics," *Speculum,* XXXIV, 1959, 201-12, and H. E. Mayer, "Zum Beurteilung Adhemars von Le Puy," *Deutsches Archiv,* 1960, No. 2, 547-55.
30. Baudri of Dol, *Historia Jerosolimitana, Pat. lat.* 166, 1069: "Episcopus et comes, Moysen et Aaron nobis reimaginantur." William of Malmesbury, *De gestis regnum anglorum* (Rerum Britannicarum Medii Aevii Scriptores, ed. Stubbs), II, 457, as quoted by the Hills, *Contemporary Accounts,* 31.
31. Médicis, *Chroniques,* I, 284. A street named for St. Giles is mentioned for the first time in 1167, according to Aymard, *Fouilles au Puy,* who bases himself on a *terrier* of the monastery of St. Peter in Le Puy not further identified. A hospital is mentioned in a document dated between 1222 and 1286 on the *carreira Sancti Aegidii.* Aymard speculates that the name refers to a road leading to Saint-Gilles in Provence or reflects in a distant fashion the donations of the cathedral of Raymond of Saint-Gilles. A tower bearing the name of Saint-Gilles was constructed in the fourteenth century, according to Médicis, *idem,* 231-32.

II The Puy Doors: Description and Style

THE WOODEN DOORS of Le Puy cathedral came to the attention of the learned public at a relatively early date, though they are passed over in silence in the oldest histories of the cathedral in favor of the lost valves of the *Porte dorée.* They are mentioned in passing, apparently for the first time, in the description of the cathedral made between 1790 and 1815 by the departmental *ingénieur-ordinaire* Antoine-Alexis Duranson, which, however, remained long unpublished.[1] Merimée reported on them in his *Notes d'un voyage en Auvergne* (1838), and his confession that they reminded him of "bas reliefs indiens ou persans" gave to them an exotic coloration which has remained an aspect of their attraction and a fairly constant thread in scholarship inspired by them.[2] *Portes arabes* or the vaguely biblical *portes de cèdre* are terms still commonly applied to them. During the reconstruction of the west bays of the cathedral beginning in 1844 the doors were removed and placed in storage. This is where they were seen in 1848 by Viollet-le-Duc, who judged only the doors of the Alhambra to be their equal and recommended that copies be substituted for them *in situ* and the originals preserved within the church or in a museum.[3] These recommendations were not carried out. In a report on the condition of the building and on the restorations which he proposed to undertake, the architect Mallay called attention to their unequal state of preservation and to traces of polychromy still to be seen on the less eroded Infancy doors. Several drawings executed to the scale of the model accompanied the text and were designed, in the author's words, to spare him a more extensive description.[4] These drawings have not been located, but one of them, showing the Infancy valves, served as the basis for E. Tudol's lithograph which appeared in Mandet and Michel's monumental *L'ancienne Auvergne et le Velay* (1848).[5] The worn, though more complete, set of doors of the St. Martin's chapel with scenes of the Passion have remained to this day comparatively less well known. Aligning this early impression with the fine watercolor copies executed by M. Petitgrand in 1889 (Fig. 5), the photographs published in Thiollier's study of 1900 and especially the cast in the Musée des Monuments Français in the Palais de Chaillot (Fig. 7), as well as later reproductions, makes it clear that the losses suffered by the doors preceded their discovery, and in spite of their almost continuous exposure, little change has occurred in their appearance since that time.[6]

A restoration undertaken in a Paris atelier in 1960 accomplished the removal of a thick layer of grime, revealing the sharp contours of heretofore blurred forms as well as the remains of polychromy earlier observed by Mallay. The incomplete Infancy doors were brought back to their original height through the addition of planks tooled to evoke the appearance of the scenes now missing (Fig. 8). The joint with the older panels is hidden by one of the iron and boss-studded strips which horizontally subdivide and brace the doors.[7] Only the very careful observer will note that the strip in question is not quite equidistant with the rest, its position not having been determined by compositional logic as elsewhere, but by the accidents of preservation.

The upper section of the door, including the batten at the center—about one half of the original design—is comparatively well preserved. There is some damage along its right edge, caused by the rubbing action of the wood against the stone jamb. Below the third metal bracing strip, the composition is incomplete along the bottom and totally lost through abrasion in the central area, but the upper parts of the design, though damaged, are still recognizable along the upper corners at the outer edges of both valves. The doors of the chapel of St. Martin showing scenes of the Passion are preserved in their entirety, with the exception of the batten at the center, which is a modern replacement (Figs. 6 and 9). However, the erosion of the surface is both more even and more drastic. The best preserved sections are again found in the upper half of the design, but we are here nearly down to bare wood. Below the center, the pattern of losses embraces the central zone of the design virtually in its entirety, while somewhat more remains along the outer and lowermost areas of the panels. All the damage suffered by the doors seems to have been the result of the natural process of erosion, specifically the cumulative effect of pressure which had to be exerted against the middle to open them, up to a level roughly corresponding to a man's height. The erosion of the fabric was more drastic in the Infancy doors, leading to an eventual fracture and to further damage along the lower edge, since, as shown in Petitgrand's watercolor and in later photographs, the remaining upper section was thereafter used to close the void (Fig. 5). The greater erosion of the surface of the Passion doors can be ascribed to the partially exposed situation of the portal of the chapel of St. Martin which adjoins an arch opening directly on to the exterior.

Each of the four valves is composed of four planks of equal width and approximately two inches thick (Text fig. 1). The wood, of a coniferous type, has been described by a well-placed authority as larch, which is in plentiful supply on the mountainous slopes of the area.[8] The planks have a half-joint profile along their congruent edges, but a firm joint by means of four loose cross tongues inserted at

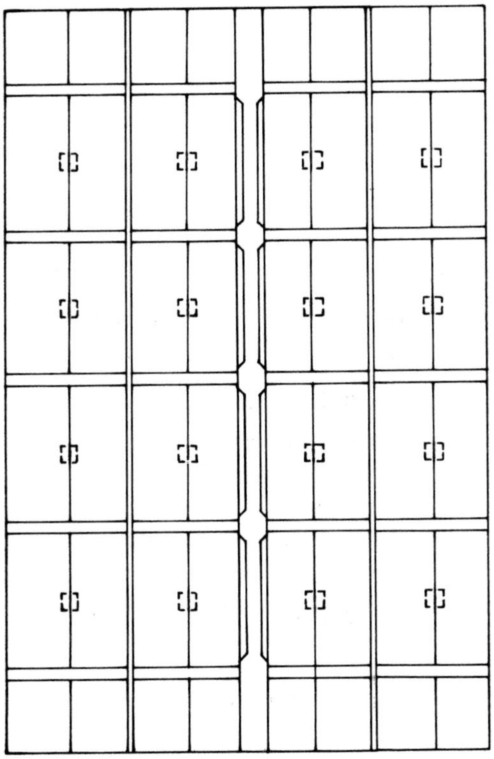

1. Wooden doors, Le Puy cathedral. Schema of assembly.

regular intervals has been realized only so far as to link the boards together in pairs. At the center of each valve, they are hinged and may be folded inward to open the doors in accordion fashion. Although the hinges, together with all the other metal fittings, were replaced in the course of the recent restoration, each of the valves seems indeed to have been designed as a combination of two semi-independent entities. Thus, while the sequence of the scenes, as well as the inscriptions, must be read horizontally across both panels, the disposition of both textual and illustrative material is such as to divide in the middle, and this interruption in the physical fabric of the work is emphasized by borders shouldering both sides of the caesura along its entire path. On the contrary, pictorial and epigraphical elements in the two sets of paired planks forming each valve lie across the joint, which has no independent compositional value. That the carving and polychromy of the doors was carried out following the assembly of the planks in sets of two seems a safe assumption.

The studded metal strips just mentioned constitute one of the problematic aspects of the design (Figs. 8 and 9). The other doors which have been attributed to the workshop are braced by metal bars on the back only. None have such fixtures on the decorated outer side (Figs. 35, 68, and 79). In the Puy doors, the sculptor has made allowance for their inclusion within the zone given to the figurative compositions and the accompanying inscriptions. But a band of blank wood is not extended across the borders, and in most instances, the metal strips awkwardly overlap and interrupt the flow of the design. This condition is rather more pronounced in the Infancy than in the Passion doors, where the interlace border has been so constructed as to terminate, in the right valve especially, short of the path of the intrusion. Although this effect was possibly not so perceptible when the polychromy of the doors was still intact, the bracing metal strips now throw the subtle play of directional forces within the composition out of balance, brutally imposing on it a pattern of strong horizontal accents.[9]

Nor do the horizontal boundaries established by the strips correspond to the internal divisions that can be drawn on the basis of the outline of figurative compositions and their accompanying inscriptions. Each valve in a complete state exhibited five sets of *tituli.* Only four of these on the more fully preserved Passion doors are sufficiently clear to be connected with specific compositions. Rightly construed, each composition must be associated with the two lines of text above it. The inscriptions below the lowest tier of scenes can no longer be read, and their relation to the scenes depicted remains unclear. The articulation of the design which communicates itself to the observer, on the other hand, is different, associating with every scene the line immediately above and below it. Each of the scenes thus appears as if provided with a frame of its own, of uniform dimensions and texture in spite of the heterogeneous parts which compose it. The sculptor clearly placed a special value on this solution and was willing to risk inconsistency and paradox for the sake of the most advantageous presentation of the individual compositions. As will be noted later, however, the polychromy of the doors initially minimized somewhat the strong visual effect of the metal bars and helped to clarify the proper relations of the lines composing each of the *tituli*.

The assertive plasticity of the batten in the middle of the door gives unusual prominence to this part. At Chamalières and at Blesle, the batten lies level with the surface of the doors, as might seem more consistent with the effect of flatness cultivated by the sculptor (Figs. 35 and 68). The desire to set the inscription recording the name of the artisan and his patron apart from the rest of the carving in the interest of greater visibility probably underlies this aspect of the design. Only the batten of the Infancy door survives, and this only in part (Figs. 7 and 8). It is held in place by nails with rounded heads of the same type, though of a somewhat larger size than those which pierce the horizontal metal strips. These nails are placed within eight pointed stars enclosed within a circle. The uppermost of these has a rounded, petaled contour, while the two below show sharp points.[10] Their location connects with the metal bars and roughly conforms to the spacing of the file of nail heads across both valves. The uppermost part of the batten is rectilinear in section. In the spaces between the nails, however, the lateral edges are given a sloping profile, leaving only the inscription in the narrow strip of wood facing the observer.

In contrast to the crowded and ornate treatment of the *tituli* attached to the individual scenes, the rendering of this text is quite straightforward. There are no ligatures and only one minor abbreviation. Rather surprisingly in view of its interest for the history of the cathedral, it was entirely overlooked in writings devoted to the church prior to the nineteenth century and seems first to have been transcribed by Longpérier and by Caillau in 1846. The first writer proposed the reading GAUZFREDUS ME FECIT PETRUS EPI *(scopus me jussit)*;[11] the second interpreted the troublesome final words as PETRO SED *(ente)*.[12] Thiollier later gave the correct and now generally accepted version: GAUZFREDUS ME F (E) CIT: PETRUS EDI *(ficavit)*.[13] There are twelve characters between the first set of nails and thirteen between the second. There was thus room in the damaged section below for an additional phrase, including perhaps a date and a laudatory formula on behalf of the two named persons. The placement of the inscription in such a conspicuous location adheres to a custom, widespread in the twelfth century, of attaching the name of the master to the portal of the church or parts of the threshold surrounding it. The inscription commemorating Gislebertus at

Autun or Girauldus at Saint-Ursin in Bourges, both located at midpoint in the tympanum, are well known examples. At Maguelone and Autry-Issards (Allier), the signatures appear on the lintel.[14] Even closer to the disposition illustrated by the Puy doors is the placement of the signature around the rim of the cast bronze door handle, as seen on one of the knockers at Saint-Julien de Brioude, and later, in another from the Cathedral of Trier.[15] The association of the doorway with yearnings for rebirth and immortality in another world are long standing in the history of religion. But these yearnings are surely buttressed here by a concomitant longing for secular fame, which, extending forward in time and space, encouraged the hope of more durable rewards.

Each valve in the two sets of doors is framed by a wide border. In their design, the sculptor makes scant use of the decorative vocabulary of stylized foliage and geometric ornament derived from ancient art which common practice might have urged on him. Only in the sequence of tri-lobed leaves separated by hollow conical projections occupying the narrow slanting edge of the batten is there an evident, though indirect reference to this traditional source–a recollection of an egg-and-dart molding. Elsewhere in the borders and in other parts of the work, the artisan was moved by a preference for motifs which could be intelligibly exploited on the surface plane and therefore harmoniously complemented his particular carving technique. This interest in ornament of a predominantly planar type, more than special considerations of ideology, engineered a sympathetic disposition toward models in several domains of artistic experience, principally low relief sculpture of the pre-Romanesque period and the decorative grammar of Islamic art.

The border of the Infancy doors, composed of Pseudo-Cufic script, has long attracted special attention (Figs. 7, 8 and 18). It consists of a short inscription continuously repeated around both valves, though complemented in two places by a kind of stylized tree. The sentence copied by the sculptor was initially read by A. de Longpérier as *Lā ilāh illā Allāh,* the Muslim profession of faith "There is no other God beside Allah." [16] A. Fikry proposed instead the reading *Mā shā' Allāh* translatable as "This is what Allah desired." [17] More recently, G. Marçais has offered the interpretation *al-Mulk lillāh:* "All power to Allah." [18] Marçais's reading presupposes the inversion of the letter *kaf* read as an *alif* by Fikry, and a rendering of the letter *mim* and final *ha* in the form frequently seen in North African and Egyptian monuments under the Fatimids. This interpretation would assign to the model employed by Gauzfredus a date in the eleventh or early twelfth century.

There is agreement within expert opinion that the treatment of Muslim epigraphy is unusually faithful and far from a mere vague echo of such forms for purely decorative effect. The open display of praise in honor of an alien God in such a context is certainly startling, but its very substance must make it doubtful that it was understood by the Auvergnat artist or by his public. The remarkable fidelity of their transcription seems to me less a sign of proficiency than of a painstaking effort to cope with the unfamiliar. Yet such a literal disposition toward the unintelligible must have been conditioned by an intuitive recognition of its worth. Knowledge that Cufic was a form of script and not mere ornament, that its brilliantly decorative convolutions elaborated a sacred or vaguely magic phraseology can be assumed to have promoted an uncommon degree of care in its transcription. Beyond a concern for accuracy in the rendering of Cufic script, the Puy sculptor, like some of his contemporaries, also shows a certain awareness of epigraphic usage within the Islamic tradition. The Infancy doors perpetuate the practice, long standing in Islamic art, of shaping the inscription to form a continuous border around an entire composition. Among the varied Romanesque quotations of Cufic script, many of them of a much more fragmentary nature, the silver gilt and repoussé altar frontal of the Arca Santa in Oviedo is close to our monument in this respect.[19] The Latin *tituli* in the doors assist the Cufic border in extending this process of epigraphic enclosure to each of the separate historiated panels in what is most likely a further reminiscence or transposition of this usage. A strikingly similar composite border of Pseudo-Cufic completed by titles in Roman capital letters frames one of the miniatures in the Beatus of Saint-Sever (Fig. 10).

The oldest recorded instance of the imitation of Cufic script in the Latin West is literal minded to a more practical end. It is encountered in the coinage of the Anglo-Saxon king Offa (757-96), which models itself on Arab issues. Some silver coins later struck on the Continent under Pippin the Short also show traces of Cufic forms in the shape of the letters which comprise the Latin legends.[20] These intrusions have no basis in considerations of taste, reflecting rather the high esteem enjoyed by Arab coins in this period, leading northern mints to model their own issues upon them, as Roman coins had served them earlier. At the beginning of the eleventh century, the Limousin chronicler Adhemar of Chabannes included a Cufic inscription in the collection of drawings of miscellaneous subjects strewn in his manuscripts, and perhaps intended to form some kind of patternbook.[21] Isolated as it is in its time, Adhemar's drawing nonetheless seems, in the perspective of subsequent developments, to inaugurate a new sensibility with both aesthetic and sociocultural dimensions in regard to the exotic script.

A true vogue for ornament based on Cufic writing manifested itself for the first time in the period which straddles the year 1100. It is illustrated by a series of examples in the art of northern Spain and the south of France, of which Spittle and Erdmann have given the fullest tabulation to date.[22] The highly ornate and occasionally extravagant letter forms encountered in the Latin epigraphy of these regions in Romanesque times constitutes another, and no less vital, dimension of its impact. The reception of Cufic in the repertory of Romanesque ornament follows several distinct channels. The appearance of imitations of the script on the imposts of Romanesque capitals or other elements of the architectural fabric is an extension of similar practice in Islamic architecture, which affected Byzantine construction as well, though at a somewhat earlier date.[23] It does not seem, however, that stonemasons in Auvergne, in contrast to those in Aquitaine and Languedoc, were touched by it. Outside the Puy doors, the examples of Pseudo-Cufic in the region—they are relatively few—occur on renderings of garments and textiles in the context of sacred imagery. A border of Pseudo-Cufic decorated the loincloth of Christ in the monumental wooden crucifix at Lavoûte-Chilhac and the cushion of the reliquary image of the enthroned Virgin of Orcival exhibits a strip of cloth treated in the same way.[29] Further west, within the scene at the beginning of the Book of Esther in the Bible of Saint-Yrieix, there is an altar cloth similarly edged by a Pseudo-Cufic border.[25] Admiration for luxury products of Byzantine and Islamic origin, assiduously collected in the treasures of Western churches, possibly mingled in these imitations with an unreflecting association of Eastern styles with the sanctuaries of the Holy Land, and consequently, with the cultural ambient of apostolic times. In the intervening centuries, the monumental topography of the eastern Mediterranean had been profoundly transformed by successive Byzantine and Arab occupations, and the postclassical accretions must have been apprehended by the Western traveler as characteristic features of the landscape from time immemorial.

Such elements of Islamic influence are particularly dramatic in appearance, though more often than not isolated and without impact on the larger design. In Gauzfredus's doors, the reminiscences of Islamic art are more substantial. They must enter into the consideration of the artist's peculiar low relief technique, which will preoccupy us in greater detail below. They are also palpable, as has been noted by previous writers, in certain of the other ornamental motifs employed on the doors.[26] In both sets of valves, a row of eight-pointed stars fills the spaces adjacent to the upper and lower sections of the border (Figs. 7 and 25, top). The shape and disposition of these ornaments is suggestive of the effect of a row of decorative nails. A relief with Christ in Majesty in Berlin, attributed to Spain and dated in the middle of the twelfth century, shows the same device.[27] It figures also among the surviving panels of the ceiling of the church of S. Millán in Segovia, Muslim work probably several decades earlier in date, and a low relief carving style analogous to our monument (Fig. 11).[28] The starry and petaled formations outlined by circles housing the nails on the batten, versions of the same design in a more elaborate state, are found on another Islamic wood carving in low relief, part of a support for the roof of the church of Santa Maria in Tarifa (Cadiz) (Fig. 12); they mark here the outer faces of the characteristic tubular shafts of Islamic corbels.[29]

The upper part of the batten, rectilinear in section, is covered on its outer side with foliage decoration cast in the form of a continuous figure eight which is described by a pair of interweaving strands (Fig. 7). The loops are filled with open palmette leaves like those which fill quarter circles in the upper corners of the scene of the traveling Magi on their way to Herod's court (Figs. 17 and 19). The hollows in between show downward-turning tri-lobed leaves disposed in symmetrical fashion on each side of the interweaving stems. Fikry and after him, Marçais, have seen here another element of the design of Islamic derivation, but the evidence is in this instance less clear-cut since this ornamental configuration was also well known to Romanesque stonemasons and sculptors.[30]

The valves of the Passion doors have borders composed of interlace, and the sculptor is here dependent clearly enough on purely indigenous sources (Figs. 9, 24, and 25). The design is constructed by joining the ends of two parallel rows of half-circles placed back to back by a network of oblique intersecting lines. This type of interlace configuration is most common. Examples abound especially within the sphere of low relief sculpture applied to chancel furniture in the eighth and ninth centuries, but a comprehensive inventory, scarcely a practical undertaking, would include contemporary and earlier illustrations in manuscripts and metalwork as well.[31] The extension of this type of ornament in sculpture forward in time beyond the Carolingian period must also be envisaged, though it does not seem that the stylistic criteria which some authors have proposed as a means of distinguishing the ninth-century examples from later productions are uniformly applicable. It is nonetheless beyond dispute that a far from negligible quantity of interlace friezes and panels conventionally dated in early medieval times were carved over a time span extending into the Romanesque period.[32] The cornice frieze of the Cathedral of Gurk in Carinthia furnishes an example fully comparable to the Puy door and datable as late as the third quarter of the twelfth century.[33] Older fragments of interlace sometime appear embedded in the masonry fabric of Romanesque buildings, but the panels which frame the windows of the eleventh-century choir at Peyrusse-Grande (Gers) are contemporaneous with the building.[34] Within central France and outlying regions, the type of ornament employed by the Puy sculptor is found in Romanesque times on the altar and lintel above the doorway leading to the St. Michael's chapel in the church of Bessuéjouls in Rouergue and around the portal of Saint-Pierre at Saint-Marcel-d'Ardèche in Vivarais, of which, unfortunately, only fragments remain.[35] Even closer at hand, the sculptor could have drawn inspiration from the carved balusters and slabs discovered in the pavement of the choir of the cathedral in the course of the reconstruction carried out by the architect A. Mimey in the year 1867 (Fig. 13). These fragments were probably once part of an altar or chancel arrangement devised for the structure preceding the present building and not necessarily dismantled after its replacement.[36] A special predilection for altar decoration in this conservative low relief style may be noted in central France, and it must be assumed as well that here as in the Midi generally, the sanctuary furniture of the Carolingian period survived to a greater extent than in the northern regions of the country, where the Norman invasions took their toll.[37]

The choice of this form of interlace ornament presented the sculptor with some difficulties which are more successfully disguised in the Pseudo-Cufic border of the Infancy doors. It lies in the nature of the design to permit unending forward progress in a single direction, but there is no way by which a corner can be gracefully turned while maintaining the basic rhythm of the pattern undisturbed. In stone sculpture, such interlace configurations are thus confined to a straight path, and where necessary, juxtaposed at a right angle to other sections rather than joined to them in an organic way. In the Puy doors, the treatment of these connections is not consistently worked out. At the lower right corner of the left valve, the sculptor attempted in one single instance to connect the horizontal and vertical strands of the border, to very ill effect. In the upper part of the panels, where alone this aspect of the border is still fully distinct, the interlace strips are extended to the upper edge in one instance and across to the sides in the other three (Fig. 9). Along the upper right side, the border terminates in a pair of symmetrically splayed tri-lobed leaves, a device which was designed to mask an excessively wide gap where the two sections of interlace abut (Fig. 25, upper right). But on the opposite edge of the same valve, the sculptor achieved the same effect through a slight deformation in the shape of the terminal interlace configuration and a leftward extension of the narrow strip of wood which defines the inner edge of the border.

Each set of doors initially exhibited eight individually framed panels with figurative compositions. Of these, the two lowermost on the Infancy side with their accompanying inscriptions are totally lost. The Passion doors are complete, but badly worn below the center, especially so in the zone comprising the central section of the third and fourth tier of scenes. Here, only a few meager details and some fragments of letters can be made out. In spite of these losses, the nature and general disposition of the subjects can be determined in most instances with a reasonable measure of accuracy. The sequence of the scenes is from the bottom to the top of the door and, in all but one case, from the left to the right of the panel. The Infancy cycle begins, in its present state, with the Annunciation to the Shepherds, followed by the Adoration of the Magi (Fig. 7). In the middle register, the three Magi on horseback are led by their star into the presence of Herod. The two compositions in the upper tier are devoted to the Massacre of the Innocents and the Presentation in the Temple. The missing scenes which initiated the sequence must have included the Nativity, preceded by the Annunciation and quite possibly, the Visitation.

The first two scenes of the Passion cycle on the doors of the chapel of St. Martin are poorly preserved, but details of the composition and parts of the *tituli* surviving leave no doubt as to their identification (Fig. 9). The scenes are not in the usual left-to-right order, showing in the opposite sense, the Resurrection of Lazarus and the Entry into Jerusalem. In a divergence from the more common cyclical pattern, the Lazarus story takes the place normally accorded to the Washing of the Feet. The following scenes are in the conventional sequence. On the third tier are shown the Last Supper and the Arrest of Christ. Here, losses are more serious since, extending both left and right of the modern batten, they embrace nearly half of each of the panels, where the remaining composition is otherwise complete in its own right. But a close reading of the traces of the carving which still survives and iconographic comparisons reduce to an acceptable level the range of uncertainty. The Carrying of the Cross, the Crucifixion, and the Three Maries at the Tomb appear on the second tier, and the series is completed with the Ascension and Descent of the Holy Spirit.

Since the internal subdivisions imposed on each valve are constant throughout, the scenes have had in various ways to be adapted to their setting. Each of the panels is, as we have already noted, divided into two parts by the borders outlining the hinged joints in the middle. Because of the accommodation made for the batten where the valves meet in closing, the innermost of the two zones is not as wide as its companion along the outer edges of the doors. These factors led the sculptor either to limit scenes to a single zone within each panel, or, where this was impractical, to give the composition the form of two semi-independent but complementary entities. The Carrying of the Cross and Crucifixion (Fig. 24), and probably the lost Annunciation and Visitation on the Infancy doors, are instances where the first solution prevails.

Elsewhere, a single event is divided into two separate moments. In the Massacre of the Innocents, we see Herod first giving his command (left) and the Killing of the Infants (right) in the adjoining zone (Fig. 18). In the Presentation in the Temple, the group of Simeon receiving the Christ Child from the Virgin is detached from the figure of the handmaiden bringing her gifts (Fig. 20). In both cases the sculptor took advantage of the unequal size of the spaces to give greater emphasis to the core of the action and set it apart from the subsidiary moment. The division of a subject usually treated as a unified composition is not, however, apprehended as an incongruity since it is consistent with the unfolding of the action in time. In the Ascension and the Descent of the Holy Spirit, the sculptor faced a different kind of problem, for these subjects are normally cast in the form of centralized compositions which effectively deny to them all potential of temporal extension (Figs. 24 and 25). Indeed, they cannot easily be conceived as subdivided into multiple episodes. But the application of the traditional schema would have meant splitting in two the vital center of the composition, or were it to have been confined to one of the two available sections, an unwelcome reduction in the size of the figures. The solution was to isolate this iconic core and give the lesser participants in the scene a separate pictorial status. Thus, the Descent of the Holy Spirit is divided into two distinct parts: one with three figures dominated in the middle by St. Peter or the Virgin Mary and corresponding to the central group in the traditional iconography; the other, with five additional disciples seated side by side, a token representation of the rest of the apostolic college (Fig. 25). In the Ascension, the sculptor adapted the composition to the configuration of the available space by consigning the witnesses to the right of the heavenly apparition and on the same level rather than below it (Fig. 24, above). It is noteworthy that in these two scenes and probably the Last Supper as well, he was willing to make a considerable sacrifice in the number of apostles customarily included as participants in order to strive for a presentation of almost emblematic concentration (Fig. 26). The subject matter, already in abbreviated state, is pushed close to the picture plane and allowed to fill virtually all of the available space. Even where the process of adjustment to the nature of the design did not involve a difficult recasting of the scene, as in the case of the Annunciation to the Shepherds and the Three Maries at the Tomb, the sculptor welcomed the opportunity to focus on the large figure of the angel isolated in its own space.

The scene of the Magi before Herod offered the sculptor a greater opportunity to demonstrate his resourcefulness (Figs. 17 and 19). The composition is the only one to extend across the width of an entire door, combining into an uninterrupted sequence the journey of the kings and their arrival at Herod's court. The depiction of each king in isolation conveys in an admirably expressive way their forward progress through a varied and fertile landscape. The fact that the panel at the outer left is wider than the other two is disguised by means of the stylized plant along the vertical right border of the scene, adding to the variation in the topography. The borders and the batten between the two valves are apprehended by the viewer as additional, and more perilous obstacles in their path. The fortuitous interruption in the center, isolating one of the Magi from his companions, also enabled the artist to treat Herod's audience as an incident separate from the journey of the Kings, yet without fundamentally interrupting the continuity of the entire sequence.

For an appreciation of the stylistic qualities of the Puy doors, comparison with the design and compositional technique of other medieval historiated doors like those of Pisa, Verona, or Spalato would seem to be a self-evident first requirement.[38] The comparatively extensive tradition of medieval doors with scenes cast or carved and fully modeled in relief tempts us to regard the much more unusual work in Le Puy as a kind of inexpensive reduction of sculpture in a grander vein. This disposition to look upon the work as sculpture, if sculpture in an impoverished state, is encouraged by the almost total loss of the polychromy, which makes us dependent on the outlines of the carving for their interpretation and offers the eye a more or less monochrome surface differentiated only in terms of light playing on the relief. Yet to see the doors primarily in this way distorts both the stylistic and technical nature of the enterprise. In their original condition, the doors would indeed have struck the casual observer more as painted panels than as carvings in relief. While the individual scenes as we know them are nearly complete so far as their basic configuration is concerned, they were not designed to be viewed without the many indications of pose, dress, and expression whose definition was entrusted to the brush. Certain formal conventions, like the pattern of intersecting boughs which establishes the ground line in the scene of the traveling Magi or the open palmette ornaments in the upper corners of the same composition, not to mention the Pseudo-Cufic and interlace border designs, have an obviously graphic ancestry (Fig. 17). Even if the artist had been disposed to cast his work in imitation of a more sculptural model, he would have had to adjust his intentions to the particular requirements of the flat surface and thus have been led to be attentive to works in a planar mode—painting and enamel work primarily—that were germane to his efforts.

The traces of the original polychromy uncovered in the cleaning of the doors in 1960 are most substantial in the upper zone of the Infancy doors, especially in the scene of the Presentation in the Temple on the upper right (Fig. 20). These vestiges of paint become progressively more rarefied as the eye travels downward. The remains of paint on the Passion doors are much less extensive, and on the upper surface, the bare wood is almost entirely exposed throughout. Where we are more fortunate, as especially in the uppermost tier of scenes in the Infancy doors, the assessment of the stylistic situation is nonetheless fraught with some difficulty. The uppermost layer of paint, along with all outlines and details of dress, features, and expression are lost. In places where the wood is fully laid bare, as in the Last Supper on the Passion doors, the definition of overlapping parts is incised in outline on the surface: the table in front of Christ and the apostles, the figure of Judas in the right foreground extending an arm forward and the feet of the seated figures on the footstool (Fig. 26). In the border on the left edge, the alternating over-and-under path of the interlace is similarly marked. This drawing is very summary and had in any case to be established anew over the heavy gesso base which was laid over the surface. Most of the contours internal to the forms and other details were left to the final stage of painting. The procedure is comparable to that observed in contemporary book illumination and was continued long afterward in panel painting. What is left in the best preserved parts is thus only a general impression of tonal relationships. The color scheme has a pronounced reddish cast. A warm vermilion predominates, with pink and a somewhat darker hue used more sparingly, as in the upper garment of the handmaiden in the Presentation (Fig. 20). White was used for flesh tones, some of the garments and skies in outdoor scenes. A dark, brownish color–it must, as in all other hues, have been more subtly differentiated in various contexts when the work left the painter's hands–is employed in an effective counterpoint with the lighter tones.

Color established certain distinctions within the design which are left unspecified in the carving. A major outline, consisting of the strip of wood which separates the scenes from the borders and the two sections of each valve from one another, is set apart in a uniform warm red. The strips which mark the horizontal subdivisions within this larger frame were clearly subordinated to it, being painted in more neutral colors and coming to rest against the vertical bands without interrupting them. This imparted to the doors in their original state a much more outspokenly architectural order than is now apparent, placing the weight of visual emphasis on the vertical. Actually, the independence of this outer frame from the adjacent matter was foreseen from the start: in the denuded Last Supper panel, a line inscribed by the stylus isolates the border in continuous fashion (Fig. 26). In the treatment of the varied subjects carved on the doors, the overriding concern of the painter was to articulate, much along the same principles, those pictorial distinctions which had been lost in the process of simplification required by the low relief technique practiced by the sculptor, yet without placing in jeopardy the particular qualities of style realized through it. Thus, the darkly colored *tituli* were sharply silhouetted against the lighter backgrounds. The horizontal strips of wood which enclose them and now seem wedded to the top and bottom of the letters were separated from them, and from the background as well, by means of a color contrasting with both. The awkward division between the two connected lines of text above each of the scenes perpetrated by the nail-studded metal strips was at least partially remedied by the uniformity of color. The pair of lines above the following scene was similarly united, but with the help of another combination of contrasting colors, thus setting it apart from the preceding and also the following.

The alternation of the fairly limited range of colors to distinguish parts of a larger whole, or to introduce variety and rhythmical pattern within a sequence of like parts, is in evidence throughout. In the border of the Infancy doors, the Pseudo-Cufic is treated in alternating colors, dark brown and red in the section adjoining the Presentation in the Temple, but apparently incorporating lighter tones further down. The interlace in the border of the Passion doors showed two continually intersecting strands, producing knots in an alternating sequence of dark brown and red, with the recesses within the knots painted in the reverse arrangement of the same colors. The polychromy in the scene of the Presentation brings into view the internal divisions within the framing arches and lends to each of them a different coloristic personality (Fig. 20). On the left side, the vermilion arch cuts in front of deep red turrets, which have single dark round windows and whitish conical roofs. The imposts beneath the arches are painted dark brown, the capitals deep red, the columns brownish, and the stepped bases in a tone matching the capitals. On the right, the arch is in the same deep red against a lighter vermilion background, reversing the order observed on the other side. The turrets have brownish roofs, the imposts are white, and brownish capitals and bases frame deep red columns. With the single exception where two areas of color meet in the background to define the horizon line, the application of the paint is made to coincide with the contour marking the frontier between raised and depressed areas. It thus reinforces the outlines instituted by the carving, though it blurs rather than strengthens the sharp stratification in two layers which the bare sculpture so clearly manifests. Here, a dark form stands forth against a lighter ground; there, the more intense color of the ground dominates the weaker island set in its midst.[39] The Passion doors alone are now exposed to view from the back. They are painted in a uniform tone of red which is laid over a gesso ground, and seems to have suffered little damage or alteration over the centuries.

Gauzfredus's technique of low relief sculpture draws immediate attention and constitutes one of the most problematic aspects of the doors. What remains of Romanesque wood carving in relief is, with the possible exception of the Scandinavian material, appallingly little, yet it conveys the impression that this technique was in no sense inescapably identified with wood sculpture as such nor indeed very common or widespread. In the more conventional productions, the treatment of relief in wood sculpture does not differ from the procedure observed in stone or bronze.[40] The elements of the design projecting from the ground are rounded and creviced, and otherwise made to impersonate volume bathed in light. In some carving of a decorative nature, like that on the south Italian casket in the Palazzo Venezia, the depth of the relief is slight and fairly uniform throughout, and thus, superficially at least, similar in its planar quality to the sculpture of the central French doors.[41] But even when striving for such a textile-like evenness of texture, the sculptor shapes and tools the raised surfaces in the accustomed manner. The south Italian wooden doors of Santa Maria in Cellis at Carsoli, which on first sight seem to exhibit the closest kinship with the Auvergnat monuments, are distinguishable from them on the same grounds.[42] Very different from this yet equally at variance with the work of the Puy atelier, is the type of carving illustrated on the hutches of Valeria at Sion and practiced as well in France and Spain.[43] The wholly ornamental patterns which decorate these pieces of ecclesiastical furniture are executed in a chip-carving technique for which some antecedents in Late Antique funerary art suggest themselves.[44] The chisel works at an angle, gouging the design onto the surface without giving it a self-standing body in relief. The manufacture of furniture and household implements with designs produced in this way continued well after the end of the Middle Ages, and, in the artisanal and folk milieu, can be followed close to our own times.[45] Something like the two-tiered, low relief technique of the Puy doors is embodied in a group of chests and other woodwork executed in Italy as well as in Central Europe during the sixteenth century, but neither stylistic nor historical connections can link this attractive material to the Auvergnat panels four centuries older.[46] More intriguing, perhaps, is the resemblance of the Puy carving style to the wooden core of certain goldsmithwork objects, revealed where the precious metal revetment has fortuitously disappeared, as for example, in the shrine of Bishop Ulger of Angers (Fig. 85).[47] The layering of the wood here and in similar pieces serves the purpose of defining the major compositional subdivisions and as a means of cradling insets in ivory or enamel. It is certainly reasonable to assume that Gauzfredus was familiar with this procedure and might have been called upon to execute wooden forms of this kind as a part of his practice. It is only too clear, however, that on the doors, the technique of low relief carving is employed in a much more ambitious way for representational ends rather than limited to the indication of arches and other framing devices.

This wider ambition as well as the crucial fact that in the doors, the carving was designed to be exposed and appreciated as such rather than hidden under a metallic and bejeweled mantle, are aspects of the work that are most closely paralleled in some examples of Coptic, and later, of Islamic decorative wood sculpture. Some of the carved panels found in the South Church at Bawit, datable around 800, already show the technique in full flower, and it is well illustrated also in an attractive carving with an archangel, possibly somewhat later in date, in the Brooklyn Museum (Fig. 14).[48] Fikry gives additional and subsequent instances of its use in Islamic art ranging from the ornamental carving of the dome niches in the mosques of Kairouan and al-Hakim in Cairo to the doors of the church of the Martorana in Palermo.[49] In Spain, the wooden ceiling of the Cordova mosque, as described by the twelfth-century geographer al-Idrisi and reconstituted with the help of remaining fragments by modern scholarship was adorned in the same way.[50] A traceried network of stylized foliage covered three sides of the supporting beams, while geometric ornament appeared on the surface of the flat boards reposing on them. Attributed to the period of al-Hakam's enlargement of the mosque (961), the ceiling was brightly painted in a scheme not without some resemblance to the Puy doors, the darker hues on the surface being set against the deep red tones employed in the recessed areas. Parts of a second wooden ceiling constituted in a similar manner surviving in the church of San Millán in Segovia have already been mentioned (Fig. 11).[51] The carved beams and panels showed, as at Cordova, starry geometric patterns and foliage in symmetrical interweaving arrangements. A Cufic invocation ran along the inner step at the base of the work. A few other examples of this kind of wood carving can be added: the fragments from one of the rooms in the "Cuartos de Granada" in the Alcazaba at Malaga[52] and those from the church of Santa Maria in Tarifa (Cadiz) (Fig. 12).[53] They demonstrate the practice of this technique by Muslim craftsmen over a period extending from the tenth to the twelfth centuries and its application to Christian and Islamic buildings without distinction. It also might be surmised that this technique was deemed especially appropriate for the decoration of ceilings, for this is the major function in which its use can be definitely documented. The tradition was evidently weakened as it made its way north, though a fourteenth-century ceiling in a building which now serves as the town hall of Brioude, a town little more than sixty kilometers northwest of Le Puy, still is clearly dependent on it.[54] The ceiling shows heraldic devices combined with a playfully fantastic imagery drawn from the repertory of Gothic drolleries, and it otherwise departs from earlier usage to the further extent that it achieves the cherished planar effect by a process of veneering rather than hollowing out of the solid wood.

Since the comparable body of Islamic wood carving is of an ornamental nature, it is with the corresponding parts of the Puy doors that its ties are strongest. The appropriation of a technique could here go hand in hand with the borrowing of formal components. In the case of the figurative illustrations, on the other hand, it would at best be possible to speak of a process of adaptation or a return, perhaps, to older, pre-Islamic sources, on historical grounds an admittedly problematic assumption (Fig. 14). Gauzfredus might have been drawn to such precedents all the more readily since the pictorial values which they would enable him to realize were being cultivated by other means in certain spheres of Romanesque art. The low relief sculpture of the doors invites comparison here first and foremost with marble encrustation work as illustrated in the decorative friezes in the choir of Lyon and Vienne cathedrals, or in some examples of church furniture, like the altar of Saint-Guilhem-le-Désert (Fig. 15).[55] The Crucifixion of the Saint-Guilhem altar and the corresponding subject of the Puy doors obviously have much in common, and it is easy to see how even such an excellent student of Auvergnat Romanesque art as the late Louis Bréhier could describe the doors as having lost their paste inlays.[56] Both kinds of work offer the viewer images similarly compressed within the boundaries of their subject matter and materially detached from the surrounding space. The origin of the technique of marble encrustation is as yet obscure, though R. Hamann pointed out that similar effects were achieved in certain types of metalwork, most notably niello and *opus interrasile,* as described in Theophilus's *De diversis artibus.*[57] We are thus dealing with a broadly shared system of formal conventions, adapted to particular materials and modes of workmanship rather than intrinsically grounded in the experience of a particular craft. Perhaps the most systematic applications of these conventions is to be found in Limousin shrines with appliqué reliefs datable in the later twelfth century and after. Because the layered structure in these works was achieved by a process of assembly rather than excision, its stylistic implications are exposed with particular clarity. We observe here again the strong massing of all representational elements of the scene, including details of landscape, which had to be detached from the background in order to be incorporated into a unified whole. The predilection for closed forms, a by-product of the same approach, is shown in the unbroken contour which encompasses the Limousin relief of the Baptism of Christ (Boston Museum), linking the arm of the Baptist to the head of Christ and the standing figure of the Saviour to the pyramidal swell of fish-laden water.[58] Similarly in the doors, figures, and staffage in various scenes tend to form closed groups, hypothetically detachable from the recessed ground. Thus, in the Killing of the Innocents (Fig. 18), the sword-wielding executioner and his two victims are joined by a continuous outline, as in the procession of five figures comprising the carrying of the Cross or the group of the Virgin and Child with Simeon and the altar in the Presentation (Fig. 20)

At the same time, the sculptor sought to render the forms most fully legible in relief and minimize the dependence on polychromy as a means of defining contours "lost" within the boundaries of the raised surfaces. Figures are wherever possible separated from the edges of the scene, even where their outline runs parallel to it. They are pushed back to an implied ground line and when their feet occasionally meet the border along the bottom, they do so on tiptoe. Solid shapes are opened up to reveal the outline of members superimposed upon them. Thus, we see Herod's feet and the hem of his garment silhouetted against the hollowed and incomplete outline of the cushion and footstool (Fig. 19), and the body of Christ brought into fuller view over the void opened up in the arms and lower section of the cross (Fig. 24, lower right). Critical gestures and attributes especially–the doves of the handmaiden in the Presentation, the upraised arm of the blessing Christ Child, Herod's command and the Magi's gesturing to the eastern star–are in this way saved from disappearance into the undifferentiated mass of the relief (Figs. 17, 19, and 20). Foliage is pierced by daylight and architecture by windows and openings which reduce its opacity and may at the same time reveal a section of roof or groundline otherwise lost from sight.

If through these skillful means, the sculptor attempted to turn to best advantage the possibilities inherent in this type of two-tiered sculpture, the variety and complexity of his compositions go in most instances well beyond comparable experiences in marble encrustation and metalwork. These are generally restricted to single standing figures, the Majestas Domini and the Crucifixion, subjects which in their conventional presentation adhered to the flat surface and could without difficulty be transposed into a low relief technique. The Puy scenes, on the other hand, are laid out in a much more relaxed pictorial style. While there is always at least a token affirmation of the surface plane, marked by the arcaded setting, or elements of furniture, landscape or ornament, the sense of recession is, in the narrative scenes at least, eagerly cultivated. Figures, as may be assumed from details of their outline, often assume rather informal poses, in three-quarter view. Major personages dominate, but not conspicuously so. The force of a long representational tradition reaching back to the early Christian period entirely overshadows in these designs the imprint left by conventions bound up with the practice of the low relief idiom. Singular in its multiple dimensions, the work enters with reluctance into the frail network of our stylistic categories.

NOTES

1. "De chaque côté dudit escalier et sur le même replat à peu près de l'entrée de l'hôpital, il est bon en passant de voir la sculpture des portes en bois des deux chapelles qui ne sont bonnes à remarquer que par la singularité tant des écritures que de divers tableaux qui y sont représentés grossièrement" (Jacotin, *Mémoire de Duranson*, 95).
2. Merimée, *Notes d'un voyage en Auvergne*, in *Notes de voyage*, ed. P.-M. Auzas, Paris, 1971, 558. The author was in Le Puy in mid-July 1837 (P. Merimée, *Correspondance générale*, ed. M. Parturier, Paris, 1941f., II, 121). He observes that the doors are "en bois de cèdre, autant que j'en ai pu juger," and this description is still widely used.
3. Viollet-le-Duc's report concerning the restorations of Mallay in which the doors are mentioned is dated August 31, 1848. It is published in Thiollier, *Architecture religieuse*, Appendix XI, 186ff. He refers to them as "Deux grandes portes en mélèze ou cèdre, datant du XIe siècle probablement."
4. A copy of Mallay's *devis* dated December 10, 1842, is found in the Archives Departementales de la Haute-Loire, V. 21, No. 3: "Je dois signaler aussi . . . des curieuses portes en bois placées à l'entrée des chapelles du grand escalier. Celle de droite est en très mauvais état, celle de gauche est bien conservée et l'on retrouverait facilement une partie des couleurs qui couvraient les sculptures: on voit que les fonds étaient rouges et les terrains jaunes. Les ornements byzantins sont assez bien ajustés et la forme des lettres est charactéristique, j'en ai joint quatre panneaux grandeur d'exécution." I have not been able to locate these drawings.
5. Earlier, a lithograph of the Infancy valves by Engelmann appeared in Taylor and Nodier's *Voyages pittoresques et romantiques dans l'ancienne France* (Auvergne, II), Paris, 1837, pl. 162b, and the same representation figures also in A. Hugo's *France historique et monumentale*, Paris, 1837, II, pl. XLVI.
6. The Petitgrand relevés were published in A. de Baudot and A. Perrault-Dabot, *Archives de la Commission des Monuments Historiques*, VI, 13, and pl. 20.
7. The restoration carried out by the late M. René Hémery is all too briefly described by F. Enaud, *Bull. mon.*, 1964, 57: "Il a découvert sous un badigeon gris uniforme fort laid l'existence de la polychromie d'origine. Les portes ont été décapées par écaillage à la lame de rasoir. Les couleurs très vives employées par l'artiste du XIIe siècle sont le blanc, le rouge de minium, le rouge de fer, le vert foncé et le bleu. Elles sont posés de façon irrégulière, tantôt sur les reliefs, tantôt sur les filets et les moulures. Cette brilliante polychromie, qui était restée jusqu'a présent ignorée, mérite d'être indiquée ici comme un exemple du parti extrêmement coloré de certaines ornementations romanes de part et d'autre des Pyrenées."

   The brief dossier in the Archives des Monuments Historiques dealing with this restoration (No. 163/1960) contains the following specifications, drawn up by M. A. J. Donzet, then Architecte en chef of the Monuments Historiques in Le Puy:

   "1. Recherches de polychromie ancienne, décapage, etc. . . .
   2. Dépose de ferrures anciennes à réparer ou conserver, conservation de clous anciens.
   3. Ferrures en restauration: 40 plates-bandes bombées de 0.55 et 50/3 avec percements de trous.
   4. Rivets, clous. Pentures à charrière simple. Pentures à charrière double.

   Upon completion of the work, the doors were to be coated "à 2 couches de peinture glycèrophalique."
8. Enaud, *loc. cit.* The matter does not seem to have been conclusively settled in the course of the restorations, for in a letter to the author dated January 13, 1971, M. Enaud declares that "il s'agit d'un bois résineux–un cèdre." On the vegetation of the region, see J. A. M. Arnaud, *Flore du Département de la Haute-Loire*, Le Puy, 1825, and more recently, L. Gachon, *L'Auvergne et le Velay*, Paris, 1948, 9ff., and bibliography, 326. The south door is 4.10 m high and 2.36 m wide (161 3/8 x 92 7/8"). The original parts of the north door measure 2.67 m by 2.33 m (105 1/8 x 91 3/4"). The wood is about 2" thick (520 mm).
9. The subdivision into horizontal fields with the help of large round-headed nails is paralleled on a group of late medieval doors in Toledo, specifically those of the monastery of San Antonio, the Carcel de Santa Hermandad, and the Palace

of Pedro the Cruel (A. F. Calvert, *Toledo. An Historical and Descriptive Account...*, London-New York, 1907, pls. 130, 202, and 402). A representation of what would appear to be the same kind of door occurs much earlier in the Beatus of Gerona (fols. 193v and 215v; J. Marqués Casanovas, C. Dubler and W. Neuss, *Sancti Beati a Liebana in Apocalypsin Codex Gerundensis*, Olten and Lausanne, 1962).

10. These designs resemble the stars in the Adoration of the Magi and the scene of the Magi before Herod. They are also recalled in the starry bosses on imposts of the *Porche du For*.

    A number of Limousin enamel hinges from portable caskets also show nail heads stylized in the form of petaled stars. Examples are listed by C. Enlart, *Les monuments des croisés dans le royaume de Jerusalem. Architecture religieuse et civile*, Paris, 1925-28, I, 180 and 195f.

11. A. de Longpérier, "De l'emploi des caractères arabes dans l'ornementation chez les peuples chrétiens de l'occident," *Revue archéologique*, 1846, 700. The same reading is given by F. Mandet, *Histoire du Velay*, Le Puy, 1862, VI, 104.

12. P. Caillau, *Les gloires de Notre-Dame du Puy*, Paris, 1846, 34-35. F. de Mély, "Nos vieilles cathédrales et leurs maîtres d'oeuvre," *Revue archéologique*, XI, 1920, 306-7, reports the existence of two other artists' signatures on the doors of the chapel of St. Martin, "Gachardus et Guiscardus." This seems to be a confusion based on a report in J. A. M. Arnaud, *Histoire du Velay*, Le Puy, 1816, II, 400, mentioning the inscription "GALBARO GUISCHARDI" on the buttress eventually constructed to contain the downward thrust of the façade.

13. Thiollier, *Architecture religieuse*, 66.

14. See for the location of artists' signatures the excellent lists and commentary provided by E. Lefèvre-Pontalis, "Répertoire des architectes, maçons, sculpteurs, charpentiers et ouvriers français au XIe et XIIe siècles," *Bull. mon.*, 73, 1911, 423-68.

15. The Brioude door knocker, which includes the inscription GERALDVS ME FECIT, is illustrated and described in Dr. Bachelier, "Sur deux inscriptions de l'église Saint-Julien de Brioude," *Almanach de Brioude*, 1952, 72-79. For the Trier handles, dated in the second half of the thirteenth century, see E. Meyer, "Frühgotische Bronzen im Erzbistum Trier," *Kunstgeschichtliche Studien für Hans Kaufmann*, Berlin, 1956, 106-11. They are inscribed with the names Nicolas and Iohannes de Bincio. The name of Master Piacentinus appears on the door knockers of the cathedral of Oristano in Sardinia, along with the date 1228 (W. Biehl, *Toskanische Plastik des frühen und hohen Mittelalters*, Leipzig, 1926, 114, note 106, and pl. 78a and b).

16. Longpérier, *loc. cit.*

17. Fikry, *Art roman du Puy*, 262ff. This prophylactic formula, used to ward off ill-luck and the Evil Eye, might be deemed especially well suited to a doorway.

18. G. Marçais, "Sur l'inscription arabe de la cathédrale du Puy," *Comptes rendus de l'Académie des Inscriptions et Belles-Lettres*, 1938, 153-62, reprinted in the author's *Mélanges d'histoire et d'archéologie de l'Occident musulman*, Algiers, 1957, I, 205-10. I am indebted to Mr. Ed Jajko, Near East Bibliographer of the Sterling Library at Yale University, for assistance on these readings.

19. See on this work P. de Pallol, *Early Medieval Art in Spain*, New York, 1966, 479, Nos. 74-76, with the older bibliography.

20. M. Bloch, "Le problème de l'or au Moyen âge," *Annales d'histoire économique et sociale*, V, 1933, 13f. and 19f. W. Levison, *England and the Continent in the Eighth Century*, Oxford, 1946, 11.

21. D. Gaborit-Chopin, "Les dessins d'Adémar de Chabannes," *Bull. arch.*, 1967, 213ff.

22. A. H. Christie, "The Development of Ornament from Arabic Script," *Burlington Magazine*, June 1922, 287-92, and July 1922, 31-41. S. D. Spittle, "Cufic Lettering and Christian Art," *Achaeological Journal*, 1954-55, 138-52. K. Erdmann, "Arabische Schriftzeichen als Ornamente in der Abendländische Kunst des Mittelalters," *Abh. der Geistes und Sozialwiss. Klasse der Akad. der Wissenschaften*, Mainz, 9, 1953. M. de Vasselot, *Les crosses limousines du XIIIe siècle*, Paris, 1941, 115-27. Longpérier's study of 1846 (see above, note 11) was a pioneering effort in its time.

23. Pseudo-Cufic ornament in Byzantine buildings has been studied by H. Megaw, "The Chronology of some Middle Byzantine Churches," *Annual of the British School at Athens*, XXXII, 1931-32, 104-9, and more recently by A. Grabar, "La décoration architecturale de l'église de la Vierge à Saint-Luc en Phocide et les débuts des influences islamiques sur l'art byzantin de Grèce," *Comptes rendus de l'Académie des Inscriptions et Belles-Lettres*, 1971, 15-37. Romanesque capitals with Pseudo-Cufic ornament are found in Toulouse, Saint-Guilhem-le-Désert, and Moissac (R. Argaud, "Sur les chapiteaux prétendus hispano-mauresques et byzantino-arabes du cloître de Moissac," *Bulletin*

de la Société archéol. du Midi de la France, IV, 1940, 17-24, and the study of Spittle cited in the preceding note).

24. F. Enaud, "Remise en état de la statue de la Vierge à l'enfant d'Orcival," *Les monuments historiques de la France,* 1961, 88. For the Lavoûte crucifix, see Chapter VIII, note 34 below.
25. Saint-Yrieix, Bibl. Mun. 1, fol. 268. On the manuscript, see D. Gaborit-Chopin, *La décoration des manuscrits à Saint-Martial de Limoges et en Limousin,* Paris-Geneva, 1969, 141f. A number of Oriental textiles are found in church treasures of Le Puy and the region. Among these are the Shroud of St. Chaffre and the griffon silk of Monastier Saint-Chaffre (Exh. Catal. *Trésors des églises de France,* Paris, 1965, Nos. 426 and 427); the fragments discovered within the altar of Saint-Michel d'Aiguilhe (F. Enaud, "Découverte d'objets et de reliquaires à Saint-Michel d'Aiguilhe," *Bull. mon.,* 1964, 37-57, and *idem, Monuments historiques de la France,* 1961, 136-40); the Chasuble of Saint-Rambert-sur-Loire, farther north (M.-Th. Picard-Schmitter, "Le chasuble de Saint-Rambert-sur-Loire," *Monuments historiques de la France,* 1966, 63-80. The inventory of the cathedral treasure made in 1444 refers to textiles whose description makes it likely that they were of Eastern origin (Médicis, *Chroniques,* I, 119-20). It may also be pertinent to mention in the present context the textiles inserted within the leaves of the Bible of Theodulph still in the cathedral treasure, and, according to a local tradition, given by Theodulph to the church (P. Hedde, "Notice sur le manuscrit de Théodulphe," *Annales Soc. Puy,* IX, 1839, 191-94. The so-called Horn of St. Hubert, an ivory oliphant formerly in the cathedral treasure and now exhibited in the Musée Crozatier, is presently considered to be of south Italian workmanship (E. Kühnel, "Die sarazenischen Olifanthorner," *Jahrbuch der Berliner Museen,* I, 1959, 44).
26. Although the "Arabic" character of the doors is commonly noted, the most detailed analysis of the Islamic elements of the design is found in Fikry, *Art roman du Puy,* 171ff., to which Marçais, *Sur l'inscription arabe,* has added some further observations.
27. W. Vöge, *Die deutsche Bildwerke und der anderen Cisalpinen Länder,* Berlin, 1910 (Königliche Museen zu Berlin. Beschreibung der Bildwerke der christl. Epochen, IV), No. 34. Th. Demmler, Berlin, Staatl. Museen. *Die Bildwerke des deutschen Museums,* III. *Die Bildwerke aus Holz, Stein und Ton,* Berlin, 1930, No. 2651, 4-5.
28. L. Torres Balbás, "Restos de una techumbre de carpínteria musulmana en la iglesia de San Millán de Segovia," *Al-Andalus,* III, 1935, 424-34, pls. 15-16.
29. E. Romero de Torres, *Catalogo monumental de España. Provincia de Càdiz,* Madrid, 1934, 311, and pl. CXLVII.
30. Marçais, *Sur l'inscription arabe,* 209-10.
31. There is a comprehensive, if superficial treatment in G. A. Küppers-Sonnenberg, "Flechtwerk, Knotenband und Knotendrachen," *Carinthia I,* 158, 1960, 479-601. Much is also to be learned on the origin and diffusion of this type of ornament in the studies of K. Ginhart, "Karolingische und frühromanische Werkstücke in Kärnten," *Carinthia I,* 1954, 205-43, and *idem,* "Die karolingische Flechtwerksteine in Kärnten," *idem,* 1942. 112-67. H. Michaelis, "Neue Studien sur Frage der Enstehung der langobardischen Steinornamentik," *Annalen der deutschen Akademie der Wissenschaften,* Berlin, VI, 1957, 525, and Th. von Bogyay, "Zum Problem der Flechtwerksteine," *Forschungen zur Kunstgeschichte und christlischen Archäologie.* III. *Karolingische und Ottonische Kunst,* Wiesbaden, 1957, 262-76, are more recent discussions. For the material in France, which has been less extensively studied, see R. de Lasteyrie, *L'architecture religieuse en France à l'époque romane,* Paris, 1929, 203ff.; P. Deschamps, "Le décor d'entrelacs carolingien et sa survivance à l'époque romane," *Comptes-rendus de l'Académie des Inscriptions et Belles-Lettres,* 1939, 387-96, and J. Hubert *L'art pré-roman,* Paris, 1938, 163ff.
32. Deschamps, *loc. cit.,* states, as do some other authors, that Carolingian interlace is almost always "à trois brins," instead of one or two in other periods. This seems to me far from certain. For the survival of interlace in Romanesque art, see also the study devoted to this question, as it affects book illumination, by G. Micheli, *L'enluminure du haut moyen âge et les influences irlandaises,* Brussels, 1939, 161ff.
33. Ginhart, *Werkstücke,* 218f., figs. 6 and 7. Additional examples are cited by this author at Zweinitz and St. Paul in Lavanthal. Another reasonably well-dated example is the border of the south transept portal tympanum of Worms cathedral, placed around 1150 (K. Nothnagel, *Staufische Architektur in Gelnhausen und Worms,* Schriften zur Staufischen Geschichte und Kunst, ed. F.

Arens, I), Göppingen, 1971, 73, 105, and pl. 35.

34. M. Durliat, "L'église de Peyrusse-Grande," *Congrès arch.*, CXXVIII, 1928, 43-54, and esp. 49, figs. 4 and 5.
35. For Bessuéjouls, see Deschamps, *Décor d'entrelacs*, 393-94, and G. Gaillard, *Rouergue roman*, Coll. Zodiaque, 1963, 188-92. Deschamps signals another lintel of the same type at Bozouls in Rouergue, thereafter published by B. de Gauléjac, "Linteau à entrelacs de l'église de Bozouls," *Bull. mon.*, 1940, 81-83. Several pilasters with interlace of Romanesque date are found at La Charité-sur-Loire (P. Deschamps, "Dalles carolingiennes incrustées dans le clocher de La Charité-sur-Loire," *Bull. mon.*, 79, 1920, 230). The Saint-Marcel d'Ardèche fragments (Mon. Hist. Photo 192.832), preserved in the local city hall, seem to be unpublished.
36. R. Gounot, *Collections lapidaires*, 124ff., Nos. BA 1 to 10. The fragments are here dated in the tenth century. The discovery was reported by Aymard in *Annales Soc. Puy.*, XXVIII, 1866-67, 613.
37. Deschamps, *Décor d'entrelacs*, 393f., notes the persistence of interlace ornament on the sculpture of capitals and gives a list of older fragments found in the region, which were earlier tabulated by Lasteyrie, *Architecture religieuse*, 195 and 204. An unpublished fragment is found in the crypt of Saint-Julien de Brioude. Another, from Saint-Allyre, is exhibited in the Museum of Clermont-Ferrand (L. Bréhier, *Nouvelles archives des missions littéraires et scientifiques*, XX, 1913, 64), and some fragments are to be seen in the crypt of Royat (Mon. Hist. Photo 35.190). Some of the material from neighboring Burgundy is published by L. Lex, "Sculptures décoratives carolingiennes de la vallée de la Basse Saône," *Bull. arch.*, 1924, 101-8.
38. We may refer to the recent study of Götz, *Bildprogramme*, 55ff., where these monuments are described and the up to date bibliography given.
39. These remarks parallel on a certain number of points the observations on Romanesque polychromy made by J. Taubert, "Studien zur Fassung romanischer Skulpturen," *Kunst des Mittelalters in Sachsen. Festschrift Wolf Schubert*, Weimar, 1967, 247-64.
40. There is as yet no single work devoted to wood carving of the Romanesque period. Typical examples of this material are found in H. Kohlhaussen, *Geschichte des deutschen Kunsthandwerks*, Munich, 1955, 60ff.; H. Kreisel, *Die Kunst des deutschen Möbels*, Munich, 1968, I, 7ff.; E. Mercer, *Furniture, 700-1700* (The Social History of Decorative Arts), London, 1969, 17ff.; J. Viaux, *Le meuble en France*, Paris, 1962, 45ff.; A. Feulner, *Kunstgeschichte des Möbels*, Berlin, 1927, 9ff.
41. P. Toesca, *Il Medioevo*, Turin, 1927, I, 1100, 1102. The casket is said to stem from the cathedral of Terracina.
42. It was Bertaux, who in his monumental *L'art dans l'Italie méridionale*, Paris, 1904, 555-57, first called attention—mistakenly, I believe—to the analogy of the Carsoli doors and those of Alba Fucense with the Puy valves, from a technical standpoint. This connection is also accepted by Fikry, *Art roman du Puy*, 178, who otherwise gives an excellent characterization of the respective qualities of these techniques (p. 176). Bertaux's photographs, especially of the Carsoli doors, are not of sufficient quality to decide the issue in a decisive way, but examination of the excellent plates in M. Moretti, *Museo nazionale d'Abruzzo nel castello cinquecentesco dell'Aquila*, L'Aquila, 1968, 3 leaves no doubt that the carving was of a rounded, modeled type, unlike that in Le Puy. For the Carsoli and Alba Fucense doors, see the entries in Götz, *Bildprogramme*, 71-78 and 275-80.
43. A. de Wolff, "The Romanesque Hutches of Valère and Sion in the Valais," *The Connoisseur*, January 1965, 39-42. For a Spanish example, see the choir stall from S. Clemente in Tahull in Barcelona (M. Olivar, *Museo d'arte di Catalogna, Barcellona*, Novara, 1963, 29.
44. On this technique, see A. Riegl, *Spätrömische Kunstindustrie*, Vienna, 1927, 314ff., and W. Holmqvist, *Kunstprobleme der Merowingerzeit*, Stockholm, 1939 (Kungl. Vitterhets Historie och Antikvitets Akademiens Handlingar, 47), 110ff.
45. Examples are found in A. Aymar and G. Charvilhat, "L'art rustique auvergnat," *Revue d'Auvergne*, XXX, 1913, 217-23, and L. Gachon, *L'Auvergne et le Velay*, Paris, 1948, 231ff.
46. G. H. Neckheim, "Flachschnittarbeiten in Kärnten. Ein Beitrag zur Volkskunst in Kärnten," *Carinthia I*, 143, 1953, 476-87. According to this author, this sixteenth-century low relief carving exhibits a "volkstumlichen Kunstempfindens" with possible reminiscences of Scandinavian and Longobard work. For other carving of the same kind of Renaissance date, see F. Watson, "The Swaffham Bulbeck Chest," *The Collector*, X, 1930, 152-57.
47. R. Hamann. "Der Schrein des heiligen Aegidius," *Marburger Jahrbuch für Kunstwissenschaft*, VI,

1931, 117-18. P.-M. Auzas, "Le trésor de la cathédrale Saint-Maurice d'Angers," *Congrès arch.*, 122, 1964, 39-42.

48. M. Chassinat, "Fouilles à Baouît," *Mémoires publiés par les membres de l'Institut français d'archéologie orientale du Caire,* XIII, 1911, pl. XI. H. Thorp, "The Carved Decorations of the North and South Church at Bawit," *Kolloquium über spätantike und frühmittelalterliche Skulptur,* II, Heidelberg, 1970 (Mainz, s.d.) 38. The relief in the Brooklyn Museum (No. 30.29), of unknown provenance, is assigned a date in the eleventh century, on grounds that are not wholly clear (Exh. Catal. *Early Christian and Byzantine Art,* Baltimore, Walters Art Gallery, 1947, No. 86).
49. Fikry, *Art roman du Puy,* 178-79. The Martorana doors, datable with the church in 1134, had earlier been compared with the Puy valves by L. Bréhier, "Nouvelles recherches sur l'histoire de la sculpture byzantine," *Nouvelles archives des missions scientifiques et littéraires,* N.S. XX, 1913, fasc. 9, 43. The merit of this comparison would seem to me arguable.
50. F. Hernández, "Arte musulmán. La techumbre de la Gran Mezquita de Córdoba," *Archivo español de arte,* IV, 1928, 191-225. G. Marçais, *L'architecture musulmane d'Occident,* Paris, 1954, 148-49.
51. L. Torres Balbás, *Al-Andalus,* 1935, 424-34. See also the same author's "Los modillones de lóbulos," *Archivo español de arte y archeologia,* XII, 1936, 1ff., and esp. 59. The monument is generally placed in the first half of the twelfth century. See also on the work I. de Ceballos-Escalera, *Segovia monumental,* Madrid, 1953, 56-60, and M. de Lozoya, "Influencias aragonesas en el Arte Segoviano," *Seminario de Arte Aragonés,* V, 1953, 7-11.
52. L. Torres Balbás, "Hallazgos en la Alcazaba de Málaga," *Al-Andalus,* II, 1934, 344-57. The Alcazaba is said to have been constructed in the middle of the eleventh century. The sculpture which concerns us was part of the ceiling in a room of unspecified function, near the Cuartos de Fromada. It was described by an eighteenth-century chronicler, Medina Conde, as "el adorno que ha quedrado de varios letreros árabes y maderas hermosamente labradas a lo morisco" (cited by Torres Balbás, 350).
53. Romero de Torres, *Provincia de Cádiz,* 311.
54. G. Paul, "Variétés héraldiques sur Brioude," *Almanach de Brioude,* 1961, 13-31, esp. 27-30. Two other late medieval wooden ceilings of the same type, at Lannsdorf and St. Martin near Hochosterwitz in Austria, are published by S. Hartwanger, "Gedanken zum Thema: Volkskunde und Bildende Kunst in Kärnten," *Carinthia I,* 100, 1951, 555.
55. L. Bégule, *Les incrustations décoratives des cathédrales de Lyon et de Vienne,* Lyon, 1905. For the Saint-Guilhem altar, see J. Vallery-Radot, "Les dates des autels de la Major de Marseille et de Saint-Guilhem-le-Désert," *Gazette des Beaux-Arts,* XX, 1938, 73-80, who proposes for the work a date in the second half of the twelfth century, in opposition to older opinion tending to connect it with a translation of the relics of St. Guilhem in 1138 (R. Hamann-McLean, "Das Lazarusgrab in Autun," *Marburger Jahrbuch für Kunstwissenschaft,* VIII-IX, 1936, 105). One of Vallery-Radot's supporting arguments for a late date is a comparison with the tomb in Autun which he places, along with earlier authors, between 1170 and 1189. However, an earlier date, in the 1130s, is now advanced for the tomb (P. Quarré, "Les sculptures du tombeau de Saint-Lazare à Autun," *Cahiers de civilisation médiévale,* V, 1962, 169-74.
56. L. Bréhier, "Les influences musulmanes dans l'art roman du Puy," *Journal des Savants,* 1936, 1-14, a review of Fikry's work. The idea that the recessed areas were once filled with paste was perhaps a natural extension of the characterization of the carving of the doors as *sculpture champlevée,* an expression used by both Fikry and Bréhier.
57. R. Hamann, *Der Schrein des heiligen Aegidius,* 122ff. H. Deckert, "Opus interrasile als vorromanische Technik," *Marburger Jahrbuch für Kunstwissenschaft,* VI, 1931, 137-52.
58. On this and related pieces, see W. Wixom, *Treasures from Medieval France,* Cleveland, 1957, 129ff., Nos. IV, 4-8.

III Description and Iconography of the Scenes

THE DESCRIPTION and comments on the iconography of the subjects represented on the Puy doors which follow proceed in the order of the narrative for each of the two cycles. The *tituli* were first partially transcribed by Mandet[1] and later recorded by Thiollier as fully as their state would allow.[2] I have, with few exceptions, adhered to the latter scholar's generally excellent readings. A restitution of the two lines below the last tier of scenes on the Passion doors does not seem possible in view of the few isolated and disconnected letters which remain.

INFANCY DOORS

1. *Annunciation to the Shepherds* (Fig. 7, bottom left)

PASTORES VOBIS ANNUN/CIO GAUDIA GENTIS [3]

Only the upper part of the composition is preserved. The left half is occupied by a haloed angel leaning slightly forward and gesturing with an extended right hand.

The pastoral topography is defined by plants rising behind the figure along the left edge of the scene. An orblike form inscribed within the segment of an arc is seen in the upper left corner. This form was not designed to represent the eastern star, which, elsewhere in the work, is given an eight-pointed configuration, but the luminous glory of the Lord which shone about (Luc. 2,9). A light-radiating quarter circle appears in the upper corner of the scene in the Echternach Codex Aureus, from which the angels make their descent,[4] and in the version of the scene of the painted ceiling at Zillis.[5] The angel's wing touches the outline of the heavenly light, drawing attention to the celestial origin of his mission. The scale and position of the figure suggests that it was the only occupant of the space.

On the right side of the composition, the heads and torsos of two shepherds can be distinguished, both identically pointing upward with one arm upraised. The scale of the figures indicated that they must have been standing on elevated terrain. The traditional iconography would require some representation of their flock, which must have been seen along the bottom of the scene. Possibly, a third shepherd on the left side of the space completed the design.

In ivory and in stone sculpture, the Annunciation to the Shepherds was generally cast in the form of a meeting between figures of equal size, the angel approaching a group of shepherds accompanied by several members of their flock. The full landscape setting preferred here is a formula much more widely traveled in painting. A second major variant in the treatment of the scene lies in the characterization of the angel who is shown either in the act of earthward flight, or, as in our composition, making his way forward on land to meet the shepherds.[6] The towering scale of the angel in relation to them is an occasional element in the pictorial tradition, strikingly exemplified in the scene of the Reichenau Pericopes of Henry II,[7] and afterward, in a late twelfth-century English Psalter in the Bodleian Library (Gough Lit. 2).[8]

2. *Adoration of the Magi* (Fig. 7, bottom right).

MISTICA JAM NATO DANT/PERSE MUNERA CHRISTO

The Virgin and Child are seated within a round-arched structure on the right section of the composition. One of the Magi, crowned and in a kneeling position, is seen in profile tendering his offering at the left. The contour of the Child is lost, save for the outline of the forearms (?) visible along the left side of the Virgin's silhouette. The otherwise full and roughly symmetrical configuration of the seated group indicates that the Virgin was shown in a frontal stance while the infant Christ was partly turned to face the prostrate king. A large star of Bethlehem dominates the scene. Virtually nothing is left of the other half of the composition on the inner (left) valve, which must have housed the other two Magi. A small section of an arch still visible at the top of the scene and more fully preserved in the nineteenth-century lithograph of Tudol shows that these two figures were incorporated within an architectural enclosure mirroring that on the right.

The representation of the Adoration within an architectural setting is based on the commentaries of Eusebius and Epiphanius of Cyprus as diffused in the West in the Apocryphal Gospels of the Pseudo-Matthew. These authors claim that the Magi made their visit, not to the grotto of the Nativity, but to the house of the Holy Family, when the Christ Child was two years old. Depictions of the Adoration in an architectural setting seem first to occur on sarcophagi of the City Gate type.[9] When the architecture was used as a frame for the entire scene and the view out-of-doors entirely eliminated, it became necessary to accommodate the star within the building itself. This was accomplished in German book illumination of the eleventh century and in works on its periphery.[10] The motif of the double arch by which the two figural groups are allocated equal spaces but ceremonially set apart also received its decisive formulation in this ambient.[11] The central support delimits a privileged sanctuary space within the structure which the Magi may either observe at a respectful distance or gingerly seek to penetrate in single file. In a number of monuments, the first king is thus shown in the course of his forward progress, halfway beyond the column. The Puy composition with a single king prostrate before the Virgin and Child while his companions wait in the neighboring intercolumniation is nearly identical to the corresponding scenes on the lintel over the central doorway of the cathedral of Ferrara [12] and the roughly contemporaneous painted ceiling at Zillis.[13] The clear differentiation in the poses of the kings seems to have been introduced in the Romanesque iconography of the Adoration, becoming very generalized by the end of the twelfth century. In the earlier decades of the same hundred years, the older formula which gave the kings equal treatment still vied with the newer type on a vigorous basis. However, the version of the scene with the first king kneeling in Adoration while the others stand behind, in some instances pointing to a star, is represented in north Italian sculpture at Ferrara and the cathedral of Piacenza,[14] and seems to be the typical form known to Romanesque sculpture in Provence and Burgundy in the second quarter of the twelfth century, appearing on a capital at Autun, the south portal at Avallon, the priory portal of Anzy-le-Duc, and the stylistically related tympanum of Neuilly-en-Donjon.[15] It is well known that in his classic *L'art religieux du XIIe siècle en France,* E. Mâle sought to account for this shift in the representation of the Adoration on the basis of the influence of liturgical drama. Although this view has not found universal acceptance, the factual observation which motivated it remains valid.[16]

The *mystica munera,* as the titulus describes the gifts of the Magi, probably alludes to the exegetical tradition, echoed also in the *Officium Stellae,* that each of the offerings recognized another aspect of Christ's mission: gold stood for kingship, frankincense for priesthood, and myrrh for sacrifice and death. The Rouen play pointedly enough speaks of the three gifts as having "in se divine mysteria." [17]

3. *The Magi Journeying to Herod's Court* (Figs. 7, 17, and 19).

PANDE SYON PUERUM CUJUS/JAM VIDIMUS ASTRUM

According to Matthew's Gospel (2, 1-7), the Magi were received by Herod on their way to Bethlehem and requested by him to make inquiries about the newborn Child. Following the Adoration, however, they were warned in a dream not to return to Herod's court (2,12), and they therefore took another road back to their homeland. Our scene can only refer to the first of these two journeys, as is indicated also by the accompanying *titulus.* It is thus evident that it is not in the right place in the sequence of events. The explanation for this was likely of a practical order: the scene, as conceived by the Puy sculptor, required more space than was afforded by the customary panel subdivided into equal halves, and thus could not be made the pendent of another subject on the corresponding zone of the opposite valve. The alternative open to him would have been to locate the journey in the tier below the Annunciation to the Shepherds and the Nativity, which, in regard to the unfolding of the narrative, would have involved even greater inconsistencies.

The three crowned horsemen are shown pointing to the star with an upraised arm as they make their way forward. The torso is turned in three-quarter view and, as indicated by the underdrawing of the first horseman still visible, the second hand was bent down and grasped the bridle of the horse. The first and third Magi are identical in size and virtually identical in contour. They must have been traced or outlined with the help of the same design. The second of the Magi is somewhat smaller; his arm is straight instead of half-bent, and there are also differences in the characterization of the horse. All of the riders were positioned in their respective spaces by anchoring the hind quarters of their mounts to the vertical border at the left of the scene at a point roughly midway between top and bottom. They give the appearance of riding at some distance from the stylized vegetation which defines the foreground.

Traces of the polychromy remaining indicate that the terrain rose to a horizon line drawn immediately beneath the foliage ornament, which fills the upper corners, leaving the torsos of the riders and heads of their horses silhouetted against the sky. Each of the spaces is provided with its own distinctive landscape setting, composed of various kinds of vegetation. The species of foliage are differentiated not so much through contrasts in the shape of stems and leaves, which are minimized, as by the variations brought to the underlying structure of the plant. In the thick carpet of vegetation which lines the base of the first two panels, the foliage is wedded to a grid of intersecting arches and so given a half-ornamental, half-botanical identity. It reposes on the lower frame of the scene like the crowning finial of a rooftop or the gable of a shrine, but it is not organically rooted in it. The neatly ordered and overlapping forms which compose this groundline are most likely a transposition of the characteristic hillocked grounds seen in twelfth-century miniatures, as, for example, in a number of the illustrations in the Albani Psalter. Although these are often barren of vegetation, they may be combined with foliage or show swirls with leafy contours. Rampant vegetation of a more organic type sprouts from this soil below the hooves of the second horseman. The softly meandering tendril with its opulent growth of tri- and quadrilobed leaves is graced by an elongated and double-pronged flower of which other specimens are seen disposed in radiating fashion in the half-circle along the right edge of the panel with the first king. The upper left corner in this panel and the lower right corner in the third are furnished with foliage of the same ostensibly active kind, firmly rooted for good measure in diminutive earth mounds. The pair of ornamental insets lying back to back in the tangent upper corners of the first and second panels offer, by contrast, vegetation of an entirely inert variety, consisting of an open palmette inscribed in a heart-shaped outline and resembling the stylized grounds of *fond vermiculé* enamels. The sculptor uses such insets for a variety of representational ends. This is the only instance, however, of the appearance on the doors of a pictorial entity without a specific denotational reference.

The oldest known representations of the Magi on the journey to Bethlehem are found in the art of the ninth century.[18] The kings are generally seen in a geographically indeterminate setting, or, in certain instances, entering a gate or portico. They may be individually differentiated and shown in animated discourse or, on the contrary, present themselves in nearly identical poses and self-contained detachment. It is the second conception of the event which prevails in Le Puy, and further, in Bonanno's doors at Pisa,[19] a capital from the valley of the Rhône in Hartford [20] and the panel embedded in the façade of Borgo San Donnino.[21] The unusual feature in the scene of our doors is the considerable place given to the view of landscape. This feature is paralleled in the depiction of the traveling Magi on a capital from St. Etienne in Toulouse (Fig. 16) [22] and a second, very similar capital from Lombez (Gers) in the Victoria and Albert Museum, where the kings are shown traversing terrain overgrown with abundant foliage.[23] Vegetation of a more stylized form is present in another version of the scene on a capital from the chapter house of St. Caprais at Agen.[24] Once again, the ceiling at Zillis comes very close to the interpretation of the subject in Le Puy within the sphere of painting.[25]

The *titulus,* in the form of a direct address by the Magi to a personified (?) Sion, does not describe the scene very accurately. It would seem to be the reflection of dialogue in a liturgical play, like the *Ordo ad representandum Herodem,* from Saint-Benoît-sur-Loire, where the Magi address a similar question to a chorus of inhabitants of Jerusalem: "Dicite vobis, O Ierosolmitani vives, ubi est expectacio gentium; ubi est qui natus est rex Iudeorum, quam signis celestibus agnitum venimus adorare." [26]

4. *The Magi before Herod* (Fig. 19)

ECCE VIDENS ARABES SE/VUS TURBATUR ERODES

The Magi on their journey and their appearance at Herod's court are customarily treated as two separate incidents. They are here conflated into a single event. Herod is seated on a high throne in an interior defined by a tri-lobed arch supported by columns resting on high bases. The ruler is half-turned and gestures to the stellar apparition. An attendant at the right appears to recoil in wonder. The scene in an unabridged state would have been completed by a group of the Magi standing before Herod and in discourse with him. There is a similar, though slightly less drastic, conflation in the lintel of the portal of Sant'Andrea in Pistoia (1166), carved by Master Gruamon and his brother Adeodatus, where a single kneeling king is introduced between Herod and the riding Magi.[27] Herod's pose and gesture closely resembles the figure of the monarch at Zillis, who is flanked by an attendant armed with a sword.[28] Did the corresponding figure in Le Puy once carry the same attribute, as might be suspected on the basis of the pose?

The tri-lobed architecture was possibly intended to suggest a royal audience hall having the form of a triple conch. It was, in other respects, designed to set the scene apart both from those involving sacred personages (Adoration of the Magi, Presentation in the Temple, Last Supper) which are placed within round arched or domical spaces, and the timbered hall with gabled roof where, at the other end of the value scale, the Massacre of the Innocents takes place. In Carolingian art, the Adoration of the Magi and the Appearance of the Magi before Herod are sometimes brought side by side in a deliberate parallelism, but both scenes are placed within similar conventional palatial settings, which seem to have been calculated to level the distinctions between the two events rather than to dramatize them.[29] The use of architecture, as in Le Puy, to qualify the nature of the subject or heighten and lessen its symbolic import seems first to have been carried out with a certain consistency in the Gospel narrative cycles of Ottonian art. The Echternach Codex Aureus offers some examples of this process throughout the Infancy narrative sequence, where the scene of the Magi appearing before Herod is in fact also set within a tri-lobed arcaded space.[30] Parallel to and perhaps even prior to the use of this form in a descriptive context, it is occasionally found as a framing device for an entire page, as for example, in several pages of the Missal of Robert of Jumièges.[31]

5. *Massacre of the Innocents* (Figs. 7 and 18)

MACTAT AB UBERIBUS/RAPTOS SINE LEGE TIRAN(US)

The slaughter of the Innocents is illustrated in two adjoining compositions, both set within a gabled structure. In the first scene, Herod is showing giving his command. The ruler is seen in profile and seated on a cushioned throne whose lower parts, not fully legible as rendered in low relief, must have been supplemented with details added by the painter. A helmeted attendant stands behind. On the right side of the composition, a figure wielding a sword and grasping a child at the wrist receives Herod's command. The second scene is no more than a modification of the first. It is dominated by a figure brandishing a sword and menacing a child whose arm he has similarly seized at the wrist. A second victim, already beheaded, lies on the ground. The disposition of the figures is once again very similar to the Massacre of the Zillis ceiling.[32]

The articulation of the subject into two distinct episodes–first Herod issuing his command and second, the killing of the Innocents–is found as early as the Rabbula Gospels of 583 and constitutes one of the major references of the Puy composition to the pictorial tradition of the Massacre.[33] The physical setting sometimes accentuates the division: Herod may be shown in his palace as his edict is rendered, while the killing itself takes place outside. But there are instances beginning with the representation on the ninth-century ivory book cover of a Metz Gospel Book in Paris

(Bibl. Nat. lat. 9393) in which Herod himself presides over the Massacre as both episodes are fused into a unified composition set before an architectural prospect.[34] The Puy version adopts an indoor setting, yet without abandoning the principle of separate incidents. The fact that the scene had to be divided in the middle clearly inhibited the design of a single and coherent interior; nowhere else on the doors does the sculptor permit an architectural member to straddle this division. The mode of the killing is also a distinctive element of various traditions. In the earlier history of the theme, the flinging about or piercing of the infants injects in it a strong note of rhetoric-ladened pathos.[35] The Puy composition, at once more dispassionate and callous, seems to have been modeled on a scene of martyrdom in which a saint first defiantly confronts authority and is then led to execution. The turbulence of combat has thus been replaced by the cold power of the judicial act. This aspect of the depiction is also made explicit in the *titulus,* which refers to Herod as "sine lege," a complaint in all probability justified but not lodged against him by the Gospels nor by general sentiment.

Of the pair of open-gabled structures in which the action takes place, that where Herod is seen issuing his decree is the more elaborate. The summit of the gable is filled by a two-pronged and multilobed ornament enclosed within the segment of an arc, a motif also employed in the scene of the Three Women at the Tomb. In the upper corners, a pair of turrets are seen on each side, the outermost with a large window, the inner unfenestrated and with a conical roof. The capitals sustaining the roof have more ample profiles than those in the corresponding position in the right half of the composition and one further distinguished through the presence of impost blocks. Open gabled structures are not depicted with great frequency in early medieval art. The frontispiece of Odbert's Psalter of Saint-Bertin offers an example.[36] Another is found toward the end of the eleventh century among the illustrations of the Salzburg Lectionary in the Morgan Library.[37]

6. *Presentation in the Temple* (Figs. 7 and 20)

ECCE SENEX GESTAT PUE/RUM QUEM PRONUS ADORAT

The composition is situated within an arcaded interior. On the right, the haloed Virgin presents the Child, whose arms are extended forward and half-raised, to Simeon. The latter prepares to receive Him with veiled hands. An altar appears between the two standing figures. In the left panel, a female figure is seen approaching with the two sacrificial birds. She is flanked by two large plants growing out of bulb-like appendages. The scene of the Presentation is traditionally set in the interior of a sanctuary, within a free-standing ciborium or in proximity of a temple structure. The interior may be so arranged as to separate by means of a column the secondary figure from the group of the Virgin and Simeon, as earlier, in the scene of the Autun Troper.[38] The double arch performs just this function in our scene, but while it localizes the event entirely indoors, the inclusion of landscape elements suggests rather that the handmaiden carrying the birds is to be seen as outside the building into which the Virgin and Child have already entered, or that this was the case in the sources available to the sculptor. The form given to the two plants seems in a curious and unaccountable way the echo of the corresponding motif in the Visitation scene of the Ratchis altar at Cividale.[39]

The grouping of the principal personages around an altar, which forms the heart of the composition, can be traced back to the early ninth-century reliquary cross of the Sancta Sanctorum.[40] Simeon is in the vast majority of representations shown with a halo. The nimbus is omitted, as in Le Puy, where the titulus refers to him only with the biblical qualification of *senex,* most notably in the Presentations of the two Ottonian cycles in the Evangelistaries of Nuremberg and the Escorial.[41] The sacrificial birds, though often carried by St. Joseph, are sometimes entrusted to a handmaiden. D. C. Schorr has suggested that his exclusion in favor of an anonymous servant girl was intended to bring out the relation of the subject to the feast day of the Purification of the Virgin.[42]

PASSION DOORS

7. *Resurrection of Lazarus* (Figs. 9 and 21)

(LA)ZAR(US) EN JUSSU DO/(MINI DE MOR) TE RESURGIT

The major outlines of the scene of the right side are still visible. The composition of the panel on the left, however, is entirely obliterated. In the foreground of the surviving composition, Lazarus is seen rising from his tomb at Christ's command. The figure is in a seated position within the tomb, with arms upraised. The rim of the tomb is tilted up and its left edge drawn in a foreshortened slant. The vertical sides are not clearly delineated in relief but apparently masked by a broad horizontal band which spans the foreground. The band perhaps showed an arcade, as on the coffin in the scene of the Three Maries at the Tomb. The silhouettes of three haloed figures appear on the left side of the composition. Their feet–three can be distinguished–rest on the same level as the rim of the tomb, suggesting that the latter was to be seen as sunken in the ground. Christ, the first in the group, is somewhat detached from the rest. His hand was extended downward to the awakening Lazarus. The right side of the composition shows a group of onlookers standing in front of an architectural prospect defined by two conical turrets in the upper right corner. A puzzling detail of the scene is the irregular trapezoidal form seen near the center, in the void between the two groups of figures. This detail is probably to be understood as the lid of the tomb, which one of the bystanders, possibly assisted by Christ, was in the process of removing from the tomb. On a capital from the church of the Magdalen at Vézelay, Christ with a forceful gesture pushes the lid up single-handedly.[43] At Saint-Benoît-sur-Loire, the task is performed by two attendants.[44]

Since the composition includes all of the required participants, what was the subject of the lost scene in the left half of the panel? The fragmentary *titulus* does not allude to a second theme. The most likely supposition is that the Resurrection of Lazarus was preceded by a scene showing Martha and Mary, the sisters of the deceased, imploring Christ to come to their aid. This incident forms part of the Lazarus representation in the early Christian cycles of the Rossano Gospels [45] and the Gospels of St. Augustine in Cambridge.[46] Later, it is included on the column of Bernward at Hildesheim,[47] on the Chichester reliefs,[48] and in the bronze doors of the Cathedral of Pisa.[49] The missing composition likely showed the two sisters kneeling before Christ, near a schematized architecture marking the site of Bethany.

8. *Entry into Jerusalem* (Figs. 9 and 22)

TURBA IACIT VESTES CUM FLO/(RIBUS) . . . [50]

Much of the left half of the composition is preserved, at least in part. In the upper right sector, Christ is represented riding on a donkey, with an arm extended in blessing. Behind Him is seen the outline, no longer fully distinct, of three haloed disciples. A small tree grows along the right edge of the scene, but the expected figure of Zacchaeus has been omitted. A second animal appears in the right foreground. According to the account of the event given in the Gospel of Matthew, Christ instructed two disciples to fetch an ass and a colt from a nearby village for His entry into the Holy City. Mark speaks of a colt only, and John only of the ass. Luke's version is that Christ instructed the disciples to bring the two beasts, but they seem to have returned only with the first. Our composition thus follows Matthew most closely in showing the second animal participating in the procession. The right section of the composition, of which a few meager traces can still be made out, must have exhibited the group of men greeting Christ at the gates of the city with palm branches and garments cast upon the ground.

The inclusion of the second beast in early medieval scenes of the Entry is not uncommon. The oldest examples are those found on early Christian sarcophagi. The young animal is generally seen ambling beside its parent and protectively nestled in its train. In the Pericopes of Henry II, it is shown in the act of suckling,[51] and in the version of the scene in the tympanum of Pompierre (Doubs), following in processional fashion with the disciples.[52] The representation of the Entry formerly seen in the south tribune of Le Puy cathedral depicted the colt nibbling at the garment thrown onto the ground by one of the men at the gate of the city.[53] The depiction of the subject in the Avila Bible[54] and on a painted altar from Sagars in the Solsona Episcopal Museum is closer to the scene of the doors in showing the animal in a similarly playful bucolic manner, straining to lead the way in the immediate foreground as the procession moves apace above it, seemingly upon higher ground.[55] The frieze of the façade at Saint-Gilles gives an unusually full account of this episode, showing the fetching of the two beasts as well as the participation of the second animal in the procession.[56] Further in the same region, the colt is included in the Entry of the lintel above the doorway at Thines,[57] on a capital of the cloister at Arles,[58] and to the north, on a capital at Saint-Maurice in Vienne.[59]

9. *Last Supper* (Figs. 9 and 26)

IMMITIS MITEM SUMIT MALE/PRODITOR (. . . .)

The surviving left section of the design focuses on the subject in a highly concentrated fashion. The scene is set within an arcaded interior. Christ is seated in the middle of a rectangular table, with St. John pressed against His side. A haloed disciple appears on each side of the central group. The feet of the figures repose on an arcaded platform found also in other versions of the Last Supper, as in the scene in Hartker's *Liber responsalis* in St. Gall,[60] and later, in Nicholas of Verdun's Klosterneuburg altar.[61] Judas, seated near the right end and on the opposite side of the table, extends his hand toward the dish, whose delineation must have been entrusted to the painter. The Last Supper with Judas on the viewer's side of the table occurs in the Burgundian lintels of Bellenaves, Nantua and Saint-Julien-de-Jonzy, and also at

Thines in Provence. For Hamann, Judas's relegation to this position denotes his loss of moral standing (*Entwürdigung)* within the community of the apostles.[62]

Since the kernel of the action is complete, the subject of the missing scene cannot be determined with absolute certainty. The lost panel perhaps only completed the existing composition with a group of additional apostles at a table and under a round arch repeating the substance of the design on the right side. The Last Supper in the painted ceiling at Zillis takes precisely this form.[63] The Pentecost scene in the Puy doors presents itself in two parts as well, an iconographically pregnant central core being set apart from the secondary participants in the action. However this may be, the concentration on the principals of the event in the remaining half of the composition should qualify the Last Supper of the Puy doors, along with the painting at Zillis as among the incunabula of the much-discussed iconic groups of St. John comforted on the bosom of Christ.[64]

Although there is no allusion to any other subject in the *titulus,* it is possible, on the other hand, that the existing depiction was completed by a subsequent incident of the Passion narrative such as the Washing of the Feet, Christ instituting the Communion, or the Agony in the Garden. The Washing of the Feet is quite frequently paired with the Last Supper in monuments within a reasonable geographic orbit of Le Puy. The two subjects appear side by side in the Romanesque lintels of Vandeins, Bellenaves, Saint-Julien-de-Jonzy, and Saint-Pons-de-Thomières, as well as in the frieze at Beaucaire.[65]

10. *Arrest of Christ* (Figs. 9 and 23)

DECIDIT HIC MALCUS A FER/RO VINDICE PETRI

The *titulus* places the emphasis not on the betrayal but on Peter's vengeful gesture. The composition in the right panel illustrates this act. In the right foreground, the haloed Peter crouches over the stumbling Malchus, whom he has seized from the rear. Left of center and on higher ground, Christ is embraced by Judas. A second pair (?) of figures, possibly helmeted, are crowded into the left corner of the scene. A group of armed men, advancing in pairs, is seen in the upper right corner. One figure carries a long-handled ax; the others wield torches, which, for lack of space, have had to be bent forward. The hilly contour of the terrain, outlined by the placement of the figures on the left side of the composition, probably serves as an indication of the Mount of Olives, which is occasionally incorporated in depictions of the Arrest.

11. *Christ before the High Priest* (?) (Fig. 23, left)

The upper part of the composition, all that remains visible on the narrower panel to the left of the Arrest, shows a double arch, each housing a single figure. That on the left is haloed, and perhaps the other as well, though the outline of the head might suggest instead some type of headdress. The stance of the figures and their relation to each other is otherwise unclear. The iconographic tradition offers several possibilities for the identification of the subject. Judas denouncing Christ to the High Priest, or after the Betrayal, returning the thirty pieces of silver, deserve some consideration. The first theme is sometimes combined with the Arrest, as in the fresco cycle of Sant'Angelo in Formis.[66] This episode is also treated in a very detailed way in the frieze of Saint-Gilles.[67] But the presence of at least one haloed personage would rule out this pair of participants. The Denial of Peter based on a possible identification of the figure under the right arch as the maid would also make a defensible case and be consistent as well with the emphasis laid on Peter in the Betrayal *titulus.* The Denial is generally set in proximity of a house or arcaded structure, and this scene is, too, occasionally combined with the Arrest. However, the absence of the rooster, which is in most cases a prominent part of the scene, makes such an identification hazardous. Still another and probably the most likely alternative would be the appearance of Christ before the High Priest.

12. *Carrying of the Cross* (Figs. 9 and 24, bottom left)

VITA CRUCIS LIGNO PATI/TUR DISCRIMINA MORTIS

Christ bearing the cross is prodded by a figure behind Him, laying a hand on His shoulder or possibly abusing Him with a switch. Three soldiers follow behind. The first wields a long-handled ax, held with both hands in front of the body. The second carries a lance, and the third, partly masked by the left edge of the composition, a hook-like weapon. The march to Calvary proceeds upward over gently sloping terrain charted only by the disposition of the moving figures. A kind of platform, possibly intended to suggest the presence of a stairway, fills the foreground at the lower right. Its vertical edge seems originally to have extended downward to the border of the panel, but was unaccountably pared off, terminating in mid-air.

13. *Crucifixion* (Fig. 24, bottom right)

The cross is planted on a small mound of earth. Its bottom widens out to form a platform upon which Christ's feet repose. The disks of the sun and the moon appear above the arms. The Virgin Mary stands on the left side, partly facing the cross, hands clasped and raised within her garment to the head in a gesture of grief. St. John stands at the right. His right arm seems to have been half-raised in front of the body, either in a gesture of acknowledgment or to cup his cheek in the hand. The figure of Christ was in a nearly frontal stance, its slight torsion fully contained within the body of the cross, and the haloed head situated at the intersection of the arms. The Cathedral once possessed a Byzantine ivory of the Crucifixion of the end of the tenth century now in a Swiss Private Collection, in which the three participants are displayed in a comparable manner.[68]

14. *The Three Maries at the Tomb* (Figs. 9 and 25, bottom)

ANGELUS ALLOQUITUR VENI/ENTES UNGERE IESUM

The composition extends over both of the adjoining halves of the panel. On the left side, the angel is seated on the lid of the open tomb. The rim of the coffin is tilted upward, revealing the shroud of the risen Christ. The exposed longer side of the monument shows a running arcaded design. Behind it and against the left border of the panel stands the domical structure of the Holy Sepulcher. Its conical roof is outlined by a broad cornice and five openings are inscribed on the visible side, two small squarish windows near the top, a larger rectangular opening at the center, and a pair of small roughly square windows near ground level. Representations of the Holy Sepulcher in scenes of the Entombment and Resurrection often show as the entrance of the structure a similarly large rectangular portal.[69] A larger arched opening, supported on columns, which adjoins the right side of the structure, is to be construed as the entrance of the grotto of the Sepulcher, which could be seen within. The angel, wings outstretched, motions with both hands to the three women. The latter are seen approaching in single file on the right panel. The details of the outline of the first figure suggest that they were carrying the customary perfume jars, and this is confirmed by the wording of the *titulus.* Two crouching soldiers, normally found at the side or immediately below the tomb, can be seen, one above the other, behind the women. The upper figure, wearing a pointed helmet, carries a short pike. In the upper left corner of the scene, the hand of God with the middle and forefinger joined in blessing, emerges from the arc of heaven. The conventional quarter-circle is itself filled by a bifurcated palmette form, which may have been intended to suggest a fiery apparition. The presence of the Divine Hand is unusual in the iconography of this scene. According to the authors of the Four Gospels, the Women were variously addressed by a single or a pair of angels or men. Their dialogue with the angel furnished the substance of a liturgical play and was an irreplaceable element of the Passion story.[70] The divine hand was perhaps designed to add incontrovertible testimony to the angel's account of the Resurrection in line with the increasing tendency in the twelfth century to give the miracle material form by showing Christ emerging from the Tomb.[71] Another possibility, which has the greater weight of likelihood on its side, is that the hand refers to the appearance of Christ to the Women, which follows the story of the Three Maries at the Tomb in the Gospel narrative. The pictorial tradition, beginning with the Gospels of Rabbula and continuing thereafter, shows the Lord addressing the women in the scene following the visit to the tomb.[72] The Puy composition would seem to conflate the two episodes.

15. *Ascension* (Figs. 9 and 24, top)

CETUS APOSTOLICUS CHRISTUM/MIRATUR EUNTEM

The scene fills the two contiguous halves of the panel. The left side is dominated by the figure of Christ, upright and, judging by the position of the feet, facing to the right at the center of a mandorla. He holds a cross in the left hand and motions upward with the right. Four additional figures occupy the spaces on each side of the mandorla. The pair in the upper zone of the composition are winged and hover along its edges. Those below, wingless, are shown recoiling in awe before the blinding apparition. The personage on the left kneels and half-prayerfully, half-protęctively, holds both hands in front of his body. That on the right, who is haloed, falls back and raises both hands in wonder. The two upper corners are masked off by the celestial quarter-circles repeatedly employed on the doors. Four haloed apostles, grouped in picturesque disarray and gesturing toward the rising Christ, appear in the right half of the composition. The type of profile ascending Christ with a cross staff, surrounded by angels, derives from the sphere of Carolingian art. The Ascension in the Bible of S. Paolo fuori le Mura furnishes an example.[73] Closer to Le Puy is the corresponding design in the Benedictional of St. Aethelwold, itself in all likelihood based on a late Carolingian model.[74]

The two halves of the composition are normally seen as one under the other rather than side by side. In this novel presentation, the idea of the mandorla situated in mid-air above the heads of the apostles is lost. The sculptor, possibly recognizing this, may have been motivated to substitute the two figures thrown back to the ground for a second pair of angels customarily placed beneath the mandorla and shown in the act of displaying or guiding it upward. But the inclusion of the two figures may also point to his acquaintance with a particular and rather uncommon strain within the iconography of the Ascension. The Ascension of the doors of Santa Sabina shows Christ about to begin his heavenward journey with the apostles strewn on the ground below Him as by a whirlwind,[75] and a similar conception prevails in the famous fifth-century ivory in Munich.[76] The formula is illustrated later in a ninth-century ivory in the treasure of Minden cathedral related to the Liuthar group, with the significant innovation that some of the apostles are seen standing while others nearer the center of the composition have fallen to the ground.[77] The Ascension in the eleventh-century Fulda Sacramentary in Bamberg and the scene incorporated in an ivory in a Freiburg Private Collection datable a few decades later, take us close to the representation of the witnesses of the miracle as it is seen in Le Puy: only the pair of figures on each side of the central axis bow or shrink back in awe, while the rest stand impassively behind them.[78] Singling out for special attention those two figures was no doubt designed to identify them as specific persons rather than types. In the Freiburg ivory and in other representations of the Ascension where such a sharpening of the iconographic focus was carried out, the central figures are generally characterized as Peter and the Virgin Mary. The same identification may also have been intended in Le Puy.

16. *Descent of the Holy Spirit* (Figs. 9 and 25, top)

IGNIS AB IGNE DEI VENI/ENS PERLUSTRAT ALUMNOS

Three seated and haloed figures are seen in the narrower left half of the composition. The personage at the center is larger in stature and shown in full frontality. His feet rest upon a footstool projecting forward to the lower boundary of the scene, and, as is implied also by the small pair of arches visible near the hem of his garment, he is seated on a throne. The flanking apostles are placed slightly farther back. Their seats were cushioned and supported by colonnettes apparently attached at each end. The scene is delimited at the top by a horizontal strip, whose contour is straight on the inside and undulating on the exterior, nearly touching the upper border. This detail of the design is a translation in relief of the luminous band which serves as a visual embodiment of the Holy Spirit. Since the undulation occurs on the outer face of the band only, it would seem that the central figure or the group as a whole were themselves to be construed as a source of spiritual radiance. The right half of the scene shows five seated apostles. The one on the left appears to be in a frontal stance, while the others face partly inward toward the center. One apostle (fourth from left) motions with hand in the same direction. The bench upon which the figures are seated rests on an architectural support consisting of an alternation of conical turrets and arches.[79] Above the apostles's heads, a horizontal band is also visible, though it is straight without and undulating within, reversing the order observed in the left scene; it is also set somewhat lower than the band on the left, its outer side corresponding to the level of the latter's inner face.

Combined, the two parts of the composition represent the center and right side of the apostolic convention in the traditional iconography of Pentecost.[80] The figure enthroned at the center may be either the Virgin Mary or St. Peter. Both are found in this position in twelfth-century Pentecost representations, and there are no decisive clues for determining which may have been intended here.

Although the particular combination and disposition of the subjects in the Puy doors is not precisely duplicated elsewhere, they offer us variations on well-known themes, exploited in other monuments of the same kind at least since the eleventh century. The same juxtaposition of Infancy and Passion scenes occurs in somewhat amplified form, in the doors of St. Mary in the Capitol in Cologne.[81] In a more compressed state, it is seen even earlier in one of the valves of Bernward's bronze doors at Hildesheim. The comparable works of twelfth century date are all of Italian origin. They include the bronze doors executed by Bonanus for the Cathedrals of Pisa and Monreale first and foremost, the doors of the Cathedral of Spalato, and those, less well publicized, of the churches of Alba Fucense and S. Maria in Cellis at Carsoli in the Abruzzi.[82] Lastly, mention should be made of the wooden doors of Gurk cathedral in Carinthia, datable around 1220, which incorporate elements of the same program within a pattern of traceried rinceaux.[83] There is much diversity among these monuments with respect to the number, the arrangement and the iconography of the individual scenes, and what they have in common is not to be attributed to a hypothetical play of internal relationships but to a general dependence upon a common tradition. The external limits of both cycles are thus fixed with a fair degree of consistency throughout: the Annunciation has as a parallel the Entry into Jerusalem at the beginning of the respective narratives, and the Presentation or Baptism marks the termination of the Infancy sequence as the Descent of the Holy Spirit concludes the story of the Passion. The air of a calculated confrontation between the two cycles may be more or less forcefully stressed. In Le Puy, Cologne, and Spalato, it is clearly set forth through their presentation as separate entities of like dimensions and format, participating on equal terms in a single compositional ensemble. It is suppressed, on the other hand, at Pisa and Monreale, where the sequence of the narrative is continuous across both valves from the beginning at the lower left to the end at the upper right.

The programmatic conception which we see illustrated in the Puy and related doors was not restricted to this usage and perhaps not initially devised for it. It is encountered earlier on ivories incorporated in book bindings, as for example, the five-partite compositions of Milan cathedral, Ravenna, and Etschmiadzin.[84] A division of Christ's biography into two distinct cycles, equal in length, identical in outward presentation and complementary in substance was instituted here around an iconic image or symbol at the center of the composition. The second of these two major cycles, however, concerns not the Passion but the sequence of miraculous deeds illustrating the public ministry of Christ. In subsequent times, central image and narrative cycle became disassociated from each other, and the diptych form came to embrace either the combination of Christ in Majesty and the Virgin and Child in isolation, or two linked upright panels with narrative scenes in the manner of the Andrews diptych or the panels in the treasury of Aachen cathedral. This disassociation did not affect the focal point of the narrative, which remained directed to the miracles preceding the events of the Passion. There is, by contrast, a pronounced liturgical coloration in the choice and combination of the scenes in our recension. Typologically, the scheme bears a close relation to diptychs with the twelve Feast days of the church year in Byzantine art, as exemplified by the eleventh-century icon in the monastery of St. Catherine on Mount Sinai, the earliest of the recorded works in this series.[85] The design of the doors of Bonanus at Pisa borrows from an icon of this kind the "transversal" arrangement of the scenes across both valves, as well as the inclusion of such subjects as the Harrowing of Hell and the concluding Koimesis. A somewhat earlier formulation of the same iconic type, which may be recognized in an ivory diptych in the treasure of Milan cathedral, presents closer analogies to the Puy doors. The scenes are disposed in vertical fashion, and the

Infancy and Passion cycles are each circumscribed within the boundaries of a single panel.[86]

The impact of the liturgy on the shape of pictorial form was doubtless not as forceful in Western medieval art as in the East,[87] but there are indications that a parallel development of paired cycles with reference to the feast days took place in the Latin world, reaching fruition in Carolingian times or in the period immediately thereafter. In the Sacramentary of Drogo, the liturgy of the major feasts is introduced by the appropriate Gospel illustrations.[88] Infancy and Passion scenes are confronted in the ivory panels of the binding of Drogo's second Gospel Book in the Bibliothèque Nationale (lat. 9388) and in a pair of ivory panels in Manchester, which are assigned to a West German workshop of the tenth century.[89] A number of ivory diptychs conforming to the same general program were executed in the Belgian or lower Rhenish territory in the eleventh century.[90] All the pieces which exemplify this type are bound up more or less directly with the production of the Court schools and its afterlife in Ottonian and Salian times.

In Le Puy, the two cycles were confined to separate sets of doors rather than valves or leaves of a single ensemble as was the case in all the programmatically related monuments, with the somewhat problematic exception of the panels at Hildesheim, which initially, at least, do not appear to have been hung together.[91] If, as we have assumed, the thresholds in which the doors were placed were designed to simulate the side entrances in a tripartite portal scheme on the façade of the cathedral, such a disposition must have been calculated in terms larger than the customary confrontation of Infancy and Passion scenes. In the iconography of church portals, the arrangement in Le Puy takes its place within the small group of monuments in which twin cycles or representative scenes from the earthly life of Christ flanked a central entrance devoted to an eschatological image of the Lord in Heaven. The most explicit formulation of such a scheme is found at Saint-Gilles, where the tympanum of the central portal–remade in the seventeenth century–was, according to a likely supposition, devoted to the Deesis, while the side portals are given over to the Incarnation and the Crucifixion, respectively.[92] This type of program may have been represented some years earlier already in the façade of the third church at Cluny. We have definite, if inadequate information, only for the middle of the three portals, dominated by the Majestas Domini. Some finds of sculpture have led to the suggestion that the north portal was devoted to the Virgin Mary.[93] The scheme as a whole is possibly reflected in an indirect way in the distribution of the subjects of the three entrances within the narthex of the church of the Magdalen at Vézelay.[94] Saint-

Lazare at Avallon in Burgundy and the cathedral of Saint-Apollinaire at Valence in the Rhône Valley offer two other examples of this pattern which should probably be added to the list. In the former structure, where the portal scheme, only partially preserved, can be fairly accurately reconstructed, the central portal presented Christ in Majesty to view. The cycles of the Infancy and the Passion were horizontally stratified rather than individually confined to separate doorways: the tympana of both lateral portals were devoted to the Infancy narration, while the story of the Passion unfolded on the lintels.[95] At Valence, elements of the two narrative sequences are found in the pair of doorways situated along the lateral walls of the church. The single portal doorway in the west was sheltered by an open porch, which constituted the lower story of a tower. Both have been entirely reconstructed, but it is likely that the nineteenth-century tympanum with Christ in Majesty now in place above this entrance merely reproduces the older disposition.[96]

The extensive pictorial cycle of the Life of Christ found on Gauzfredus's doors is without parallel in the territory of Velay, where Romanesque sculpture of a narrative type is quite rare. In both Auvergne to the northwest and in the valley of the Rhône to the east, however, the cyclical presentation of the Infancy and the Passion of Christ was a major preoccupation for the sculptor. In Auvergne, the tendency was to display these cycles on the capitals of the choir, as, for example, in the churches of Notre-Dame-du-Port in Clermont-Ferrand, Saint-Paul at Issoire, and Saint-Nectaire, and only secondarily in the decoration of portals.[97] The opposite holds true for Provence and the Rhône Valley, to which Le Puy thus seems to give the better part of its allegiance. Many, indeed most, of the individual episodes illustrated on the doors find an echo in the first flowering of sculpture of this artistic province during the second quarter of the twelfth century. At this time, the construction of the cathedral displays some evidence of contact with the architecture of the same region. Although such associations are of necessity too vague to firmly locate the monument in a concrete network of historical relations, they are bound to have some general implications for questions of dating and affiliation. They tend to accentuate the Mediterranean dimension of the work, already suggested in the typology by its closest iconographic parallels, all of Italian origin. Here, judging by the surviving monuments at Carsoli and Alba Fucense, elaborately historiated doors were not the exclusive privilege of important cathedral centers, but could be found in comparatively unimportant village churches. Have we in Le Puy only an isolated and somewhat wayward product of the same tradition?

NOTES

1. Mandet, *Histoire du Velay, loc. cit.*
2. Thiollier, *Architecture religieuse,* 65, Götz, *Bildprogramme,* 83-84. The abbreviations have been justified
3. To be compared to the *titulus* of the corresponding scene in the Echternach Pericopes in Bremen: PASTORES PRIMI COGNOSCUNT GAUDIA MUNDI (J. Plotzek, *Das Perikopenbuch Heinrichs III. in Bremen und seine Stellung innerhalb der Echternacher Buchmalerei,* Cologne, Diss., 1970, 135-36.
4. P. Metz, *The Golden Gospels of Echternach,* London, 1957, 29.
5. E. Poeschel, *Die romanischen Deckengemälde von Zillis,* Erlenbach-Zurich, 1941, pl. 48, No. 5.
6. G. Schiller, *Ikonographie der christlichen Kunst,* I, Gütersloh, 1966, 95ff.
7. Munich, Bayerische Staatsbibl. lat. 4452, fol. 8v.
8. *Scenes from the Life of Christ in English Manuscripts* (Bodleian Library Picture Book No. 5), Oxford, 1951, 3, No. 6.
9. Basic surveys of the iconography of the Adoration are found in H. Kehrer, *Die heiligen Drei Könige in Literatur und Kunst,* Leipzig, 1908-9; G. Millet, *Recherches sur l'iconographie de l'Evangile aux XIVe, XVe, et XVIe siècles,* Paris, 1916; G. Vézin, *L'adoration et le cycle des mages dans l'art chrétien primitif,* Paris, 1950; Schiller, *Ikonographie,* I, 105ff.
10. A large star within the building occupied by the Virgin and Child appears in Munich, Bayerische Staatsbibl. lat. 4452, fol. 17 (Pericopes of Henry II); lat. 4453, fol. 29 (Evangelistary of Otto III); Cologne, Dombibl. Ms. 218, fol. 22 (Gospels of Limburg an der Hardt) all reproduced by Kehrer, *Heilige Drei Könige,* II, figs. 110-12. A series of illustrations follows the scene in the Poussay Gospels (Bibl. Nat. lat. 10514, fol. 18v) in showing the star superimposed on the architecture, neither wholly within or without.
11. Munich, Bayerische Staatsbibl. lat 4453, fol. 29 (Evangelistary of Otto III); Berlin, Staatliche Museen, Kupferstichkabinett Cod. 78 A. 2, fol. 13v (Evangelistary of Henry IV?); Paris, Bibl. Nat. lat. 18005, fol. 34v (Sacramentary, Use of St. Maximin, Trier); Fulda, Hess. Landesbibl. Cod. Aa 35, fol. 60v (Weingarten Collectary) articulate the scene by means of an arcade in this manner.
12. R. Jullian, *L'éveil de la sculpture italienne. La sculpture romane dans l'Italie du Nord,* Paris, 1945, 114, pl. XLIV, 1.
13. Poeschel, *Zillis,* 86, Nos. 70-73.
14. Jullian, *Eveil de la sculpture italienne,* 145.
15. The Burgundian examples are conveniently grouped in G. Beaudequin, "Les représentations sculptées de l'Adoration des Mages dans l'ancien diocèse d'Autun à l'époque romane," *Cahiers de civilisation médiévale,* III, 1960, 48ff.
16. E. Mâle. *L'art religieux du XIIe siècle en France,* Paris, 1922, 139ff., restating the author's earlier "Les influences du drame liturgique sur la sculpture romane," *Revue de l'art,* XXII, 1907, 81-92. The argument is found little later in Kehrer, *Heilige Drei Könige,* II, 129ff., who refers to the "französische Schauspiel Typus." On the question of the influence of the liturgical theater on art, see also O. Paecht, *The Rise of Pictorial Narrative in Twelfth-Century England,* Oxford, 1962, 33ff.
17. K. Young, *The Drama of the Medieval Church,* Oxford, 1933, II, 44, who quotes from the Rouen play: "Tria sunt munera pretiosa quae obtulerunt Magi Domino in die ista, et habent in se divina mysteria . . ."
18. Vézin, *L'adoration,* 91ff., gives as the earliest representation the scene in the Sacramentary of Drogo (fol. 34v), but there are contemporaneous examples in Byzantine art. The question of origin is in dispute. See Schiller, *Ikonographie,* I, 109ff.
19. A. Boeckler, *Die Bronzetüren des Bonanus von Pisa und des Barisanus von Trani,* Berlin, 1953 (Die frühmittelalterlichen Bronzetüren, IV), 12.
20. W. Cahn, "Romanesque Sculpture in American Collections. I. Hartford," *Gesta,* VI, 1967, 49, No. 4. The riding Magi on separate pilaster capitals in the choir of Lyon cathedral follow in the same iconographical pattern.
21. G. de Francovich, *Benedetto Antelami,* Milan-Florence, 1952, 329; II, fig. 402.
22. P. Mesplé, *Toulouse, Musée des Augustins, Les sculptures romanes,* Paris, 1961, No. 88.
23. P. Mesplé, "Chapiteaux du cloître de Lombez," *Revue des arts,* 1958, 177-83.
24. R. Crozet, "Saint-Caprais d'Agen," *Congrès arch.,* CXXVII, 1969, 96.

25. Poeschel, *Zillis,* 87, Nos. 75-77.
26. Young, *Drama of the Medieval Church,* II, 85.
27. W. Biehl, *Toskanische Plastik des frühen und hohen Mittelalters,* Leipzig, 1926, 51, pl. 56b.
28. Poeschel, *Zillis,* 69, No. 86.
29. Kehrer, *Heilige Drei Könige,* II, 103ff. Vézin, *Adoration,* 47ff.
20. Metz, *Golden Gospels,* 29.
31. Rouen, Bibl. Mun. Ms. 274. V. Leroquais, *Sacramentaires et missels manuscrits,* I, 99. A list of architectural representations where the tri-lobed form occurs is given by C. Kelleher, *Illumination at Saint-Bertin at Saint-Omer under the Abbacy of Odbert,* Univ. of London, Diss., 1968, 118-19, who states that "although the trefoil arch was rarely used elsewhere, it seems to have been fairly popular in Anglo-Saxon art."
32. Poeschel, *Zillis,* 87, Nos. 85-88.
33. C. Cecchelli, G. Furlani, and M. Salmi, *The Rabbula Gospels,* Olten-Lausanne, 1959, 55 (Bibl. Laur. Syriac Ms. Plut. 1, Pars Aut. No. 56, fol. 4v).
34. A. Goldschmidt, *Die Elfenbeinskulpturen aus der Zeit der karolingischen und sächsischen Kaiser,* Berlin, 1914, I, 40, No. 72, pl. XXIX.
35. The comment of E. Baldwin Smith, *Early Christian Iconography,* Princeton, 1918, 59, that the depiction of the Massacre ". . . where the children are killed at the point of a sword, is, in its unqualified realism the product of the coarser cult of a declining Empire" is surely inappropriate.
36. Boulogne-sur-Mer, Bibl. Mun., Ms. 20, fol. 2v. Kelleher, *Illumination at Saint-Bertin,* 53, 230, does not comment in detail on this feature. An earlier example is the writing Gregory within an open-gabled structure in the Psalter of Charles the Bald (Bibl. Nat. lat. 1152, fol. 4).
37. Pierpont Morgan Library Ms. 780, fol. 1v (Annunciation of Joseph), and 27v (Last Supper).
38. Bibl. de l'Arsenal, Ms. 1169. H. Martin and P. Lauer, *Les principaux manuscrits à peintures de la Bibliothèque de l'Arsenal à Paris,* Paris, 1929, 12, pl. III.
39. J. Hubert, J. Porcher, and W. F. Volbach, *L'Europe des Invasions,* Paris, 1968, 258.
40. P. Lasko, *Ars Sacra, 800-1200,* Harmondsworth, 1972, 55.
41. Metz, *Codex aureus Epternacensis,* 30; A. Boeckler, *Das Goldene Evangelienbuch Heinrichs III,* Berlin, 1933, 73, pl. 113. For the group as a whole, see also J. Plotzek, *Das Perikopenbuch Heinrichs III., in Bremen,* 130ff.
42. D. C. Schorr, "The Iconographic Development of the Presentation in the Temple," *Art Bulletin,* XXVIII, 1946, 17-32. For the iconography of the Presentation, see also H. von Errfa, "Darbringung," *Reallexikon zur Deutsche Kunstgeschichte,* III, 1057-76.
43. F. Salet and J. Adhémar, *La Madeleine de Vézelay,* Melun, 1948, 200, No. 38.
44. Correctly identified, I believe, by Schiller, *Ikonographie,* I, 184, and fig. 575, though this capital stems from the transept of the church rather than from the porch, as stated here. Earlier authors had generally interpreted the scene as a miracle of St. Benedict (J. M. Berland, *Clarté de Saint-Benoît,* Cahiers de l'Atelier du Coeur Meurtry, s.d., 16, and fig. 22; G. Chenesseau, *L'abbaye de Fleury à Saint-Benoît-sur-Loire,* Paris, 1931, 218.
45. Schiller, *Ikonographie,* I, 189, and fig. 565.
46. F. Wormald, *The Miniatures of the Gospels of St. Augustine,* Cambridge, 1954, pl. IV, No. 4.
47. R. Wesenberg, *Bernwardinische Plastik,* Berlin, 1955, 124.
48. G. Zarnecki, "The Chichester Reliefs," *Archaeological Journal,* CX, 1953, 106-19. For the iconography of the Awakening of Lazarus, see also E. Mâle, "La résurrection de Lazare dans l'art," *Revue des arts,* 1951, I, 44ff., and more recently, R. Darmstaedter, *Die Auferweckung des Lazarus in der altchristlichen und byzantinischen Kunst,* Bern, 1955.
49. Boeckler, *Die Bronzetüren des Bonanus,* 14.
50. My rendering departs from Thiollier, *Architecture religieuse,* 65, who gives TURBA JAL . . . -CESES . . . FLO. . . . I note that this emendation agrees with the reading found in the notes of Baron de Guilhermy, Bibl. Nat. fr. 6106, fol. 278.
51. Munich, Bayerische Staatsbibl. lat. 4452, fol. 78.
52. Müller-Dietrich, *Romanische Skulptur in Lothringen,* 92f., 99.
53. Deschamps and Thibout, *Peinture murale,* 54, fig. 11.
54. W. Cook, "The Earliest Painted Panels of Catalonia," *Art Bulletin,* 1927-28, pl. opp. p. 177, fig. 39 (Madrid, Bib. Nac. Ms. E.R. 8, fol. 324v).
55. Cook, *idem,* fig. 29.
56. R. Hamann, *Die Abteikirche von Saint-Gilles und ihre künstlerische Nachfolge,* Berlin, 1955, 147f., and II, pls. 46-50. For the iconography of the entry, see further E. Dinkler, *Der Einzug in Jerusalem. Ikonographische Untersuchungen im Anschluss an ein bisher unbekanntes Sarkophagfragment* (Veröff. Arbeitsgemeinschaft für Forschung des Landes Nordrhein-Westfalen, 167), Cologne, 1970; E. Kantorowicz, "The 'King's Advent' and the Enigmatic Panels in the Doors of Santa Sabina," *Art Bulletin,* XXVI, 1944, 207-31, reprinted in the author's

Selected Studies, Locust Valley, N. Y., 1965, 37-75.

57. Hamann, *Abteikirche,* 273.
58. *Idem,* 212, fig. 248.
59. *Idem,* 229, fig. 281, L. Bégule, *L'église Saint-Maurice, ancienne, cathédrale de Vienne,* Paris, 1914, No. 24, 19-20.
60. St. Gall, Stiftsbibl., Cod. 390/1, fol. 183. A. Merton, *Die Buchmalerei von St. Gallen von neunten bis zum elften Jahrhundert,* Leipzig, 1912, 70, and pl. LXVIII, 1. The idea that the Last Supper took place in a room on an upper floor probably underlies this device. A two-story chapel in Jerusalem, in the upper room of which the event was said to have occurred, was shown to pilgrims. (C. Heitz, "Réflexions sur l'architecture clunisienne," *Revue de l'art,* XV, 1972, 34, and note 19).
61. F. Röhrig, *Der Verduner Altar,* Vienna, 1959, 70-71, No. II/7.
62. Hamann, *Abteikirche,* 340ff.
63. Poeschel, *Zillis,* 91, Nos. 136-37.
64. For this subject, see H. Wentzel, "Christus-Johannes Gruppe," *Reallexikon zur deutschen Kunstgeschichte,* III, 658-62, and the summary, with a comprehensive bibliography, given by J. de Coo, *Museum Mayer van den Bergh. Catalogus 2,* Antwerp, 1960, 87ff, No. 2094.

    It might be noted that on a capital from the cloister of La Daurade in Toulouse, the group of Christ and St. John is also isolated on one of the faces of the block (Mesplé, *Sculptures romanes,* No. 125.)
65. Hamann, *Abteikirche* 184ff, 338-39, 346.
66. A. Moppert-Schmidt, *Die Fresken von S. Angelo in Formis,* Zurich, 1967, 84.
67. Hamann, *Abteikirche,* 81ff., and II, pl. 54.
68. P. Bloch, H.Schnitzler, and W.F. Volbach, *Skulpturen, Sammlung E. und M. Kofler-Truniger, Luzern,* Lucerne-Stuttgart, 1964, 12-13, No. 5.8. The crucifixion is also found on the end wall of the Salle des Morts along the eastern wing of the cloister.
69. See for example the Fulda Sacramentary in Bamberg (Staatsbibl. Cod. Lit. I [A. II. 52], fol. 70), or that in Göttingen (Universitätsbibl. Cod. Theol. 231, fol. 65v), where the opening is in fact the entire front wall of the structure (H. Schnitzler, "Fulda oder Reichenau," *Wallraf-Richartz Jahrbuch,* XIX, 1957, 97ff.). Such wide openings are also found on ivories with the Resurrection, as for example the ninth-century panels in Florence and Munich (Goldschmidt, *Elfenbeinskulpturen,* I, Nos. 9 and 130).
70. Young, *Drama of the Medieval Church,* I, 239ff.
71. See on the iconography P. Bloch, "Das Reichenauer Einzelblatt mit den Frauen am Grabe im Hessischen Landesmuseum Darmstadt," *Kunst in Hessen und am Mittelrhein,* III, 1963, 24-43; F. Rademacher, "Zu den frühesten Darstellungen der Auferstehung Christi," *Zeitschrift für Kunstgeschichte,* 1965, 195ff. The isolation of the soldiers on the right side of the composition is found on several versions of the scene within the conventionally designated Reichenau cycle discussed by Bloch (Berlin, Staatl. Museen Kupferstichkab. A. II. 78; Würzburg, Universitätsbibl. Mp. th. q.5; Utrecht Archiepiscopal Museum Cod. 3). Here, however, the women approach the tomb depicted at the center of the scene from the left.

    The placement of the soldiers one above the other as a kind of spatial shorthand can be seen also in the Resurrection of the Beaucaire frieze and in the scene of the tympanum of Condrieu (Hamann, *Abteikirche,* 333-34).
72. Fol. 13. Cecchelli, Furlani, and Salmi, *The Rabbula Gospels,* 69-71. The reference is to Mt. XXVIII, 9-10.
73. Bible of S. Paolo, fol. 292v. H. Schade, "Studien zu der karolingischen Bilderbibel aus St. Paul vor den Mauern in Rom," *Wallraf-Richartz Jahrbuch,* XXII, 1960, 24ff.
74. Brit. Mus. Add. 49.598, fol. 64v. F. Wormald, *The Benedictional of St. Ethelwold,* London, 1959, 12. For the iconography of the Ascension, see the studies of E. DeWald, "The Iconography of the Ascension," *American Journal of Archeology,* XIX, 1915, 277ff., No. 3; H. Gutberlet, *Die Himmelfart Christi in der Bildende Kunst,* Strasbourg, 1934; G. Kretschmar, "Himmelfart und Pfingsten," *Zeitschrift für Kunstgeschichte,* 65, 1954-55, 209ff.
75. S. Tsuji, "Les portes de Sainte-Sabine. Particularités de l'iconographie de l'Ascension," *Cahiers arch.,* XIII, 1962, 13-28.
76. F. Volbach, *Early Christian Art,* New York, 1961, 328-29, No. 93.
77. Goldschmidt, *Elfenbeinskulpturen,* I, No. 65.
78. *Idem,* III, No. 306. For the miniature (Bamberg, Staatl. Bibl. Lit. 1, fol. 81), see Schnitzler, *Fulda oder Reichenau,* 101, fig. 50, and 100-102 for the iconographic type in general.
79. The drawing published by Fikry, *Art roman du Puy,* 175, and fig. 232 is inaccurate, as is his characterization of this alternation as "un registre de polylobes."
80. A. Grabar, "Le schéma iconographique de la Pentecôte," *Seminarium Kondakovianum,* Prague,

II, 1928, 223ff. S. Seeliger, *Die Ikonographie des Pfingstenwunders,* Munich, 1956. M. Schapiro, *The Parma Ildefonsus,* New York, 1964, 43.

81. To the bibliography on the doors of St. Mary in the Capitol given by Götz, *Bildprogramme,* 67-68, should now be added R. Wesenberg, *Frühe Mittelalterliche Bildwerke,* Düsseldorf, 1972, 27ff.
82. Götz, *idem,* 58ff. Treated here under the heading "Reine Christusviten."
83. Götz, *idem,* 169ff., and K. Ginhart and B. Grimschitz, *Der Dom zu Gurk,* Vienna, 1910, 54ff.
84. F. Volbach, *Elfenbeinarbeiten der Spätantike und des frühen Mittelalters,* Mainz, 1952, Nos. 119, 125, and 142. F. Steenbock, *Die kirchliche Prachteinband im frühen Mittelalter,* Berlin, 1965, Nos. 5, 8, and 11.
85. K. Weitzmann, "Byzantine Miniature and Icon Painting in the Eleventh Century," *Proceedings of the XIIIth International Congress of Byzantine Studies,* Oxford, 1967, 207-24, reprinted in *Studies in Classical and Byzantine Manuscript Illumination,* Chicago, 1971, 271ff., esp. 293.
86. A. Goldschmidt and K. Weitzmann, *Die byzantinischen Elfenbeinskulpturen des X.-XIII. Jahrhunderts,* Berlin, 1930-34, II, Nos. 42a and b. Steenbock, *Kirchliche Prachteinband,* 112-13, No. 35.
87. On the cycle of the feast days, see Millet, *Recherches sur l'iconographie de l'Evangile,* 15ff; W. Kermer, *Studien zum Diptychon in der sakralen Malerei,* Diss., Tübingen, 1967, 134ff.; T. A. Ismaïlova, "L'iconographie du cycle des fêtes d'un groupe de codex arméniens d'Asie mineure," *Revue des études arméniennes,* 1967, N.S. IV, 125-66.
88. Paris, Bibl. Nat. lat. 9428. W. Koehler, *Die Schule von Metz* (Die karolingischen Miniaturen, III), Berlin, 1960, 153ff.
89. Goldschmidt, *Elfenbeinskulpturen,* I, 27a and b; Steenbock, *Kirchliche Prachteinband,* 210-11, No. 110.
90. Goldschmidt, *Idem,* II, Nos. 52-53, 55-56, 62, 63-64.
91. Wesenberg, *Bernwardinische Plastik,* Berlin, 1955, 65.
92. Hamann, *Abteikirche,* 89ff. On the other hand, Fliche regards the relief of Christ in Majesty presently in place over the central door as a clumsy restoration (or replacement?) of the original, presumably reflecting the same subject (*Aigues-Mortes et Saint-Gilles,* Petites Monographies des Grands Edifices, Paris, s.d., 89).
93. K. J. Conant, *Cluny. Les églises et la maison du chef d'ordre,* Mâcon, 1968, 100: "Des fragments de deux ou trois baldaquins trouvés dans le voisinage du petit portail nord suggèrent pour ce portail une Madone en Majesté accompagnée de deux saints."
94. Salet and Adhémar, *La Madeleine de Vézelay,* 113ff.
95. J. Vallery-Radot, "L'iconographie et le style des trois portails de Saint-Lazare d'Avallon," *Gazette des Beaux-Arts,* LII, 1958, 23-24.
96. Perrot, *Bulletin de la Société départementale d'archéologie et de Statistique de la Drôme,* LIX, 1925, 57-58. For the side portals, see Abbé Didelot, "Portes historiées récemment découvertes à la cathédrale de Valence," *idem,* XVI, 1882, 182-208 and 282-323
97. L. Bréhier, "Les épisodes de la Passion dans la sculpture romane d'Auvergne," *Gazette des Beaux-Arts,* LXXI, 1925, 48-72.

IV The Place of the Doors in the History of the Cathedral

IN THE LATE YEARS of the eleventh century and throughout the twelfth, Le Puy was the site of extensive building activity. In addition to the cathedral and its immediate dependencies, the modern visitor can still see as evidence of this construction the church of Saint-Michel d'Aiguilhe perched high on its rock,[1] the chapel of Saint-Clair or "Temple of Diana" immediately below,[2] the portal of the Hôtel Dieu,[3] and in the suburb of Espaly, the church of Saint-Marcel.[4] Documentary sources and other archaeological evidence further amplify the picture.[5] Yet few, if any, firm dates can be given to provide a secure foundation for a chronology of Romanesque architecture and sculpture in the city. The rebuilding of the cathedral itself seems to have gone entirely unrecorded by contemporary witnesses. From the sixteenth century onward and the earliest efforts of modern historiography, it was believed that the present structure was initially erected by the first bishops of Le Puy in late Roman times.[6] The histories of Odo of Gissey (1644) and Bochart de Sarron (1693) are largely monuments to the zeal of the cathedral clergy in defending this claim.[7] The faith of the canons in their cause was sustained by the absence of contrary information and by a few chance finds. In 1598, according to Gissey, an inscription (*escripteau*) was discovered near the main altar giving as the date of consecration the year 465.[8] The tenth-century Sacramentary of the Cathedral (Bibl. Nat. Lat. 2294) designated as the original builders five bishop saints "*qui construxerunt domino permittente domum beatae virginis Mariae."* [9] The votive inscription of one of these, Scutarius, which appears on the gabled slab now serving as the lintel over the portal within the *Porche du For* on the south side of the choir, singled him out from his companions as the "architect" of the structure.[10] The force of this testimony was apparently sufficient to outweigh the discordant evidence of the inscription on the wooden doors, which went unreported and was not taken into account until the beginning of modern archaeology. When in 1677, in the course of his passage through Le Puy, the learned Benedictine Dom Claude Estiennot was invited by the canons to write a history of the cathedral, he politely but firmly declined, fearing only half-humorously that his treatment of local pious legends would not be well received.[11]

The original documents in the cartulary of the cathedral are no longer extant, but several digests are known and a number of charters were published in full before their loss. These documents make it possible to witness, beginning in the second half of the eleventh century, a steady increase in the Chapter's holdings in land and other sources of revenue. In 1062, Count Bernard of Bigorre placed his territories in the hands of Notre-Dame du Puy and promised to pay an annual rent of sixty *sols morlaas* in perpetuity.[12] Shortly thereafter, Bernard Turmapaler, count of Armagnac and Gascogne, imitated his example.[13] In 1075, the town of Lez was received from Artaldus of Paillars, and the Chapter was favored on the same terms as Santiago de Compostela with a cash gift in the testament of Count Raymond Berenger of Barcelona.[14] As we have noted earlier, Count Bernard IV of Toulouse donated to the cathedral a number of estates on the eve of his departure on the first Crusade, in which, together with Bishop Adhemar de Monteil, he was to play a leading role. Further acquisitions are recorded in 1134 under Bishop Humbert of Albon.[15] One year earlier, the same figure joined in an appeal for assistance on behalf of the *hospitium* located on the north side of the cathedral, *"et eius adheret gradibus."* [16] There is here one of the rare topographical allusions to the unusual site on which the structure stands, but it is impossible to say on the basis of this text whether the church, to which the stairs in question led, is the present building, and if so, to determine how much of it had been completed at the time.

In the same year, Humbert obtained from the king of France a charter giving him and his successors extensive rights of justice and taxation in the town and forbidding the erection of fortresses without his permission in a wide tract of land between the Rhône and the Allier.[17] This concession, which must incidentally have given him control over the supply of stonemasons and quarries within the same territory, was strictly speaking only a confirmation of a grant initially made by the ephemeral Austrasian prince Raoul in 936. However, the changed social and economic circumstances of the moment no doubt conferred on the new and rather more detailed document a significance of its own. Historians of the Capetian monarchy have recognized in it a consequential step in the extension of its influence beyond its old domains.[18] The benefits of royal tutelage on the ecclesiastical side were sizable enough, and the terms of the charter of 1134 were confirmed by Louis VII in 1146 and 1158.[19] The alliance between the king and the episcopal see was further strengthened when in 1162, Louis intervened in the strife between the Chapter and its turbulent neighbors, the lords of Polignac.[20] This action no doubt enhanced the power and economic resources of the cathedral by removing from prominence a rival of stature whose appetite for feudal prerogatives and gain could only be exercised at its expense. In the course of the same years which saw this consolidation of its position, the finances of the cathedral must also have been bolstered by rewards derived from the renown of its miraculous image of the Virgin, celebrated and recommended to pilgrims on their way to Compostela in the *Codex Calixtinus.*

The cult image of the cathedral, destroyed in the French Revolution, was rumored in local tradition to have been brought from the Holy Land by St. Louis. Late copies and graphic documents show the statue almost entirely concealed in elaborate vestments of post-medieval date, but the lengthy and quite acute description made by an eighteenth-century observer, Faujas de Saint-Fond, should leave little doubt that the work was a Romanesque image of the Virgin like those for which Auvergne has become especially known.[21] A number of twelfth-century statues still preserved in churches of the region of Le Puy possibly offer a reflection of the lost monument. Its appearance might be connected with the change in designation of the site of the cathedral from *Anicium* to *Podium Sanctae Mariae,* which is documented for the first time in the early years of the eleventh century.[22] An image of the Virgin, possibly identical with the lost work, definitely stood in the sanctuary by the year 1095.[23]

These accretions to the patrimony of the see—solicited or otherwise—presuppose the existence of increased obligations which the realization of a huge building program explains well enough. That the cathedral treasury was indeed under a strain is suggested by a papal brief of 1155, which forbids Bishop Peter III to exact money from widows seeking to remarry.[24] A document of 1134, unfortunately known only through a brief seventeenth-century paraphrase, has a possible bearing on the question of construction around this time. In that year, according to Gissey, Raimond of Saint-Quentin, a canon of the cathedral, made a donation to the chapter "de certains bastiments . . . pour luy édifier un dortoir." [25] What part of the cathedral precinct might have been designated for this project remains uncertain, nor can we be sure that it was ever carried out. Bochart de Sarron, who depends on Gissey, but might have had access to the original document, qualifies the donation as "pour la fabrique d'une des galeries du cloître capitulaire." [26] In the present complex, the most likely site for a dormitory would be that now occupied by the *bâtiment des Clergeons* on the eastern arm of the cloister and abutting the end wall of the north transept, from which the canons would have had convenient access to the choir (Fig. 32).[27] There are obvious implications for the chronology of the building in this asssumption, for it must be supposed that a construction in the cloister could have been initiated only after the erection of at least the perimeter walls on the northern side of the cathedral.

If, as the document of 1134 suggests, the construction of the cathedral was well underway by that date, when was the enterprise begun? The sources are entirely mute on this point. Gissey reports that according to a tradition current in his time, the doorway sheltered by the *Porche du For* on the south transept arm was constructed in connection with Pope Urban II's halt in Le Puy on his way to the Council of Clermont and for the express purpose of permitting the pope to make a suitable entry into the cathedral.[28] Urban II celebrated the feast day of the Assumption of the Virgin on August 15, 1095, in Le Puy, following his dedication of the cathedral of Valence some ten days earlier. On August 18, he was at La Chaise-Dieu to consecrate the new Romanesque church there.[29] There is no record of a similar ceremony for Le Puy at this time. Indeed, we have it on the authority of the liturgical books of the cathedral that the *dedicatio ecclesiae* was celebrated on July 11, and consequently not on any possible anniversary of the papal visit.[30] The tradition reported by Gissey is thus unverifiable, and M. R. Gounot has made the very pertinent observation that it may have been inspired by a misconstruction of the abbreviation PA(ter) PA(triae) in the inscription of the doorway.[31] Yet we cannot overlook the fact that the doorway, of late Roman origin, was set into the masonry of the present building, and the possibility that a misreading of the inscription into a papal greeting may have been a cause of this. Taken at face value and on the not altogether inconceivable chance that it might still embody a kernel of truth, Gissey's report would suggest that by 1095, at least the eastern parts of the church including the apse and substantial parts of the transept were already standing.

These disappointingly tentative conjectures need to be examined in relation to the testimony of the inscription of the Infancy doors, which constitutes the most explicit, if by no means a self-explanatory piece of evidence on the authorship and date of construction of the building to have come down to us (Fig. 7). Attention must focus here not on Gauzfredus, the maker of the doors, but on Petrus, whose name is followed by a word which can only be completed as EDI(ficavit). There has been some discussion concerning the identity of this second figure, who might have been either a bishop of Le Puy, or more literally, the architect or *maître d'oeuvre,* who carried out the construction of the cathedral. There does not seem to be any way to settle this question conclusively, but since in medieval usage, the role of builder tended to be personified by the hierarchical head of the enterprise, the first suggestion has much the greater degree of plausibility. This is also how modern authors have understood it. In the list of Le Puy bishops, the name Peter occurs four times before the end of the twelfth century.[32] Among the most detailed studies on the cathedral that have appeared to date, Peter II (1053-73) has had the support of A. Fikry,[33] while N. Thiollier believed the inscription to refer to Peter III (1145-55) or Peter IV (1155-89).[34] The gap between the two positions is vexatiously large, but thus far, no really decisive evidence has been brought forth in favor of either side. The situation is made more complicated by the fact, on which there has long been general agreement, that the building of the cathedral involved several campaigns and extended over a fairly substantial period of time. Thus, the identity of the builder cannot be considered unless a prior understanding is reached on the division of labor which the term *edificavit* should be taken to express. Applying the seemingly unanswerable data furnished by the inscription to the edifice as a whole has had the effect of forcing all argument into twin procrustean beds: an early and a late chronology, neither of which fits the picture presented by the archaeological evidence very comfortably. It is, perhaps, not unreasonable to suppose that the construction of the church might have been initiated in the third quarter of the eleventh century, but the documentary evidence already set forth and the stylistic evidence to follow make it most unlikely that the edifice could have been brought anywhere near completion by 1073. Thus if the inscription of the doors refers to Peter II, this must be first and foremost to commemorate his role as founder and prime mover. Peter III and Peter IV, on the other hand, could have been involved in the construction only when it was already well under way. To identify one as builder and associate his name with the sculptor of our doors, which could have been installed only after the erection of the middle bays of the edifice, is to ascribe to him a major share in its completion. The inscription tells us only one thing with a fair measure of clarity: by 1189 at the latest, the doors were finished and probably in place.

The cathedral has been so extensively restored that analysis must often founder on the absence of reliable archaeological data (Fig. 30). Some repairs to the vaults of the two western bays proved necessary as early as the first half of the fourteenth century, and subsequent times also left their mark on the structure.[35] None more so than the buoyant revival following the troubled era of the French Revolution and its aftermath. The work done under the supervision of Aymon Mallay between 1844 and

1855 is fairly well documented, chiefly through the architect's own reports and drawings.[36] Mallay was impelled by the poor condition in which he found the building and by motives of a less practical sort to dismantle and reconstruct in their entirety the two nave bays adjoining the crossing as well as the two westernmost bays. Only the middle section of the nave (bays 3 and 4) were left standing, though certainly not untouched. Mallay also reconstructed the upper stories of the extraordinary tower adjoining the east end of the north aisle and substituted a dome of his own design for the octagonal tower over the crossing. The work of restoration was continued around 1865 by Auguste Mimey, who was responsible for the drastic alteration of the choir.[37] Precariously perched on its high volcanic outcropping, the building seemed from the start to defy the physical limits of its material constitution, and like other creations flawed by such tensions—Leonardo's *Last Supper* comes to mind—it has had to pay a heavy price for the solicitude of later generations.

Prior to the major restorations of the nineteenth century, the oldest part of the cathedral was the chevet, which Mimey razed and reconstructed without regard to the original design.[38] It was apparently square in plan, but diagonal walls mounted within the corners transformed the interior into a somewhat irregular heptagonal apse. The space, vaulted by a half-dome, was illuminated by a single window at the center of the east wall, and possibly a pair of additional openings in the lateral walls. The structure was much lower in height than the present vessel and clearly ill-married to it. The masonry, of small and roughly squared blocks of volcanic stone, was enlivened in the upper parts by polychromatic elements, and at its base and cornice, by fragments of Gallo-Roman sculpture. Varying dates have been assigned to its construction. Some nineteenth-century critics were persuaded that it might be a remnant of the first cathedral of Le Puy, possibly constructed in the late fourth or early fifth century, but more recent opinion has tended to view it as an early Romanesque structure.[39] The mention in published descriptions of a blind arcade within the apse and of a triple arch framing the window on the outer face of the eastern terminal wall would seem to constitute an argument in favor of the same hypothesis. The characterization of the masonry calls to mind the coloristic walls of ragged volcanic stone and imbricated reliefs of the churches of Saint-Romain-le-Puy and Champagne (Ardèche).[40]

The eastern masses of the cathedral consisting of the crossing, the transept with the two adjoining nave bays, and the lower stories of the free-standing steeple in the east belong to a second building campaign, at a somewhat later time than the first. In spite of the drastic restoration, these parts offer some scope for typological analysis. As it appears on Mallay's drawing made before restoration, the transept presented itself on the exterior as a rather stark and inarticulate volume (Fig. 29). The crossing was crowned by an octagonal tower pierced by a double-arched window on each of its sides. Buttresses marked the angles. The truncated appearance of the tower on the drawing and on the summary view of the eastern parts of the cathedral made by the architect Moiselet suggests that the structure initially rose at least one story higher. The design thus adhered to the Auvergnat type exemplified by the towers of Saint-Saturnin, Notre-Dame-du-Port in Clermont-Ferrand or Saint-Julien de Brioude which have two stories with double-arched openings beneath a crowning spire.[41]

Tribunes, filling the transept arms in their entirety, connect the internal articulation of the sanctuary space with a series of buildings dated from the second half of the eleventh century to the first quarter of the twelfth century, which, following the precedent of St. Michael at Hildesheim, and ultimately, of Angilbert's church at Centula, embody this motif. The cathedral of Bayeux, dedicated in 1077, has the virtue of being a parallel particularly well localized in time.[42] Each of the end walls of the transept houses a pair of apsidal niches. Uncomfortably squeezed together and partly intersected by the masonry of the east and western walls, each of these additionally embraces a pair of semicircular recesses flanking the central axis. There are niches similarly lodged in the arms of the transept at St. George in Cologne, at Süsteren, and in the church of the Holy Trinity at Essen.[43] The latter building, which Grodecki regards as the model formulation, presumably belongs to a campaign of construction datable between 1039 and 1051. In these Ottonian buildings, however, the niches are situated within polygonal walls, or, as at Essen, within a slightly inward projection of the masonry, thus helping to soften the angular contour of the inner wall path. In Le Puy, on the other hand, the niches lie parallel to each other on the unbroken surface offered by the end walls, and they are enlarged to the size of full-standing chapels. The effect suggests a comparison with the pair of larger niches on each face of the straight bay preceding the apse of St. Vincent at Cardona, completed in 1040.[44] The importance assumed by this unusual feature in the cathedral was likely intended to compensate for the absence of a developed choir or ambulatory with radiating chapels.

The apparent connection of the design of the transept with architectural schemes well beyond the confines of Central France is reinforced by observations on the derivation of the capitals and of the important sequence of frescoes in the tribunes of the northern arm. The capitals constitute two fairly homogeneous groups: some are of the Corinthian type, with broad and undetailed leaves; the others, well represented especially among the smaller blocks set in the embrasures of the wall fabric and employed also in the jambs of the chapels of St. Martin and St. Giles, have been given in Fikry's discussion the designation *chapiteaux ajourés.*[45] These capitals have a cubic basket, tapering down to a much narrower and rounded neck. The form itself is veiled by a dense network of highly stylized foliage, punctuated by deep interstices, of which the constituent element is an elongated and gently convoluting tendril terminating in a tri-lobed leaf. Fikry's analysis lays forceful stress on the influence of Islamic art in this sculpture. Along with other aspects of the architecture of the cathedral and the carving of the doors, it is also for him strong evidence of the central role which he would assign to Le Puy in the diffusion of Islamic elements in Romanesque art north of the Pyrenees.[46] Unfortunately, the chronology of the monuments in which this type of sculpture manifests itself is in most instances as imprecise as that of the cathedral. Outside Le Puy, *ajouré* capitals are found on the outer wall of the chevet at Saint-Guilhem-le-Désert, whose construction is thought to have followed a dedication of the church in 1076.[47] A group of capitals in the Issoudun Museum, other carvings in the same vein, stems from the abbey of Notre Dame in the town, which was reconstructed during the eleventh century and apparently standing by 1081.[48] Another series of capitals connected with this style from the church of l'Ile Barbe near Lyon are conventionally assigned to the end of the eleventh century,[49] while other variants of the type around the cornice line of the choir of St. James at Béziers,[50] in the jambs of the north doorway of Saint-Julien de Brioude,[51] and in the choir of Saint-Cerneuf at Billom probably belong to the end of the first quarter of the twelfth century at the earliest.[52] Among the finest specimens of such sculpture are the corbels of the chapel of Sainte-Croix at Montmajour, which may be somewhat later still.[53] The distribution of the *ajouré* capitals within Le Puy cathedral embraces the same wide chronological span, extending over parts of the structure belonging to building campaigns separated by an appreciable period of time, from the crossing to the perimeter wall of the two western nave bays.

The walls of both transept tribunes were originally covered with frescoes but those on the south side were destroyed in the course of Mallay's restorations, though copies of some of the scenes remain.[54] The paintings on the north side, still preserved in part, are best known through the gigantic iconic image of St. Michael on the pier at the angle of the north and west walls. The very loosely structured scheme included additional large standing figures; below them (?), oblong panels with scenes of the Bible and, it is thought, scenes of saints' martyrdom. The selection and arrangement of the subjects from the Old and New Testaments was governed by a typological system whose interest has been underscored by A. Grabar.[55] Both the style and certain aspects of the iconography of these paintings point in this case to the sphere of provincial Byzantine art. The sigma-shaped table with Christ seated at one end in the

Last Supper of the south tribune follows the conventional Byzantine formula. Michael is clad in the imperial *loros*. Monumental images of the archangels similarly attired are found in a number of the rock-cut churches in Apulia. The mosaics of Torcello in the second half of the eleventh century offer a pair of additional examples. Others appear in Catalonia at a somewhat later date. In Le Puy, however, the iconography has been so modified to bring it into conformity with the Western preference for the archangel in a combatting stance: instead of a globe and standard, he wields a lance and tramples a dragon underfoot.[56] Although the style is not exactly duplicated elsewhere, the boldly simplified and static masses which mark the painter's idiom recall in a striking way certain frescoes of northern Italy, those of St. Peter and Ursus at Aosta (Piedmont), first and foremost. The Aosta paintings have been dated as early as the end of the tenth century and as late as the beginning of the twelfth.[57] The related monuments are nearer to the latter date. There does not seem to be any hope of dating the paintings in Le Puy more precisely on the basis of style alone. Leaning on the identification of Bishop Peter II as the builder of the cathedral, scholarly consensus, following Deschamps and Thibout, has found not implausible the idea that they were executed in the second half of the eleventh century.[58]

The eastern sector of the cathedral includes two additional structures of note, the tower standing against the northern flank of the terminal wall of the choir and the baptistery located a short distance to the northeast. As originally noted by Viollet-le-Duc, the design of the tower belongs to the series of steeples illustrated at Brantôme, in the cathedral of Limoges and elsewhere in Limousin.[59] In these towers, the first story is pierced by barrel-vaulted, intersecting passages opening in the middle of the four sides. The square mass of the first two or three tiers sustains an octagonal shaft. The transition between the base and the upper stories of the tower involves a gradual setback which is accomplished by means of gables set at the center of each face. Since the initial identification of the type, the list of related monuments has increased in length and the problem of affiliation grown in complexity.[60] The Limoges steeple, which apparently survived the burning of the cathedral in 1105, is thought to be the oldest work in the group.[61] Only the two lower stories of the original structure, however, still stand, and these are encased on three sides by later masonry. The tower rises over a vaulted chamber at ground level, which was initially open on all four sides. Four columns standing in isolation within the spaces defined by the heavy corner piers took up the stress concentrated toward the center by the inward tapering mass of the upper stories. The base of the steeple of Le Puy cathedral is similar in plan, and other aspects of its design may also have been anticipated at Limoges, though this can no longer be proved.

The Le Puy steeple had another, and probably closer relation in the tower, now destroyed, of the cathedral of Valence.[62] At Valence, too, the plan of the open porch at ground level showed four detached supporting shafts. As in Le Puy, the same plan was repeated on the second tier, the shafts being planted in the same position as those below, at the four points marking the intersection of the barrel vaults. The elevation, best recorded in a lithograph by A. Dauzats, shows in both structures the same motif of paired windows with trefoil arches squeezed between two short buttresses in the middle of the third story. Above this point, the similarity between the two designs ceases. While the multiplication of setbacks and gables confers on the steeple of Le Puy a sculptural and jaggedly picturesque appearance, the tower of Valence presented a largely cubic and unbroken silhouette. The change in plan reveals a shift in the designer's allegiance from the Limousin tradition represented by the steeple of Le Puy to the architecture of the Rhône Valley. The towers of Saint-Peter and Saint-André-le-Bas in Vienne furnish near parallels for the shape of the structure in its completed form, the grouping of windows framed by colonnettes set singly or in pairs, and the clear differentiation of floor levels by means of corbel friezes and pilaster strips.[63] Drawings of a substantial body of decorative sculpture removed from the tower securely place the work within the sphere of developments in an axis reaching from Provence to the region of Lyon from the third decade of the twelfth century onward.[64]

The construction of Valence cathedral is said to have been initiated by Pope Urban II, who presided over a dedication in 1095. The Chronicle of the bishops of Valence states that the building was completed in its entirety by Bishop Goutard, who died in 1107.[65] But no recent student of the monument has been able to concur, and it is generally agreed that the bulk of the work on the edifice must have been accomplished after that date.[66] Like Notre-Dame du Puy it has been much restored, and the progress of construction in time can be no more than roughly charted. If the date of dedication can be taken as a point of departure, the middle decades of the twelfth century should have found the masons in the advanced stages of their labor. The sculpture of the two side portals is excellent work in a Rhodanian manner, which on a comparative basis, must be assumed to have been executed in the period around 1150. Saint-André-le-Bas, under construction in 1152, provides a chronological term of reference for the advanced stages in the building of the tower. Valence would thus seem to be a somewhat younger contemporary of Le Puy cathedral, an inference which sets the chronology of the eastern parts of the older monument within relatively strict outer boundaries.

It may be recalled here that in his influential paper on the diffusion of Muslim elements in Romanesque art, E. Mâle attributed to Le Puy and to the Velay generally an influence on Valence well beyond the single quotation represented by the lower stories of the tower.[67] Among these elements, the most widely dispersed, and hence, those which it is most difficult to place within an intelligible pattern of affinity are polylobed arches and polychrome masonry, of which the two cathedrals both offer examples.[68] However, some architectural features at Valence foreign to regional practice, like the arcade framing the upper windows on the exterior of the choir with its alternation of round and polylobed forms, and the sequence of blind arches alternately round and mitered beneath the cornice on the lateral walls of the nave can be more readily localized and have rightly been connected with central France. The first of these devices is seen at clerestory level along the exterior of the nave at Chamalières-sur-Loire and will therefore preoccupy us at greater length below. The second recalls the arcades with a similar alternation applied to the transept end-walls at Issoire, Saint-Etienne de Nevers, Ennezat, and other buildings of Auvergne and nearby areas.[69]

The group of capitals removed from the tower of Le Puy during the restorations of the nineteenth century ought to figure in any consideration of the chronology of the structure. If the results of R. Gounot's investigations concerning the original position of these capitals can be accepted, we would be in possession of a rough sampling of sculpture extending from the base of the third story to a point immediately below the crowning pinnacle.[70] This sculpture is homogeneous in style and does not show any marked formal progression corresponding to possible stages in the construction of the tower. It is also wholly different from the decorative carving within the eastern parts of the cathedral. In the place of an unwavering concentration on stylized foliage, the capitals of the tower show a wide range of vegetal, zoomorphic, and figurative imagery. Two capitals with the four cardinal virtues personified by a standing figure offer a schematic version of the theme later taken up in the portal of the Hôtel-Dieu and in the doorway at Bourg-Argental (Loire) (Fig. 89).[71] In the tower sculpture, the subjects stand in clear relief against flat backgrounds and the peculiarly blank and elongated blocks appear as if stripped of all reminiscence of the conventional articulation proper to their architectural function. Within the precinct of the cathedral, the style of these carvings is most nearly approximated in some of the capitals of the cloister, notably that with the symbols of the Evangelists at the angle of the north and east galleries. There is thus reason to believe that work on the building of the tower was interrupted for a time after the completion of the lower stories, or, in more general terms, that the structure was erected over a fairly substantial period of time.[72]

From the crossing, the construction of the cathedral proceeded westward with the same spare and ponderous masses in evidence in the interior of the immediately adjoining bays (Figs. 30 and 27, right). Massive cruciform piers, unqualified by responds or moldings, sustain the first two of a file of octopartite domes on trumps.[73] Mallay's drawings of the lateral exterior elevations would make it appear that before his restorations, the outer walls were equally stark in their effect (Figs. 29 and 31). However, the unadorned quality of the walls along the two bays closest to the crossing, especially on the northern side, does not represent the situation accurately, and is due either to the artist's use of a graphic shorthand, or more likely, to a wish to show the building as legend helped him to imagine it in an earlier state, emphasizing the reputed antiquity of the sanctuary space and of the eastern parts as a whole. In any case, the structure of the windows and the bold, if somewhat fussy, colorism of the walls now in evidence can be shown to have been a part of the original design. The recessed spaces between and above the clerestory windows, subdivided by colonnettes and papered with polychrome encrustation were sketched and described by Viollet-le-Duc prior to the eighteenth-century reconstruction.[74] They are in evidence also along the upper part of the east wall of the north transept (Fig. 32). Such recessed quadrangular panels housing colonnettes are found on a number of Auvergnat churches, though by preference along the upper wall of the choir. Saint-Nectaire is taken by critics to be the earliest in the group and dated around 1080, while St. Paul at Issoire, assumed to constitute its latest member, is placed in the period 1130-50.[75]

A distinct change in the stylistic fabric of the structure occurs in the two following and middle bays (Bays 3 and 4), which were left standing by Mallay though certainly thoroughly renovated (Figs. 29, 30, and 31). Once again, Mallay's drawing is at variance in some important details with the structure in its present form, though in this instance, it is the drawing which seems the more trustworthy. In the drawing of the southern elevation, the cornice molding of the upper aisle wall is continuous from the junction of the transept and the nave through the end of the western edge of the buttress dividing the fourth and third bays. The windows are not identical but of much the same type, with the pointed arch in evidence throughout. In the present building, the middle bays are framed by heavy buttresses, and the windows are clearly distinguished from those in the two eastern bays. Probably guided by the view, several times reiterated in his writings, that the cathedral was constructed in three distinct stages, the restorer emphasized the break between the eastern flank and the middle bays of the nave. On the northern flank, the remodeling appears to have been less drastic, even if the division between the middle and eastern bays is again more forcefully stressed in the fabric of the building than in the drawing. The large circular window in the aisle wall of the fourth bay is explained by the close proximity of the lean-to-roof of the west arm of the cloister (Figs. 31 and 32). The window probably replaced an earlier, more conventional round arched opening.

We do not, unfortunately, possess any views of the interior prior to the restoration. Here, the change in style in the middle bays makes itself sharply felt (Fig. 27). Pointed arches span the nave and mark the lateral progression of the arcades. Their fastidiously articulated profiles contrast with the unbroken contours of the round arches in the two bays farther east. The surfaces of the domical vaults are no longer bare but ringed at their base by a network of colonnettes grouped in pairs beside the arched openings on the major axes and set in the four corners beneath the trumps. Several other examples of this kind of design are known. It is employed over the crossing at Saint-Martin d'Ainay in Lyon, a church begun in 1102 and dedicated four years later by Pope Paschal II, though probably completed at least a decade later.[76] It is seen as well in the corresponding location at Saint-Philibert de Tournus, and at Saint-Sorlin-en-Bugey. The chronology of Tournus is still in dispute, but critics tend to agree in the association of the eastern parts, along with the crossing tower, with a "second dedication" of the church by Callixtus II in 1120.[77] The version of the *parti* at Tournus is somewhat more elaborate than that at Ainay and Le Puy, involving the insertion of an additional colonnette at a point halfway between the windows and the base of the trumps, but it would obviously be hazardous to draw any inferences from this on the question of dating. Saint-Sorlin at Bugey shows the motif in reduced form, with only a single colonnette in each of the four corners, perhaps as a result of a reconstruction of the crossing tower in the middle of the twelfth century. The original structure has been dated, on rather slight evidence, in the period straddling the first and second decades of the same hundred years.[78]

Below the cupolas, the new element in the design appears in the zone of the triforium, which shows in each bay a blind arcade of three arches, the central one more deeply recessed than those on its sides (Figs. 27, left, and 28). M. P. Quarré has pointed out that the same design is found in the bay of the nave closest to the crossing at Saint-Julien de Brioude. This is all that remains of the Romanesque triforium of the church, the rest having been reconstructed along with the vaults of the nave in the middle of the thirteenth century. It is sufficient, however, to invite the supposition that in its original state, the nave of Brioude may have had domical vaults, and was more closely allied than heretofore thought to the Cathedral of Le Puy.[79] The design of the triforium in the two churches calls for comparison with the "false triforia" in Burgundian churches in the following of the third church at Cluny, on which it almost certainly depends. The more pronounced recession of the central arch in the triforium of the Auvergnat churches is most reasonably construed as a transcription in simplified form of the intermediate tier in the nave elevations of Autun and Paray-le-Monial, where the corresponding space is pierced by a window. Saint-Julien de Brioude is like Le Puy, a building without a documented history. According to the most authoritative analysis based on style, the oldest part of the existing church is the ground story of the narthex, possibly erected at the end of the eleventh century, and followed closely by the adjoining bays of the nave. The four nave bays closest to the crossing are thought to have been constructed as late as the middle years of the twelfth century.[80]

The two western bays of the cathedral mark yet another distinct stage in the edification of the monument. The flat termination of the western face of the piers against which the second bay is joined suggests, as we have already noted, that it was originally intended to erect a façade at this point (Fig. 30).[81] At ground level in the open porch below, it is apparent that the thresholds of the lateral chapels below the aisles of the third bay are not on the same axis as the spaces sheltering them to the west. Within the vessel above, the architecture is of a somewhat lighter effect than in the preceding bays, though there are once again continuities as well as contrasts. The most striking change is in the form of the piers, which are cruciform, with slim colonnettes inserted *en délit* in the four angles. In a nominal way, these link up visually with the molding of the arch above the imposts. The motif is in all likelihood another element derived from Burgundian architecture, which provides a close parallel in the structure of the piers of the Cathedral of Langres.[82] The colonnettes here sustain ribs of roughly the same breadth applied to Gothic quadripartite vaults, a procedure which the domical vaults of Le Puy necessarily rendered impractical. The third bay in the south aisle is unexpectedly rib-vaulted. The ribs have the rounded and rather plump section of the more archaic type. If these ribs were part of the original building, which must remain uncertain, we should have here some incidental evidence of the penetration of early Gothic architecture into central France.[83] Saint-Amable at Riom and Saint-Pourçain-sur-Sioule, the two most accomplished buildings in the new style in central France, belong to the later decades of the twelfth century.[84] Closer to Le Puy, the vaults under the crossing at Brioude, remodeled in the third quarter of the twelfth century (?) show ribs closely comparable to those of the cathedral.[85]

The sculpture of the capitals constitutes an extension of the *ajouré* type seen in the older parts of the building, but a kind of trellis weave may now be laid over the surface, or pulled apart at the corners and in the center to form roundels containing figures in bust length or other subjects (Fig. 33). These capitals appear to have been worked over in the restorations of the nineteenth century and are unsuitable for stylistic analysis. But there are capitals in the same style which have been left untouched in the enigmatic chapel of Saint-Clair outside Le Puy and in the church of Saint-Martin at Polignac, some three kilometers north of the city (Fig. 34).[86] In 1128, with the approval of Bishop Humbert, this church was given to the abbey of Pébrac, which installed canons there. Additional benefactions were made by him in 1142.[87] Although the documents preserve no record of building activity, these dates might well mark out the progress of construction in time.

In most other respects, the architecture of the two western bays holds no surprises. The domical vaults show the same system of applied colonnettes as in the preceding two bays. In the form of the nave arcades and aisle windows, there is even a return to the round arch, and a more ponderous system of moluration is introduced. No doubt, the daring thrust of the western mass of the building into space is in itself a novelty of dramatic proportions. The nature of the topography was obviously a major factor in the choice of a design in two stories, with the façade harboring a monumental porch serving simultaneously as an entrance and as the substructure of a room at upper level, where a western choir or *choeur St. André* was formerly installed. But the architect may well have been attracted to this solution through familiarity with monuments of the 1140s and 1150s like Notre-Dame de Soissons and Saint-Leu d'Esserent, which, with their open porches extending to the full width of the façade and surmounted by a hall of equal dimensions, constitute the nearest typological parallels.[88] In Auvergne, the church of Châtel-Montagne was, like Notre-Dame du Puy, enlarged subsequent to its completion through the addition in the west of a two-storied entrance porch incorporation stairs. This addition is thought to have been made around 1150.[89]

These rough coordinates of style portray the construction of the cathedral as having unfolded in three stages from the second half of the eleventh century through the middle of the twelfth. Setting aside the old choir, which might well have been a remnant of an older edifice, it remains to be determined what part of the cathedral now standing can be credited to the single builder named in the inscription of the Infancy doors. There is a reasonable likelihood that the eastern masses of the church inclusive of the two nave bays adjoining the crossing were planned and executed in part during the later eleventh century. The range of comparable architectural, sculptural, and painterly evidence available to us encompasses within its chronological limits the period of Peter II's tenure, though not altogether comfortably so. Only by advancing strong claims on behalf of the originality and influence of the cathedral would it be possible to maintain that these eastern parts stood complete by 1073. Such claims are not wholly implausible, but their full vindication could ultimately be secured only with the help of a very literal and by no means an incontrovertible reading of the inscription.

Nevertheless, Peter II is the only bishop of Le Puy to whom the inscription could with reason apply. Perhaps, having planned and begun the new church, his role loomed larger in the local consciousness than it does to us now. In addition to the church, he was possibly involved in the construction of the baptistery, a building almost entirely undocumented in the sources, but which on archaeological grounds must be assumed to antedate much of the cathedral architectural complex to the west.[90] It is also tempting to lay to his initiative the onset of work on the cloister. This fine ensemble, as has long been noted, is not homogeneous. Its oldest segment, consisting of the arcade along the northern side of the church, shows capitals of an unusual type, not found elsewhere in the region, and sometimes considered to be stones of pre-Romanesque times reused.[91] They are, in fact, adaptations of provincial Byzantine models, closely comparable in their conception to certain of the "two-tier" capitals found in San Marco in Venice, and thus arguably still datable in the second half of the eleventh century.[92] The wording of the inscription in a complete state might well have elaborated further on the bishop's accomplishment, or, conversely, qualified his role in a more limited sense than is now implied by what remains. But even the apparently unambiguous sense conveyed to us by the word *edificavit* is not necessarily to be taken at face value. Little of Valence cathedral, as we have seen, was constructed by the man remembered for it in the dedicatory inscription and even more explicitly in the episcopal chronicle, which does not hesitate to affirm that he erected the building *"a primo lapide ad summum."*[93] Other examples of the same inflation of the achievement and personality of the founder in the historiography of medieval institutions could be given.[94]

With the middle bays of the nave, we are, in comparative terms again, in a period at least a generation later. The typology of the vaults, the fastidious moluration, and the unmistakable references to the architecture of Burgundy and the Rhône Valley all point toward the end of the first quarter of the twelfth century. There are at this and in the succeeding time some other traces of Rhodanian influence in the art of the cathedral. A decorative roundel with a fantastic animal embedded above the entrance at the northeastern extremity of the cloister recalls the frequent use of similar medallions in the architecture of the Rhône Valley and the contiguous geographic zone to the north, as for example, in the cloister of Aix-en-Provence, at Saint-Donat-sur-l'Herbasse and at Cluny.[95] The portal of the chapter house off the middle of the eastern arm of the cloister is framed by undulating columns similar to those, somewhat better known, of the cloister of Saint-Guilhem-le-Désert.[96] The brilliant octagonal crossing tower at Monastier-Saint-Chaffre, less than twenty kilometers southwest of Le Puy is of the purest Burgundian design and was perhaps erected with the help of masons dispatched from Cluny.[97] The change in aesthetic orientation illustrated in the second building campaign of the cathedral also parallels in a suggestive way the shifting pattern of episcopal appointments. Whereas Peter II and his predecessor Stephen II (1030-53) were members of a prominent Auvergnat family, the Mercoeurs, the roots of Adhemar of Monteil (1087?-98) were in the Rhône Valley, near the present-day Montélimar.[98] Adhemar was followed in office by Pontius of Tournon (1102-12) of whom little is known, but who may be inferred to have had roots in the same region.[99] Pontius-Maurice, his successor, was a Montboissier, and thus again of eminent Auvergnat stock. But with the influential Humbert of Albon (1127-44), the succession passed to a member of an important Viennois family whose major offshoots were the counts of Grenoble.[100] In the light of our proposed chronology, it was Humbert or his immediate predecessor who brought the monument to the state of its initial completion.

It is generally agreed that between the construction of the middle and western pair of bays, some time must have elapsed. How much time is a question open to debate, though any suggestion must come to terms with the sustained but not markedly discontinuous pace of stylistic progress which characterizes the structure as the eye proceeds from the middle to the western end wall. The frescoes of the entrance porch in the fourth bay, which were executed in the period around the year 1200, might be taken as a terminal date for the completion of the work, since they are unlikely to have been carried out while building activity on the western bays was still in progress. The incidental clues furnished on the basis of comparisons would also tend to situate the final stage of construction in the second half of the twelfth century. The builders involved in this final campaign must have found the wooden doors already in place, since it does not seem conceivable that the two chapels flanking the entrance could have been left exposed to the elements for a period encompassing at least a generation.

NOTES

1. Thiollier, *Architecture religieuse,* 73ff. Fikry, *Art roman du Puy,* 33ff. *St.-Michel d'Aiguilhe. Commémoration du millénaire,* Le Puy, 1962. The chapel was founded in 962 (*Gallia Christ.,* II, 695), but later enlarged at a time close to the building of the cathedral, judging by the analogies between the towers of the respective buildings.
2. Thiollier, *Architecture religieuse,* 70ff. U. Rouchon, "La chapelle octogonale d'Aiguilhe ou temple de Diane," *Mém. et Procès-Verbaux,* 1902-3, 113-41. Fikry, *Art roman du Puy,* 39ff. The original function and date of this structure have been the subject of much discussion. Thiollier believed that he had found a mention of the chapel as a dependency of the Hôtel-Dieu in a document with the date 1088, but Fikry holds that the reference is vague and inconclusive.
3. There is as yet no detailed study of this monument. The sculpture from the site has been inventoried and the portal hypothetically reconstituted by R. Gounot, *Collections lapidaires,* 197ff.
4. A. Fayard, "Les premiers évêques du Puy," *Cahiers de la Haute-Loire,* I, 1966, 17ff. The oldest mention of the church seems to be that found in a charter of 1177, when a certain Cormac d'Espaly concluded a transaction recorded "iuxta ecclesiam Sancti Marcelli" (A. Jacotin, *Preuves de la maison de Polignac,* Paris, I, 1907, 125). See also Thiollier, *Architecture religieuse,* 113-14.
5. For fragments of architectural sculpture of unspecified provenance found in the city, see Gounot, *Collections lapidaires,* 209ff. Topographical surveys are found in A. Boudon-Lashermes, *Le vieux Puy. La vie d'autrefois au Puy-en-Velay,* Saint-Etienne, 1912; A. Aymard, *Les origines de la ville du Puy,* Le Puy, 1855, and *idem, Fouilles au Puy.* Romanesque churches for which some archaeological evidence exists are Saint-Barthélemy, the chief Templar house; Saint-Georges, a collegiate church mentioned in a charter of 1089 (A. Fayard, *Saint-Hilaire au Puy et l'église Saint-Georges,* Le Puy, 1968, 32 and 61ff.), of which the few remaining parts are now incorporated into the chapel of the Grand Séminaire; the parish church of Saint Vosy, of which the last vestiges were seen by Thiollier around the turn of the century; and Saint-Pierre-le-Vieux, the remaining parts of which are incorporated in the sacristy of the Pères Observantins (Thiollier, *Architecture religieuse,* 76-77).
6. The legends concerning the foundation of the cathedral and the miraculous events surrounding its construction are found in Pierre Odin's *Fondation de la saincte église et singulier oratoire de Nostre-Dame du Puy,* and Mathurin des Roys, *Histoire de Notre-Dame du Puy en Velay,* Lyon, 1523. Both of these works have been reprinted by Ch. Rocher, "Les vieilles histoires de Notre-Dame du Puy," *Mém. et Procès-Verbaux,* V, 1886-87, 1ff. and 45ff.
7. Odo de Gissey, *Discours historiques de la très ancienne dévotion de Nostre Dame du Puy,* Le Puy, 1644. Th. Bochart de Sarron, *Histoire de l'église angélique de Notre Dame du Puy,* Le Puy, 1693.
8. Gissey, *Discours historiques,* 625.
9. On the historicity of these figures and the early episcopal lists, see L. Duchesne, *Fastes épiscopaux de l'ancienne Gaule,* Paris, 1900, II, 55-58, and Fayard, *Premiers évêques,* 17-70. Writing in the mid-sixteenth century, Médicis transcribed the same account of the establishment of the see from a now lost Lectionary of the cathedral (*Chroniques,* ed. Chassaing, I, 7ff.). Gissey, on the other hand, observes cautiously, but shrewdly that "On croy que ce bastiment soit antique, si est-ce qu'il tient plus du moderne, et Gottique . . ." (p. 85).
10. The evidence concerning this figure, which has inspired a copious bibliography, is carefully examined by Gounot, *Collections lapidaires,* 104ff. His identification as the builder of the first cathedral is based on the interpretation of the inscription . . . PISO SENATUR ARTIFEX (or . . . PIS SENATUR ARTEFEX) found on a fragmentary lintel discovered in the nineteenth century in a garden near the cathedral, and restored by Aymard as follows: *(Scutarius e)pis(c)o(pus) senatur artefex fecit.* This reading is accepted neither by E. Le Blant, *Sarcophages paléochrétiens de la Gaule,* Paris, 1886, II, 573, nor by Gounot, *Collections lapidaires,* 112.
11. Estiennot's amusing letter to Mabillon in 1677 states that he did not wish to get involved with the "traditions du saint Prépuce" and the dedication of the church "par les saints anges," alluding to two of the most cherished legends promoted by

the cathedral (A. Lascombe, "Correspondence Bénédictine," *Tablettes hist.*, III, 1872-73, 520-21).

12. Charter first published by P. de Marca, *Histoire du Béarn*, Paris, 1640, 810-11 and also found in DeVic and Vaissete, *Histoire générale du Languedoc*, III, 345. It is analyzed by Ch. Rocher, "Les rapports de l'église du Puy avec la ville de Girone en Espagne et le Comté de Bigorre," *Tablettes hist.*, III, 1872-73, 350ff., and No. IV, 473-74.
13. De Marca, *Histoire du Béarn*, 811. Rocher, *Rapports*, No. V, 475.
14. DeVic and Vaissete, *Histoire générale du Languedoc*, V, 622-23, and 747. Rocher, *Rapports*, 476-77, Nos. VI and VII. Vaissete casts some doubt on the authenticity of this donation (III, 345).
15. *Gallia Christ.*, II, 705.
16. *Gallia Christ.*, II, 704. The document is found in Bibl Nat., Recueil Doat 117, fol. 367, and commented on by Thiollier, *Architecture religieuse*, 29.
17. DeVic and Vaissete, *Histoire générale du Languedoc*, V, 1002.
18. M. Pacaut, *Louis VII et son royaume*, Paris, 1964, 85-86.
19. *Gallia Christ.*, II, Instrum. 231. A. Luchaire, *Etudes sur les actes de Louis VII*, Paris, 230. 1885, Nos. 185, 158-59, and 405.
20. Bouquet, *Recueil des historiens des Gaules*, XIV, 465-68. Pacaut, *Louis VII*, 169, 171.
21. Faujas de Saint-Fond, *Volcans éteints*, 417-28. The history of the statue is traced by I. H. Forsyth, *The Throne of Wisdom. Wood Sculptures of the Madonna in Romanesque France*, Princeton, 1972, 103ff.
22. Rocher, *Vieilles histoires*, xvi-xvii. The oldest explicit mention of the new name seems to be a passage in the *Liber miraculorum sanctae Fidis* compiled by the *scholasticus* Bernard of Angers some time after 1013: "Namque peregre profecti sunt nuper quidem ex nostris Andecavinis orationis causa ad illustrem et populosam illam urbem, quam, pene deleto antiquiore nomine, quod Anicium ni fallor fuisse videtur, nunc Podium Sanctae Mariae vulgares appellant" (*Liber miraculorum*, ed. A. Bouillet, Paris, 1897, 30). It is taken up again in a bull of Leo IX of 1051: "ecclesia Aniciensi, quae et Vellaviensis seu Podium Sanctae Mariae dicitur" (*Tablettes hist.*, I, 218). The date 1077 given by G. and P. Paul, *Notre-Dame du Puy. Essai historique et archéologique*, Le Puy, 1950, 6, for the first appearance of the name is probably a misprint.
23. As noted by Forsyth, *Throne of Wisdom*, 104, it is stipulated in the donation of Raymond of Saint-Gilles that a candle should burn on his behalf both day and night before the image of the Virgin on the altar ("ante Dei Genitricis venerandam imaginem super altare ardeat"). It may be supposed that the image in question was the statue described by Faujas and destroyed during the French Revolution.
24. Bibl. Nat. Coll. Languedoc 47, fol. 243.
25. Gissey, *Discours historiques*, 105. The name Saint-Quentin probably refers to a *castrum* listed among the possessions of the cathedral in a privilege issued by Clement IV in 1267 (Médicis, *Chroniques*, I, 80) and located in the community of Saint-Quentin-Chaspinhac, northwest of Le Puy (A. Chassaing, *Dictionnaire topographique du Département de la Haute-Loire*, Paris, 1907, 260). The Saint-Quentin clan is mentioned with some frequency in Le Puy documents and seems to have occupied an influential position in the town. Bozo and Ymbert of Saint Quentin, both described as *milites* also made donations to the cathedral, as recorded in a thirteenth-century obituary preserved only in part (P.-M. Fournier, "Fragments d'un obituaire d'une église du Puy," *Bull. hist.*, IX, 1924, 72-82).
26. Bochart de Sarron, *Histoire de l'église angélique*, 98.
27. There is as yet no reliable archaeological survey of this building, which is still undergoing piecemeal restoration. See F. Enaud, *Peintures murales*, 35ff.
28. Gissey, *Discours historiques*, 327-28: "De cette arrivée Pontificale au Puy, je n'ay appris autre chose, sinon que la porte murée de l'église Notre-Dame (qui regarde le Fort, et laquelle entre en la Sacristie) fut expressement faicte pour donner entrée au grand Pape."
29. R. Crozet, "Le voyage d'Urbain II en France (1095-96) et son importance au point de vue archéologique," *Annales du midi*, 1937, 42-69, and esp. 57. The author surmises that Urban did not perform any ceremony in Le Puy nor in Clermont, in spite of his close relations with Adhemar of Monteil.
30. Chassaing, *Calendrier de l'église du Puy*, 284.
31. Gounot, *Collections lapidaires*, 104ff.
32. A list of bishops is given by Médicis, *Chroniques*, I, 142-43, and with reference to the documents, in *Gallia Christ.*, II, 687ff. More extended treatment, with important corrections, is found in J. Payrard, *Nouvel épiscopologe du Velay*, Le Puy, 1891, and L. Pascal, *Bibliographie du Velay et de la Haute-Loire*, Le Puy, 1903, 605ff., with the sources.
33. Fikry, *Art roman du Puy*, 282-83. Earlier, the same opinion was put forth by Longpérier, *De l'emploi des caractères arabes*, 701, and by A. Aymard,

Annales Soc. Puy, XIV, 1849, 211, who were attracted by the idea that Peter might also have commissioned the door at Lavoûte-Chilhac, where he was buried. Fikry's thesis was rejected by Bréhier (*Journal des Savants,* 1936, 16) in favor of Peter III or IV, but it seems otherwise to have gained a wide measure of support. See, for example, L. Grodecki, "La sculpture en France au XIe siècle. Etat de questions," *L'information à l'histoire de l'art,* III, 1958, 102.

34. Thiollier, *Architecture religieuse,* 64-66. This was also the opinion, earlier, of Mandet (*Histoire du Velay, loc. cit.*), and it was found again most recently in Götz, *Bildprogramme,* 88.
35. The history of the restorations is set forth by Thiollier, *Architecture religieuse,* 30ff., and more summarily by G. and P. Paul, *Notre-Dame du Puy,* 63ff., as well as Gounot, *Collections lapidaires,* 142ff. G. Brassart, *La façade de la cathédrale du Puy,* Montbrison, 1938, argues on the basis of an unpublished drawing by Dupérac (Bibl. Nat., Estampes, Topographie de la France, Va. 85) that the façade of the cathedral and the first two bays were added to the structure not earlier than the late sixteenth or early seventeenth century. Although this is scarcely to be taken seriously, some details from the ornamental corbels near the upper cornice of the façade published by this author suggest that some repairs, not otherwise documented, were probably made at that time.

    Since 1900, the date of Thiollier's publication, repairs to the cathedral have continued, but without materially affecting the basic design of the monument.
36. In addition to various reports on work in progress and proposals, Mallay wrote three monographic studies on the cathedral. The most detailed is that published by Thiollier with the title "Monographie de la cathédrale du Puy. Manuscrit de l'architecte Mallay," *Mém. et Procès-Verbaux,* XII, 1902-3. A shorter version was published in *Annales scientifiques et littéraires de l'Auvergne,* XVI, 1843, 381-401. The third, seen by Thiollier in the Archives du Ministère des Cultes and bearing the author's (?) note "Inutile," stands between these two studies. It is now part of the Le Puy dossier in the Archives Nationales, F19 1832. The working documents, correspondence, and accounts of Mallay are found in the Archives Départementales de la Haute-Loire under the following headings: Nos. 157. O.XII (Cathédrale du Puy, Restauration, Expropriation); 3.V.20 (Vues. Correspondance concernant sculptures et fresques de la cathédrale, 1844-58); 3.V.21 (Travaux-Réparations, 1844-1928). Other papers are found in the Archives Nationales, Nos. F19 7823 and 7824, as well as in the Archives des Monuments Historiques. Unfortunately, the drawings to which Mallay alludes have in many cases been separated from these documents and could not be found.
37. Thiollier, *Architecture religieuse,* 32, 35. Mimey's work is unfortunately poorly documented.
38. The principal source for the appearance of the old choir and for the discoveries made when it was razed is A. Aymard, "Découverte d'antiquités éffectuée à la Cathédrale du Puy en 1865 et 1866," *Annales Soc. Puy,* XXVIII, 1866-67, 599-655, which is not always free of ambiguity. A drawing said to have been made by the architect Moiselet in 1840 also illustrates Thiollier's discussion (*Architecture religieuse,* 36). His reconstruction, however, relies largely on the drawing of Mallay (*idem,* 29, and G. and P. Paul, *Notre-Dame du Puy,* pl. VII). It is criticized by Gounot, *Collections lapidaires,* who argues that this represents Mallay's proposed alterations rather than the original appearance of the structure.
39. Thiollier, *Architecture religieuse,* 28 and 38, who does not make too great a distinction between the chevet and transept, assigns to both a date in the second half of the eleventh century. Dealing with the chevet in particular (*idem,* 61), he concedes its archaic character but finds it difficult to believe that it could be earlier than 1050. Gounot, *Collections lapidaires,* 142-43 and 150, opines in favor of a pre-Romanesque date for the core of the structure, but holds that the upper parts must subsequently have been considerably remodeled.
40. N. and J.-Ph. Thiollier, "Saint-Romain-le-Puy," *Congrès arch.,* XCVIII, 1936, 161-205. N. Thiollier, "L'église de Champagne (Ardèche)," *idem,* LXXXVI, 1925, 128-45.
41. The latest reconstruction of the original tower is by Gounot, *Collections lapidaires,* pl. LI. For the crossing towers of Auvergnat churches, see D. Jalabert, *Clochers de France,* Paris, 1968, 21-22. G. Nicot, *La basilique de Saint-Julien de Brioude,* Clermont-Ferrand, 1967, 74ff.
42. J. Hubert, "La vie commune des clercs et l'archéologie," *La vita commune del clero nei secoli XI e XII* (Miscellanea del Centro di Studi Medioevali), Milan, 1962, 90-111; P. Héliot, "Les abbatiales de Saint-Sever et de Preuilly-sur-Claise: les tribunes de transept et l'emplacement des

choristes dans les églises romanes," *Bulletin de la Société Nationale des Antiquaires de France,* 1965, 200-236 take up the history of this *parti* and speculate on its function. For Bayeux, see most recently R. Liess, *Der frühromanische Kirchenbau des 11. Jahrhunderts in der Normandie,* Munich, 1967, 139ff. and 146-47.

43. L. Grodecki, *L'architecture ottonienne,* Paris, 1958, 60-61, 110-111 and 252.
44. W. M. Whitehill, *Spanish Romanesque Architecture of the Eleventh Century,* Oxford, 1941, 45-51. The author cites for comparison the choir of S. Paragorio at Noli (J. Puig y Cadafalch, *La géographie et les origines du premier art roman,* Paris, 1935, 210 and 324-25) and the foundations uncovered by MM. Moreau and Genermont in the choir of St. Pierre at Souvigny (M. Deshoulières, "Souvigny," *Congrès arch.,* CI, 1938, 130-31).
45. Fikry, *Art roman du Puy,* 147ff.
46. Fikry's investigation of Islamic influence in French Romanesque art is the most detailed contribution to a discussion apparently initiated by E. Mâle in his two papers, "La mosquée de Cordoue et les églises de l'Auvergne et du Velay," *Revue de l'art ancien et moderne,* XXX, 1911, 81-89, and "L'Espagne arabe et l'art roman," *Revue des Deux-Mondes,* 1923 (reprinted in his *Art et artistes du moyen âge,* Paris, 1927, 39-88). Other studies concerned with the same problem are E. Lambert, "Les voutes nervées hispano-musulmanes du XIe siècle et leur influence possible sur l'art chrétien," *Hesperis,* 1928, 147-75, and the same author's "L'art hispano-mauresque et l'art roman," *idem,* XVII, 1933, 29-33; C. Enlart, "L'église du Wast en Boulonnais et son portail arabe," *Gazette des Beaux-Arts,* II, 1927, 1-11; M. Aubert, "Bibliographie critique" added to R. de Lasteyrie, *Architecture religieuse à l'époque romane,* 758ff.; H. Focillon, *Art d'Occident,* Paris, 1938, 76f.; C. Daras, "Réflexions sur les influences arabes dans la décoration romane des églises charentaises," *Mélanges en l'honneur de Réné Crozet,* Paris, 1966, II, 751ff. Fikry's treatment of Le Puy as the center from which elements of Islamic origin in French art were derived was doubted, in my opinion rightly, in L. Bréhier's perceptive review already mentioned (*Journal des Savants,* 1936, 5ff.). See also his *L'art en France des invasions barbares à l'époque romane,* Paris, 1930, 90. Criticism from another perspective is found in F. García Romo, "Influencias hispano-musulmanas y mozárabes en general y en el románico francés del siglo XI," *Arte español,* 1953, 163-95, and 1954, 33-57, esp. 180-81, and 184 in the first section of this essay.
47. J. Vallery-Radot, "L'église de Saint-Guilhem-le-Désert," *Congrès arch.,* 1951, 156-80.
48. R. Crozet, *L'art roman en Berry,* Paris, 1932, 234-36. The date is based on a church council held there at this time (E. Hubert, *Le Bas-Berry. Châteauroux et Déols,* Paris, 1930, 48-50). L. Grodecki, "Les débuts de la sculpture romane en Normandie. Bernay," *Bull. mon.,* 108, 1950, 27. Both Crozet and Grodecki refer to the style of the carving as Byzantine in origin.
49. A number of these capitals were reemployed in the restoration of the church of St. Martin d'Ainay in Lyon during the nineteenth century (M.-M. Cottinet, "La sculpture carolingienne et le décor roman à l'Ile-Barbe," *Bull. arch.,* 1943-45, 589-99. No firm date for the construction of L'Ile Barbe seems to have come down. It has been claimed, however, that a chapel, Notre-Dame de Grace, was erected in 1070 by Abbot Ogerius (Abbé Roux, "Précis historiques sur L'Ile Barbe," *Bull. mon.,* 1844, 65ff.). R. Jullian, "Sculpture lyonnaise et sculpture viennoise à l'époque romane," *Mélanges Crozet,* I, 563-68, also places the beginning of reconstruction of the abbey around 1070.
50. P. Lablaude, "Saint-Jacques de Béziers," *Congrès arch.,* 108, 339-42. The apse is here tentatively dated at the beginning of the twelfth century.
51. Two of these capitals are reproduced by Fikry, *Art roman du Puy,* fig. 224, and they seem otherwise to have gone unstudied.
52. A. Rhein, "Billom," *Congrès arch.,* 1924, 112ff., esp. 123. These carvings are not mentioned by Fikry.
53. E. Labande, *Congrès arch.,* 1909, I, 165-68. The date 1019 once applied to the chapel was refuted by A. Brutails, "Note sur la date de la chapelle Sainte-Croix de Montmajour," *Comptes rendus de l'Académie des Inscriptions et Belles-Lettres,* 1898, 64-70, in favor of the late twelfth century, while Labande prefers the first three decades of the thirteenth. F. Benoît, *L'abbaye de Montmajour,* Paris, 1928 (Petites Monographies des Grands Edifices), 47ff., opines tentatively in favor of the second half of the twelfth. The late twelfth century is proposed by the latest student of the building, P. Pontus, *L'abbaye de Montmajour,* Paris, 1967, 46.

Two other monuments cited by Fikry in his discussion of the *ajouré* type, Saint-Martin at Brive and the Hôtel de Ville of Saint-Antonin, do not belong to the series at all. For the first, see M.-M.

Macary, *Sculpture romane en Bas-Limousin,* Périgueux, 1966, 78ff., and R. Moeller in *Renaissance of the Twelfth Century,* ed. S. Scher, Providence, 1969, 56-59. The capitals of the gallery zone of the building at Saint-Antonin have been recently discussed within the framework of lower Languedoc sculpture by L. Seidel, "Romanesque Capitals from the Vicinity of Narbonne," *Gesta,* XI/1, 1972, 43-44. Both buildings would seem to belong to the second quarter of the twelfth century.

54. These copies, formerly in the collection of P. Grellet de la Deyte and now exhibited in the Musée Crozatier in Le Puy, have never been fully or adequately published. A few specimens are found in L. Giron, *Peintures murales de la Haute-Loire,* Paris, 1911, 3-6, and others are reproduced through the medium of poor pen sketches in M. Thibout and P. Deschamps, *La peinture murale en France,* Paris, 1951, 54-59. The copies in the Musée des Monuments Français in the Palais de Chaillot were made subsequent to the restorations and concern only the paintings in the tribune of the north transept, which are still extant. Mallay gives a summary description in his *Monographie de la cathédrale,* 168-71. A full bibliography is found in R. Mesuret, *Les peintures murales du sud-ouest de la France,* Paris, 1967, 147-50.

55. A. Grabar, "Notes sur les peintures de l'Auvergne," *Bulletin de la Société Nationale des Antiquaires de France,* 1957, 162-64, reprinted in his collected studies *L'art de la fin de l'antiquité et du moyen âge,* Paris, 1968, II, 1045-46.

56. A. Grabar, "Le pantocrator vêtu à l'antique et les archanges en costume impérial," *Atti del V. Congresso internazionale di Studi Bizantini,* Rome, 1936, II, 142ff., and more recently, C. Lamy-Lassalle, "Les archanges en costume impérial dans la peinture murale italienne," *Synthronon,* 1968, 189-98.

57. N. Gabrielli, *Le pitture romaniche* (Repertorio delle cose d'arte del Piemonte), Turin, 1944, 4-8, dates these frescoes in the end of the tenth century or the first third of the eleventh, a view endorsed by O. Demus, *Romanesque Mural Painting,* London, 1970, 291-92. In his review of Gabrielli's monograph, A. Grabar, "Fresques d'Aoste et l'étude des peintures romanes," *Critica d'arte,* XXX, 1949, 50-51 (reprinted in *L'art de la fin de l'antiquité et du moyen âge,* II, 1021ff.), argues that they should be placed instead "à une époque plus avancée, au XIIe ou, plutôt, à la fin du XIe siècle." The related paintings to which we refer are the frescoes of Roccaforte-Mondovi (Gabrielli, 55ff.) and somewhat more distantly, those of Oleggio (*idem,* 41ff.) Grabar cites as Italian parallels for the Puy transept tribune paintings the frescoes of the chapel of San Siro at Novara and the chapel of S. Eldrado at Novalese ("Peintures murales, notes critiques," *Cahiers archéologiques,* VI, 1952, 178-79. These have most recently been placed in the middle of the thirteenth century (Demus, *Mural Painting,* 311-12). C. R. Dodwell, *European Painting, 800-1200,* Harmondsworth, 1971, 183, alludes in connection with the Puy paintings to Italian influences in general terms.

58. Demus, *Mural Painting,* No. 106, 416, "can see no substantial objection" to the opinion of Deschamps and Thibout that the paintings date from the middle of the eleventh century, while Dodwell, *European Painting, loc cit.,* opines for the second half of the century. Grabar, on the other hand, initially referred to them as clumsy imitations of Byzantine paintings of the twelfth century (*Cahiers arch.,* 1952, 177), but in his article of 1957 cited in note 57 above, made the earlier date his own. His erstwhile opinion provoked a rejoinder by Deschamps and Thibout, "A propos de nos plus anciennes peintures murales," *Bull. mon.,* 1953, 387-91.

59. E. Viollet-le-Duc, *Dictionnaire raisonné de l'architecture française du XIe au XVIe siècle,* Paris, 1861, s.v. "Clocher," III, 196f.

60. J. Vallery-Radot, "De Limoges à Brantôme, au Puy et à Valence," *Gazette des Beaux-Arts,* 1929, I, 265-84. *Idem, Eglises romanes de France. Filiation et échanges d'influence,* Paris, 1930, 152ff., and another study by the same author, "La limite méridionale de l'école romane de Bourgogne," *Bull. mon.,* 1936, 303ff. Jalabert, *Clochers de France,* 21ff.

61. R. Fage, "Le clocher limousin à l'époque romane," *Bull. mon.,* LXXI, 262-86, and *idem, La cathédrale de Limoges* (Petites Monographies des Grands Edifices), Paris, 1926, 23. Vallery-Radot, *De Limoges à Brantôme* adds to the group the steeple of Saint-Martial at Limoges, as depicted on a drawing published by A. Rostand, "Un dessin inédit du clocher de Saint-Martial de Limoges," *Bull. mon.,* LXXXIII, 1924, 172.

62. Vallery-Radot, *De Limoges à Brantôme,* 282f. On the steeple of Valence, see N. and F. Thiollier, "L'ancien clocher de la cathédrale de Valence," *Revue de l'art chrétien,* January 1902, 31-40, and *Architecture religieuse,* 58, where the connection of this monument with Le Puy is also stressed, as it was earlier in Mâle's already quoted essay *L'Espagne arabe et l'art roman,* 69-72.

63. E. Albrand, *L'église et le cloître de Saint-André-le-Bas à Vienne,* Vienne, 1961. J. Formigé, "Abbaye de Saint-André-le-Bas," *Congrès arch.,* LXXXVI, 1925, 73ff. *Idem,* "Abbaye de Saint-Pierre," *op.cit.* 89ff.
64. These drawings are published by F. and N. Thiollier, *Ancien clocher,* 38-39. The carvings themselves which must have been among the most handsome works of the classicizing style, are said to be lost.
65. J. de Font-Réaulx, "Les chroniques des évêques de Valence," *Bulletin de la Société départementale d'archéologie et de statistique de la Drôme,* 1926, 112-13.
66. Ch. Perrot and N. Thiollier, "Valence," *Congrès arch.,* 1925, 227-48, and especially 236ff. Ch. Perrot, "La cathédrale Saint-Apollinaire de Valence," *Bulletin de la Société départementale d'archéologie,* 1922ff., 56ff.
67. Mâle, *L'Espagne arabe et l'art roman, loc cit.*
68. Since Mâle, and after him, Fikry, considered these questions, scholarly concern with them has considerably extended the bibliography. On polylobed arches, see P. Héliot, "Les arcs polylobés de l'Aquitaine et des régions limitrophes," *Bull. mon.,* 1946, 75-89. A. de Laborderie, "Les arcs festonnés et polylobés dans l'art roman limousin," *Fédération des Sociétés savantes du Centre de la France,* Moulins, 1934-39, 141-62. R. Crozet, "Les arcs polylobés et festonnés en Berry," *idem,* 26-28. E. Vergnolle, "Les arcs polylobés dans le Centre-Ouest de la France, Limousin, Poitou, Angoumois," *L'information à l'histoire de l'art,* November-December 1969, 217ff., concludes that while it is now accepted that this motif is of Muslim origin, the paths by which it was diffused are as yet far from clear.

    As regards the origin of polychromed masonry, it is doubtful whether a straightforward derivation from Islamic art can be accepted, as was judiciously pointed out by Bréhier, who called attention to the role of this technique in Carolingian architecture (*Journal des Savants,* 1936). A similar approach is taken by V. Lassalle, "L'origine antique de l'appareil polychrome roman dans la région lyonnaise," *Bulletin des Musées et Monuments lyonnais,* 1963, 4, 127-38, and *idem, L'influence antique dans l'art roman provençal,* Paris, 1970, 21, who stresses the role of antique *opus reticulatum.* For a recent survey of the problem, see M. Cagiano de Azevedo, "Policromia e polimateria nelle opere d'arte della tarda antichita e dell'alto medioevo," *Felix Ravenna,* I, 1970, 223-59.
69. J. Vallery-Radot, *La limite méridionale,* 302-3, finds persuasive the idea that Le Puy, or churches related to it, may be the source of the polylobed arches in the Rhône Valley. He also notes the presence of the Auvergnat motif of the triple arch, round at the ends and mitered in the middle, on one of the transept end-walls at L'Ile Barbe.
70. Gounot, *Collections lapidaires,* 156ff.
71. Gounot, *idem,* 203, and O. Beigbeder, *Forez-Velay roman,* Collection Zodiaque, 1962, 51. Virtues also appear on the doorway along the north side of the church of Saint-Pierre at Vienne (J. Formigé, "Abbaye de Saint-Pierre," *Congrès arch.,* LXXXVI, 1951, 91), and closer to Le Puy, on the west portal at Monastier-Saint-Chaffre, where an inscription on the impost block, perhaps referring to the standing figures on one of the capitals on the right splay, may be read ECCE FIGURA PRUDENCIE and ECCE FIGURA CARITATIS (Thiollier, *Architecture religieuse,* 121).
72. Viollet-le-Duc, *Dictionnaire,* III, 300-301, dated the tower toward the end of the eleventh century. Vallery-Radot, *De Limoges à Brantôme,* 280, places it in the twelfth.
73. Thiollier, *Architecture religieuse,* 58, notes that only three monuments in Romanesque France are vaulted with a file of domes on trumps: Champagne (Ardèche), Saint-Hilaire in Poitiers, and Le Puy cathedral. Examples of domes on trumps in isolated form over the crossing, are, of course, frequent. It seems to me doubtful that the three instances where this mode of vaulting is applied to the entire nave exemplify a pattern of affiliation. Nonetheless, a case has been made for a connection between Le Puy and Saint-Hilaire, based also on the relation of the transfer of the body of that saint from Poitiers to Le Puy, an event which is situated in the wake of the Norman invasions of the later ninth century (Fayard, *Saint-Hilaire au Puy,* 6ff.). The nature of this connection has, however, been variously interpreted. Fikry characteristically takes the vaults of Saint-Hilaire to be derived from those of Le Puy. This was also the opinion earlier of J. Berthelé, "De quelques influences auvergnates et périgourdines dans les églises romanes du Poitou et de la Saintonge," *Revue de l'art chrétien,* 1888, 51-67. In his *L'art roman en Poitou,* Paris, 1948, 87, on the other hand, R. Crozet asserts the precedence of Saint-Hilaire, where the vaults are thought to have been installed toward the end of the eleventh century. A repertory of French Romanesque domed churches, with bibliography, is given by R. Chappuis, "Eglises romanes françaises comportant plu-

sieurs coupoles," *Mémoires de la Société archéologique et historique de la Charente,* 1968, 109-38.

74. *Dictionnaire,* V, 372. Thiollier, *Architecture religieuse,* pl. 17, shows Viollet-le-Duc's drawing of the cloister with a view of the northern side of the cathedral.
75. P. Frankl, *Frühmittelalterliche und romanische Baukunst,* Wildpark-Potsdam, 1926, 150ff., and K. C. Conant, *Carolingian and Romanesque Architecture,* Harmondsworth, 1959, 176, seem to concur on the rough chronology of these buildings, for which little in the way of firm documentary evidence exists.
76. A. Chagny, *La basilique, ancienne abbatiale, de Saint-Martin d'Ainay,* Lyon, 1935. M. Deshoulières, "Ainay," *Congrès arch.,* 1935, 98ff., and *idem,* "Les trompes des coupoles romanes en France," *Bull. arch.,* 1927, where this writer assumes that the construction might have been completed around 1120. The dedication charter (*Gallia Christ.,* IV, 236) of 1106 states that the church took four years to build. Fikry supposed that the example of Le Puy might have inspired Ainay (*Art roman du Puy,* 89ff.). This view was rejected by M. Aubert, "Les plus anciennes croisés d'ogives," *Bull. mon.,* 1934, 496, who doubted the early date proposed by that author for the completion of the cathedral. Aubert's reservations are shared by Vallery-Radot, *La limite méridionale,* 305.
77. J. Virey, *L'église Saint-Philibert de Tournus,* Paris, 1952 (Petites monographies des grands édifices). J. Vallery-Radot, *Saint-Philibert de Tournus,* Paris, 1955. Although these authors disagree on a number of important points, both take the dome of the crossing and the straight bays of the choir to have been comprised in the dedication of 1120. According to Vallery-Radot, Tournus takes Ainay for a model.
78. P. de Truchis, "L'église romane de Saint-Sorlin de Bugey," *Bull. mon.,* 1914, 88-106, esp. 99ff., and Deshoulières, *Trompes de coupoles,* 375.
79. P. Quarré, "Saint-Julien de Brioude et l'art roman auvergnat," *Almanach de Brioude,* 40, 1960, 59-72. In regard to the possibility that Brioude may originally have been vaulted with a series of domes, Quarré develops an earlier suggestion by M. Donzet, *Les monuments historiques de la France,* 1958, 177.
80. E. Lefèvre-Pontalis, "Les dates de Saint-Julien de Brioude," *Congrès arch.,* 1904, 542-55.
81. Thiollier, *Architecture religieuse,* 34 and 40-41.
82. W. Schlink, *Zwischen Cluny und Clairvaux,* Berlin, 97ff. and 105ff. The motif is the subject of a thorough study by J. Bony, "Origines des piles gothiques à fûts en délit," *Gedenkschrift Ernst Gall,* Munich-Berlin, 95-122, who does not, however, allude to its occurrence in Le Puy.
83. Thiollier, *Architecture religieuse,* 40, sees in these ribs an addition to the original structure, but does not comment on their possible date. P. Quarré (see below, note 87) cautiously accepts them as part of the initial work "pour autant que les restaurations n'aient pas modifié l'état primitif." De Guilhermy's opinion is of special interest since he visited the cathedral first in 1836, before Mallay's reconstruction, and again in 1861. Unfortunately, it is not absolutely certain that his observation that "la voute de la troisième travée est croisée de quatre grosses nervures rondes, du XIIIe siècle" belongs to the first of these visits (Bibl. Nat. fr. 6106, 277).
84. E. Morand, "La date de construction du choeur de Saint-Amable de Riom," *Bull. mon.,* CXXII, 1964, 171-175. For Saint-Pourçain, see A. Lapeyre, *Des façades occidentales de Saint-Denis et de Chartres aux portails de Laon,* Mâcon, 1960, 123f. On the problem generally, P. Pradel, "L'apparition de l'art gothique en Bourbonnais," *Bull. mon.,* 1936, 405ff., and L. Bréhier, "L'église de Montpensier et la question de la durée de l'art roman auvergnat," *Revue d'Auvergne,* 1907, 415ff.
85. This observation is due to Quarré, *Saint-Julien de Brioude,* 68. The crossing with these vaults is placed toward the end of the twelfth century by Lefèvre-Pontalis, *Congrès arch.,* 1904, 553. Among the oldest rib vaults in the region are those of the Cistercian church of La Bénissons-Dieu, which have been dated around 1170 (R. Branner, *Burgundian Gothic Architecture,* London, 1960, 16, 114).
86. Thiollier, *Architecture religieuse,* 41, and 130-32.
87. J. B. Payrard, *Cartularium sive terrarium Piperacensis,* Le Puy, 1875, LXXVII, 18-20.
88. See on this type P. Héliot, "Remarques sur l'abbatiale de St. Germer de Fly et sur les blocs de façade du XIIe siècle," *Bull. mon.,* 1956, 100-11, and *idem,* "Les églises de l'abbaye Notre-Dame à Soissons et l'architecture romane dans le nord de la France capétienne," *Revue belge d'archéologie,* 1968, 77ff.
89. E. Lefèvre-Pontalis, "L'église de Châtel-Montagne," *Bull. mon.,* 1905, 505-17.
90. Thiollier, *Architecture religieuse,* 68-70, and *Congrès*

arch., 1904, 23-26. The structure, which merits more detailed investigation than it has thus far received, is placed by this author around the middle of the eleventh century or even somewhat earlier.

91. Gounot, *Collections lapidaires*, 185-86, is a recent *mise au point*. Thiollier, *Architecture religieuse*, 47ff., dates this section of the cloister in the late eleventh century or early twelfth century. It is surely not older than the northern aisle wall of the church against which it leans. The most advanced work in the cloister, found along the western arcade, is thought to date around 1160 (H. A. von Stockhausen, "Die romanischen Kreuzgänge der Provence. II. Die Plastik," *Marburger Jahrbuch für Kunstwissenschaft*, VIII-IX, 1936, 145-47, with suggestive comparisons to the cloister of Saint-Donat-sur-l'Herbasse, Drôme).
92. F. Ongania, *La basilica di San Marco in Venezia*, Venice, 1881, V, part 1, Nos. 15, 81, and 120; part 3, Nos. H2 and H3, pls. 207 and 208. The combination of birds at the corners and human heads in the place of the rosette illustrated in Le Puy is seen on one of the capitals adjoining the entrance of the north transept arm within the atrium of San Marco. O. Demus, *The Church of San Marco in Venice*, Washington, 1960, 76-77, has argued that the entire northern wing of the atrium and lateral façade were reconstructed in the thirteenth century, but the capitals of the transept portal clearly belong to the edifice dedicated in 1067.
93. See above, note 65.
94. St. Hugh of Cluny was said on his death in 1109 to have had his new church "a fundamentis construxerat" (*Bibliotheca Cluniacensis*, 518), but the structure was at that date still far from complete (F. Salet, "Cluny III," *Bull. mon.*, 1968, 276). In connection with the façades of Modena and Cremona cathedrals, which appear to be dated by much older inscriptions reused, T. Krautheimer-Hess remarks that "Innerhalb der magischen Vorstellungswelt des Mittelalters wäre es durchaus Denkbar das man den einmal mit grossen Pomp geweihten Bau auch nach seinem Einsturz und Trotz veränderten architektonischen Bedingungen als weiterhin existent angesehen hätte." ("Die figurale Plastik der Ostlombardei von 1100 bis 1178," *Marburger Jahrbuch für Kunstwissenschaft*, IV, 1928, 245.)
95. For the Provençal examples, see Stockhausen, *Kreuzgänge*, 183. Some Burgundian examples are disscussed by L. Seidel, *Gesta*, XI/1, 1972, Nos. 6-7. A study of these medallions on French buildings would usefully complement the studies of H. G. Franz, "Das Medaillon als architektonisches Schmuckmotiv in der Italienischen Romanik," *Forschungen und Fortschritte*, 1957, 118-25, and *idem*, "Das Schmuckmedaillon in der Baukunst des Mittelalters in Italien, Byzanz und dem Islamischen Orient," *Zeitschrift für Kunstwissenschaft*, 1959, 111-38.
96. J. Rorimer, *The Cloisters. The Building and the Collection of Medieval Art*, New York, 1951, 16-21, and R. Hamann, "Ein unbekannter Figurenzyklus in St. Guilhem-le-Désert," *Marburger Jahrbuch für Kunstwissenschaft*, II, 1925-26, 87.
97. Thiollier, *Architecture religieuse*, 119-24, and *idem*, *Congrès arch.*, 1904. See also below, Chapter V, note 117.
98. See on Adhemar the studies cited in Chapter I, note 29, and in summary, L. Bréhier, "Adhemar de Monteil," *Dictionnaire d'histoire et de géographie ecclésiastique*, I, 552-55. The successor of Peter II and Adhemar's predecessor Stephen III of Polignac ruled for only four years before being deposed in 1077.
99. Pascal, *Bibliographie du Velay*, 650-51, and P.-R. Gaussin, *L'abbaye de la Chaise-Dieu*, Paris, 1962, 139-45.
100. Pascal, *idem*, 652-54, and Ch. Rocher, "Humbert d'Albon, évêque du Puy (1127-44)," *Annuaire de la Haute-Loire*, XII, 1880, 3-51.

V Chamalières

THE DOORS OF THE CHURCH of Chamalières-sur-Loire are in terms of scale, variety of workmanship and pictorial elaboration the most ambitious of the three iconographically related central French monuments whose low relief wood-carving technique links them to Gauzfredus's doors (Figs. 35 and 36). Until 1892, when they were removed for safekeeping to the interior of the church, they hung in the round arched western portal of the church (Fig. 38). Since that time, they have been permanently mounted against a walled-in doorway in the first western bay of the southern lateral wall. The upper parts of the doors are comparatively well preserved, but below midpoint, much of the original fabric has been lost. Some of these losses occurred at a time fairly remote from our own. Because the large size of the doors made it difficult to maneuver them, its two valves were joined together and a smaller doorway installed in the lower section of the right panel (Fig. 35).[1] The spaces both left and right of this opening are crudely covered with boards transversely laid in an effort to strengthen the weakened threshold. The monument was discovered at a comparatively early date and was well documented thereafter. First brought to general attention by Mandet in 1862,[2] it was more carefully described by the architect Normand[3] and later by N. Thiollier.[4] A careful watercolor copy made by Normand in 1852 is fairly reliable so far as the existing parts are concerned, but quite fanciful in its restoration of those parts of the design, then, as now, already missing. Other *relevés* by M. Petitgrand (1888)[5] who restored the church, and E. Noirot (1896)[6] do not add much to the picture but support the conclusion that the appearance of the work since its discovery has been more or less unchanged. A number of good photographs made in a raking light when the present installation was in progress reveal some details of the design not so clearly visible to the unassisted eye (Figs. 39 and 40), and others show the rear side of the panels now hidden to view.

Each valve comprising the doors consists of four pine (*pinus silvestris*) planks laterally fastened, the three narrower ones through half-joints (Text figs. 2 and 3).[7] The two outer pair of planks are wider and also somewhat thicker than the rest. The vertical parts of the border are carved directly onto them. The upper and lower sections of the border design, however, are executed on separate and thinner boards, mitered at the ends and mounted against the backing planks with the unsparing use of nails. This procedure made possible the carving of the design to take advantage of the direction of the grain of the wood and provided some needed lateral reinforcement as well. The cross and the design surrounding it as well as the neighboring elements below are also executed on separate panels. Lamination to the three thinner vertical boards evens out the fabric to the thickness of the outer planks. The execution of the joinery is most precise, leaving the surface uniform and without irregularities. On the back, the wood was left in an unfinished state, roughly but evenly hewn with the chisel. Each valve is braced laterally with the help of three forged iron bars. The upper and lowermost of these and a third horseshoe-shaped tie in the middle have rings at their outer extremities by which the doors were suspended in place and could swing open. The right valve is equipped with a batten preserved roughly to midpoint, which met the inner edge of the left valve in a half-joint when the doors were closed. In the process of anchoring the batten to its mooring, some losses occurred along the inner edge of the right valve. Damage is most readily apparent in the panel with imbricated circles on the upper left side of the cross (Fig. 35).

Each valve, like the other two doors in the group, is dominated by a large Greek cross located at the top. The crosses are formed by a pair of boards locked in the middle through notched joints and secured to each other by the attachments of the central of five projecting lobes (Text figs. 2 and 3). Below the cross, there are two oblong panels with designs carved in low relief, separated by a latticework construction (Figs. 35 and 39). The latter is formed by interlocking strips, grooved along the horizontal edges and house-joined in the same manner as the two larger crosses. The upper and lower extremities of the shorter vertical strips are fastened to the panels above and below them through a beveled mortice and tenon joint. Under the second oblong panel, diapered lozenge and starry patterns were incised directly onto the vertical backing boards in an area covering some 80 cm. in depth (Figs. 40 and 45).

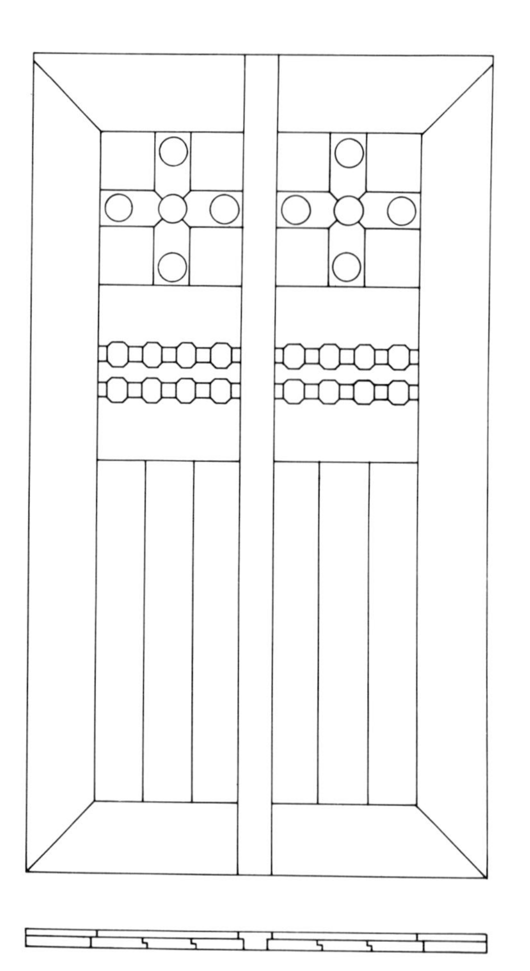

2. Wooden doors, Chamalières-sur-Loire. Schema of assembly

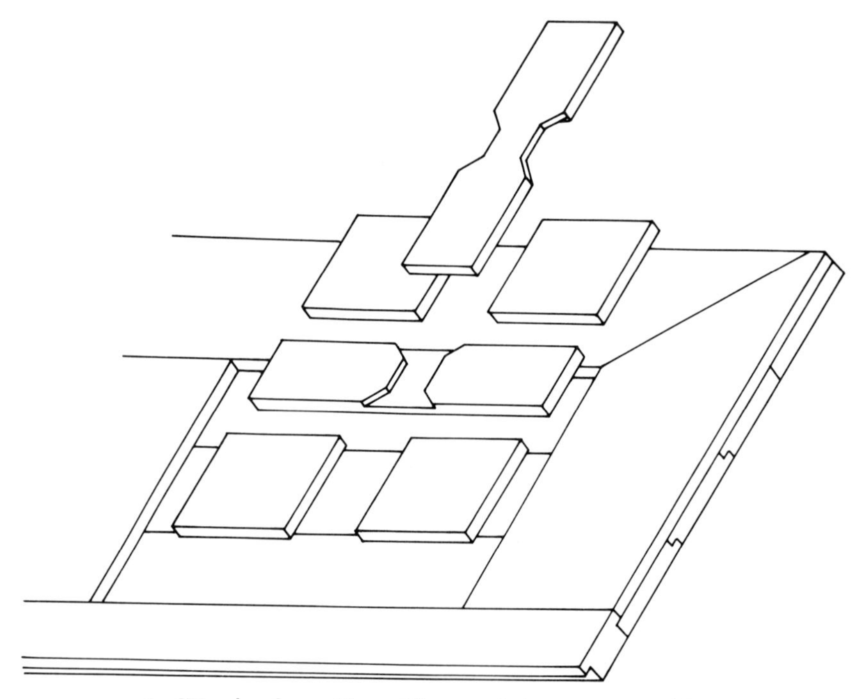

3. Wooden doors, Chamalières-sur-Loire. Cross assembly

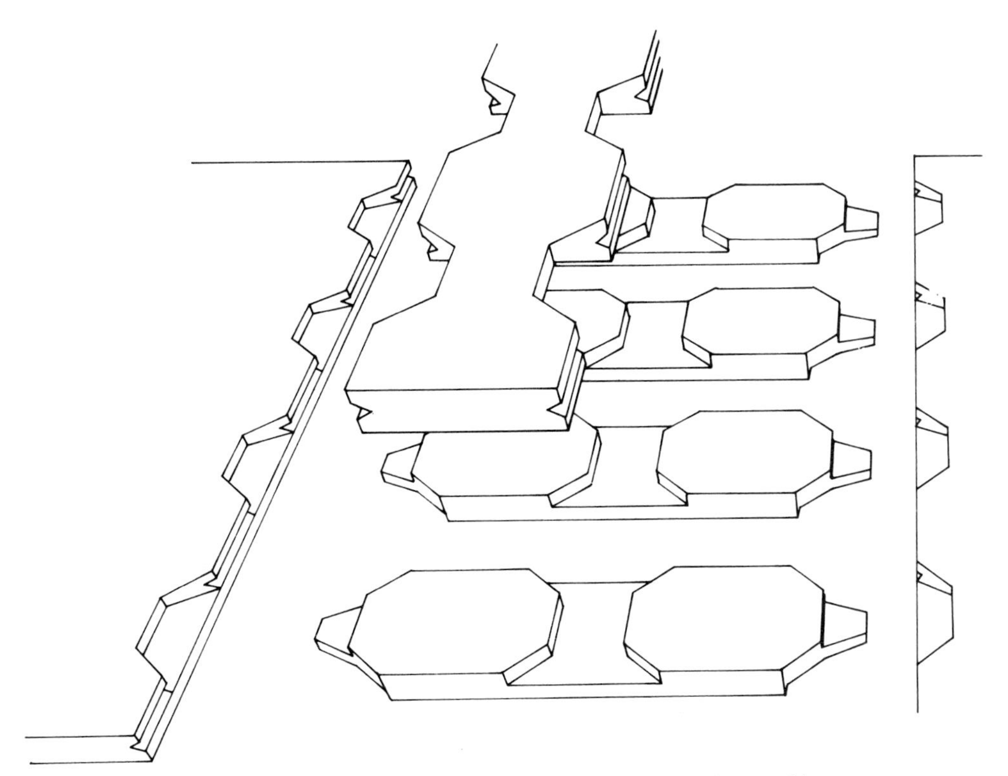

4. Wooden doors, Chamalières-sur-Loire. Latticework assembly.

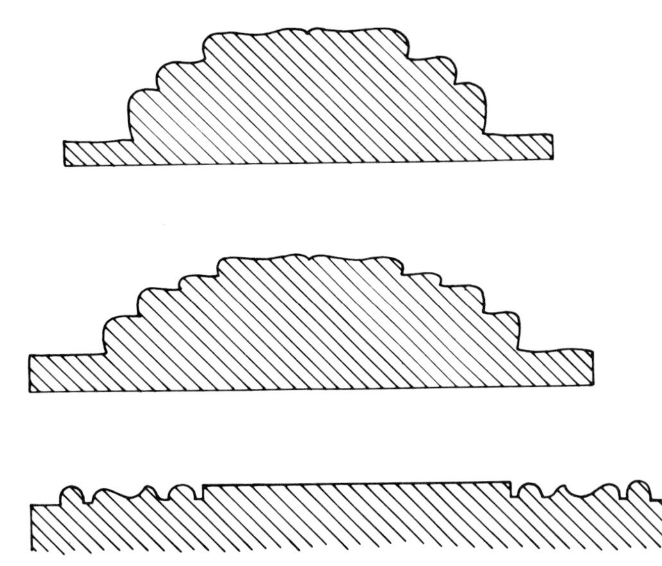

5. Wooden doors, Chamalières-sur-Loire. Sections, Cross arms lobes (top); Cross central lobe (center); batten (bottom)

Below this point, nothing is now visible, though some traces of the original design may be left under the boards nailed onto the surface in the later alteration of the doors. Normand and Petitgrand, who did not record the existence of these ornamental patterns, erroneously reconstituted the design of the lower half of the doors as a procession in reverse order of the motifs found at the top. It is, on the contrary, quite clear that as in the related doors of Blesle and Lavoûte-Chilhac, the lower sections received an expressively subordinate treatment, comparable to the simulated textile hangings and paneling of the dado zone in the apse of wall painting compositions.

Since the doors, though rectangular in format, were installed in a round-arched opening, those parts of the work protected by the masonry have retained their polychromy virtually intact. The two spandrel-shaped zones directly affected embrace principally the two corner sections of the stylized palmette border (Figs. 41-42). The flat outer border was painted in a solid blue color. The recessed ground is bright red. The foliage and the interweaving outline which encloses it are treated in a shade of the same color made lighter by in-painting with white accents, alternating with parts done in blue, which are similarly modeled with a lighter tone. The modeling clarifies the internal structure of the leaves as well as the alternating pattern of overlapping forms within the design as a whole. Shading in the leaves is by means of light lines laid down in parallel fashion against a darker ground on one side, while the "negative" effect of the same scheme, showing darker lines in reserve against a lighter ground, appears in the facing half of the plant. The interweaving tendrils are also shaded in an alternation juxtaposing a dark sequence against a lighter one. Thus, at the center, a rather loosely painted wavy line is rendered in off-white against a dark background, while in the adjoining zone, it is shown in a dark hue against a lighter ground. Faint traces of the same general color scheme also appear in the zone just below the semicircular outline representing the contour of the portal arch, which was partially protected from the effect of weathering by the overhang of the masonry. Seen in its totality, this choice of colors would seem to have been of a more limited range than that of the Puy doors. The well-preserved traces of surface modeling are nonetheless of the highest interest, not only in themselves, but as a possible record of the finishing layer of the polychromy in the other doors of the group, which, even in the best preserved sections of the Puy valves, is found wanting.

The imposing border, whose width was no doubt dictated in part by the need to neutralize the stresses generated by the large scale of the work, houses a design of unusual refinement and complexity (Figs. 35, 36, and 39). It is constructed like an unending chain whose links consist of two strands of even width describing a space shaped like a mandorla and intertwined at the ends where tri-lobed leaves cross each other or join at the tips in flowerlike forms. In its more common variant, as seen in the upper part of the batten in the Puy Infancy doors (Fig. 7), this type of design affects a simple twisting loop, sprouting symmetrical leaves of a nondescript species. The Chamalières version exploits more fully the opportunity for interweaving and mutually countermanding forms, paralleling the sculptor's penchant for interlace knots and interlocking circles. Limousin and Aquitanian manuscripts offer some useful analogies for the characterization of the foliage, which is of a palmette derivation. Webs of a more open, less rigidly structured kind, formed of long-stemmed plants with multilobed leaves occur in the initials of books more or less contemporaneous with the second Saint-Martial Bible of Limoges like the Homiliary in the Bibliothèque Nationale (lat. 3785), the somewhat earlier Troper (lat. 1121), and a Homiliary possibly attributable to Figeac (lat. 3783) (Fig. 44). As in the borders of the Puy and Blesle doors, the sharp break between vertical and horizontal directions involve some difficulties at the corners, where the consistency of the pattern breaks down, leading the sculptor into makeshift arrangements that differ from side to side (Figs. 35 and 36). The design seems to have continued around the bottom, where vague traces of its general outline are still visible, but the path which it took in its transition from the sides to the bottom can no longer be followed.

Within the space circumscribed by the border, the latticework strip separating the pair of oblong panels below the crosses and the two roughly square patterned fields at the bottom of the design, as now preserved, complete the inventory of purely ornamental form exploited by the sculptor. The two latticed grids are constructed with the help of four vertical strips of wood which come to grip a single horizontal board of equal width at equidistant points by means of interlocking joints. The shorter vertical pieces have tapering ends which are inserted into hollows hewn into the contiguous planks and fastened to them and to the backing boards behind by means of nails (Text figs. 2 and 4). The edges of these planks as well as those of the strip of wood dividing the space between them are deeply grooved, probably for the purpose of simplifying and making more accurate the process of assembly. It is not impossible, on the other hand, that the open squares within the grid were initially designed to house panels, which the grooves would have served to hold in place. The type of latticework construction incorporated in the Chamalières doors is encountered in both Islamic art and in the Latin West, though the examples known to us are later in date than our monument, and tend to take the form of large all-over patterns in which structural and decorative functions are closely allied. The doors of Sainte-Croix at Gannat and those of the church of Blassac, south of Brioude, neither of them earlier than the advanced years of the fourteenth century, offer illustrations of this kind of joinery in Auvergne.[8] But one of the full page prefatory designs in the Codex Vigilianus, dated 976, which seems to represent the same pattern as drawn in line suggests that the underlying woodwork technique may be a good deal older than the evidence now available.[9]

The nails, whose pyramidal heads aggressively jut forth, have an unusual and not always welcome prominence in the design. In spite of the refined workmanship evidenced in the carving and the joinery, no effort was made to take their necessary presence into account, or arrange them, as was sometimes done elsewhere, in regular patterns. The overriding concern of the artisan was to ensure the solidity of the fabric. Thus, he did not hesitate, as, for example, along the diagonal joints at the extremities of the upper border, to plant a row of nails across the foliage and, for good measure, to invade the adjoining space with a few additional ones (Fig. 41). Where there was greater room for maneuver, however, an attempt was made to minimize the interference of the nail heads with the design. The nails set in a row at the center of the upper border are placed in hollows within the stylized vegetation. Those in the oblong panels above and below the latticework grid conscientiously avoid trespassing on the depiction of confronted animals, to the extent that their position may seem haphazard (Figs. 39, 40). But within the geometric devices along the upper arms of the crosses, they were on the contrary, and with some forethought, incorporated into the framework of the ornament. The arrangement of the colors on the polychromed surface of the panels made possible other emphases or combinations.

The zones of ornament below the second pair of oblong panels, carved directly onto the backing planks, are unfortunately so worn that only the rough configuration of the design is still distinct (Figs. 40 and 45). On the left side, the space was subdivided by intersecting diagonals alternately overlapping or passing under each other. Each of the lozenge-shaped areas thus delineated is filled by an open palmette leaf, tri-lobed and slotted in the middle, like the plant which marks the upper right corner of the border. The leaves were arranged in radial patterns, each in a group of four facing toward a common center. A capital inserted on the right side of the doorway on the northern side of the church at Chamalières, leading to the cloister, shows ornament of a related type (Figs. 40 and 47). On the right valve, there are nine starlike flowers disposed in three equal rows. Their outline is now quite indistinct, but it is still possible to make out the scalloped silhouette of the form with its deep slits penetrating from the four corners and probably also from the middle of each side toward the center (Fig. 45). The lower section of the door at Lavoûte-Chilhac shows an appreciably drier version of the same motif, just as the panel immediately below the inscription offers an echo of the open palmette leaf pattern on the left valve. The design in a more full-bodied state, as it presented itself at Chamalières, must have resembled the starry blossoms set in rows as moldings around the portal of the Manécanterie in Lyon [10] or along the cornice of the tower of Saint-Restitut (Drôme).[11] Single specimens are found at closer range under the cornice of the cloister of Le Puy cathedral: petaled devices, lobed at the outer edge and radiating from a central core (Fig. 48).[12]

The decorative treatment of the door below these richly textured areas is not known. It is clear on the basis of the photographs taken at the turn of the century that the carving directly on the backing planks came to an end at a point represented by the lower edge of the three rows of starry flowers and the corresponding position in the pattern of lozenges on the left valve (Fig. 40). Below, the wood appears to be blank, and if additional decoration existed at one time, which seems very likely, it must have been carved on boards nailed to the surface, as in the upper part of the doors. The artisan must have sought thereby to provide additional reinforcement for the vulnerable lower zone of the work. But it seems at least equally probable that through the recessed interval just below the center of the valves and the evenly distributed pattern of decoration assigned to it, he sought to isolate the pictorial matter above as a self-standing composition and ideographic entity.

How this ensemble of seemingly disparate images should be described and interpreted raises some thorny questions. Unlike the imagery of the Puy doors, which make direct reference to the Gospel narrative and could well be taken as a paraphrase of it, the Chamalières representations and those in the related valves at Blesle and Lavoûte-Chilhac belong to an allusive order of expression that has no specific literary source. It is even very doubtful whether the syntactic links between various elements which form a part of the design are such that they were intended to articulate a thoroughly explicit structure of meaning. We are dealing not with the description of events, even symbolic ones, but with an anthology of signs with a variable and sometimes astoundingly wide denotational range.[13]

The dominant element in the design is the large Greek cross at the top of each valve. The crosses are formed by a pair of interlocking, cross-jointed boards. Each of the arms of the cross bears an identically turned wooden lobe fastened to the background with the help of four nails placed along the edges (Fig. 35 and Text figs. 3, 5). A somewhat larger disk, more elaborate in profile, covers the joint at the center. The longer sides of each of the cross arms as well as the edges of the contiguous panels are finished off with a cable molding. The effect simulates the appearance of a goldsmithwork object encrusted with precious stones or cabochons and edged with twisted wire. The outward face of the eighth-century purse reliquary of Saint-Bonnet

Avalouze (Fig. 49),[14] the *placa franca* attached to the Caja de los Agates donated by King Fruela to the Camera Santa in Oviedo,[15] or one of the panels with a jeweled cross datable around the year 1000 and reemployed on the crown of the reliquary of St. Oswald in Hildesheim approximate the kind of work which must have served the sculptor as a point of departure.[16]

Early medieval jeweled crosses of the Greek type in an isolated state commonly exhibit flanging or curving arms and the wholly rectilinear outline of the Chamalières cross is much less widespread.[17] Several of the Longobard gold leaf crosses embrace this form,[18] as does the cross seen on the breast of the male figure in the group from Belval in Nancy. This emblem has been described as a badge identifying the wearer as a pilgrim to the Holy Land, and more recently, as a pectoral cross.[19] The rectilinear shape is more frequently encountered in those instances where, as at Chamalières, the cross is not an independent entity but serves simultaneously as a numinous sign and as a space-defining agent within a larger pictorial whole.[20] But for an irreducible margin of uncertainty, we should conclude that while the Chamalières cross embodies the material qualities of a real object with an unusual degree of precision, its outward shape avoids close reference to a particularly hallowed exemplar as well as to a version of the symbol in wide circulation.

The five lobes which transpose the appearance of jewelry in their settings into monumental form show the artisan at his most literal minded. The number and position of the jewels tell us that in true scale, the object which they might have decorated would have been a cross of small size, of a vestimentary type. Recent scholarship has tended to see in stones arranged in this fashion on early medieval crosses a purposefully conceived iconographic program. It is articulated around an all-powerful luminous presence at the center of the design, which on barbarian jewelry may be represented by a bearded and wide-eyed mask, a cameo or medallion of a divinity or imperial personage. An Apocalyptic vision of the Lord seated in heaven in the midst of a rainbow and in appearance "like to a jasper stone or a sardius . . . like an emerald" (Apoc. 4,3) would seem to be almost literally realized. The jewels on the four arms elaborate a complex quaternity symbolism.[21] The central stone or medallion is generally somewhat larger or of a different shape than those on the outer periphery of the cross. This usage is faithfully echoed at Chamalières. Some variants of the theme of the Majestas Domini are cast in the same schematic mold. The place at the center of the design is occupied, as in the Cross of Justin II in the Vatican, by the *agnus dei,* while medallions on the four arms may show adoring figures of the evangelists or their symbols.

Well before Chamalières, practical reasons could dictate the use of draftsmanly substitutes for real jewels. Surely the most common of these is a series of incised concentric circles found in the appropriate position on a variety of small crosses which have been found throughout Western Europe (Fig. 46).[22] A Byzantine altar (?) cross in Munich has more substantial substitute gems in the form of mechanically executed ridged ornaments.[23] The quality of impersonal precision cultivated in these devices, more immediately striking than the imitation of outward appearance, remains an active concern in the rendering at Chamalières.

The crosses are surrounded by square panels each showing a different motif. The panels above the transversal arms of the crosses exhibit geometric constructions, while animals appear in the zone below, which can more readily be construed as the bearer of a groundline. The figure of the cross surrounded by four self-contained yet subordinate images resembles the more familiar schema in which the symbols of the evangelists occupy the spaces around the miraculous sign. This partly programmatic, partly diagrammatic use of the cross seems first to have been initiated in Hiberno-Saxon art, though it was to be perpetuated on the Continent through the tenth and eleventh centuries. It may be seen as a special form of the Majestas Domini, dispensing, contrary to the norm in this iconographic theme, with the physical presence of the enthroned Christ.[24] But the clear distinction established at Chamalières between the imagery of the upper and lower tiers of subjects, which is maintained also in the related doors at Blesle, adheres more faithfully to those images of the cross set in a paradisiac or symbolic landscape. In such images, the areas above the transversal arms of the cross may show stylized disks or similar motifs approximating the sun and the moon, while the spaces below are reserved for stylized vegetation or animals in symmetrical combination.[25] The earliest versions of this theme, which at the same time represent its most comprehensive formulation, are found in early Christian apsidal decoration. They were luxuriant landscapes like that commissioned by Paulinus of Nola around 400 for the Basilica Apostolorum attached to the tomb of St. Felix [26] or the mid-sixth-century mosaic in S. Apollinare in Classe outside Ravenna,[27] with the elements bearing the symbolic weight of the composition—lambs in procession, palm trees, aster-laden heavens still deployed within the fiction of a natural setting. The jeweled cross in the sky is incorporated into the same tissue of verisimilitude, itself thinly spun over a rigidly axialized compositional framework and made to unfold within the conventional formulas of late Roman pictorial rhetoric. The schematic reduction of these complex inventions which appears on our group of doors grossly dramatizes these demonstrative stresses, leaving intact only an emblematic core: the celestial apparition suspended above a layered arrangement of earth and sky.

In the upper left panel of the left valve, there is an interlace knot interpenetrated by a pair of circles; the flanking panel on the opposite side of the cross arm shows the same motif, but with a single circle along the outer periphery and a kind of radial efflorescence at the center (Figs. 36 and 39).[28] On the right valve the upper panel on the left side shows a construction of seven interlocking circles, one at the center and six around the circumference (Figs. 35 and 36). The plump, eight-pointed flower or star which appears on the right side strikes a mildly inconsistent note through its total opacity and its sluggishness of contour. The representation of the animals in the squares of the lower tier have much the same discrete and impersonal quality. Spanning the central space, however, is a linked entity embodied by the much-traveled motif of the centaur aiming his bow at a stag. On its right appears a fantastic winged creature with a single pair of feet, probably to be identified as a dragon. On the left, there is a quadruped unfortunately too damaged for more definite identification. None of the three nineteenth-century copies, where the animals are not rendered very faithfully, are of any assistance for this purpose.

The two oblong panels under the crosses have suffered greater wear and those below the latticework strips show only faint traces of their erstwhile compositions (Figs. 35 and 36). On the basis of the evidence provided by the upper panel on the right valve, in slightly better condition than the others, the panels were outlined by raised borders. Each of the three in which the design can still be distinguished, and likely the fourth as well, show a pair of confronted animals or combatants. In view of the care taken by the artisan in the placement of the nails, however, their doubled number and even spacing in the lost scene on the lower left side suggests that this composition may have differed somewhat from the others. It is in any case at once noticeable that in the three scenes remaining, variation presides in the choice of subject matter in spite of a common allegiance to the format of paired men or zoomorphs in confrontation. In the upper panel on the right valve, two helmeted horsemen cross lances in combat. Their weapons, locked in the crook of the arms, simultaneously strike and are checked by their opponents' shield. The composition in the lower panel shows a horseman in close combat with a many-headed monster. The surging beast has a single pair of forepaws and a curling tail. Four birdlike heads extend like turrets from an elongated body, the torso under the first one sprouting in addition a short pair of outstretched wings. On the left valve, two quadrupeds, horses or dogs (?), stand confronted in the upper panel (Fig. 39). The scene below, likely another paired group of animals or men in confrontation, is entirely lost.

This anthology of subjects, represented also in the doors of Blesle and Lavoûte-Chilhac, is drawn from a fairly circumscribed, and, on the whole, conservative range of Romanesque ornamental imagery. Interlace knots, stars, and other constructions of interlocking or intersecting arcs are part of that fund of formal inventions which it owes to Late Roman art in the provinces of the Empire and the era of the Migrations. The classicizing impulses of the ninth century were not to be inimical to these motifs, which found their way into Carolingian goldsmithwork, book illumination, and especially low relief stone sculpture.[29] In the fabric of Romanesque buildings, interlace knots manifest themselves with a certain frequency in the form of metopes embedded in isolated state or continuous series in the mass of the wall. The placement of these carvings within the architectural setting is often of a most casual kind, so that the reuse of older pieces as spoils may be suspected. But the extensive sequence of such plaques set around the cornice line along the outer wall of the apse of such churches as Moirax (Lot-et-Garonne),[30] Marignac (Charente-Mar.) (Fig. 51),[31] or in Velay, at Brioude,[32] are an intrinsic part of the sculptural decoration of these buildings. Within these and similar series, the motif of the interlace knot with interpenetrating single or double circles is inevitably represented, sometimes by more than one example. While the other ornamental constructions on our doors, variants of a generic type susceptible to endless permutations, are only sporadically encountered in the same form, the interlace knots were clearly objects of special fascination. We see them used not only in a decorative context, but within situations freighted with particular symbolic implications. In churches throughout France, they seem occasionally to have been used as antefixes surmounting the gable of the façade.[33] At Saint-Geniès de Chateaumeillant in Berry [34] and Saint-André de Bernis in Provence,[35] interlace knots flank the major entrance portal. In the mosaic pavement of Sordes (Landes), the panel before the main altar shows two such knots, one inserted within the other and surrounded by pairs of birds or quadrupeds.[36] Knots also figure prominently in other mosaic pavements of south and central France. In the choir of Saint-Paul-Trois-Châteaux, they alternate with medallions showing Evangelist symbols and are combined with rosettes and target-like constructions around a depiction of the city of Jerusalem.[37] At Die in Provence, they are distributed along with a variety of rosettes and star patterns in a luxuriant landscape irrigated by the Four Rivers of Paradise.[38] The example in the middle of the sloping roof of a sarcophagus at Benet (Vendée) is of special interest, since the design is flanked on one side by a fantastic animal, an aspect of the imagery also at Chamalières (Fig. 52).

The motif itself and its diverse usages seem to straddle the dividing line which customarily separates the realms of the purely ornamental from the iconographically pregnant. Construed with emphasis on its major vertical and horizontal axes, it has sometimes been interpreted as a Greek cross with curving arms.[39] Normand's rendering of the device in his proposed reconstruction of the doors would seem to embrace the same idea. But its representational status is ambiguous and apt to be determined by its concrete situation: in a capital at Cunault, it is part of an Annunciation and possibly to be understood as a star or source of light.[40] This is also one of the possible readings of those interlace configurations placed on the arms of the eighth- or ninth-century cross in the treasury of Sens cathedral (Fig. 50),[41] or in the four fields between the cross arms on one of the faces of the purse reliquary of Saint-Bonnet-Avalouze (Corrèze), (Fig. 49). In the context of goldsmithwork, these configurations convey the effect of encrusted precious stones and may indeed have been intended as a convenient substitute for them, though surely more an abstraction of their luminous brilliance than an imitation of their outward appearance. Much the same connotations, as we have seen, can be attached to the interlace knots at Chamalières.

These interpretations are not readily applicable to the depictions at Sorde, Die, and Saint-Paul-Trois-Châteaux, nor to those instances where the motif is seen in isolation, divorced from all narrative or symbolic connections. Another level of significance is perhaps to be discovered in the endlessly interlocking and well-regulated pattern of the design, which may indeed arouse in the observer the impression of a knot. We are thrown here into the shadowy zone of magical speculation almost universally inspired by knotwork patterns, which, if it did not touch the loftiest reaches of religious thought, nonetheless entered with much of the pseudo-scientific lore of Late Antiquity into the recesses of medieval practical wisdom.[42] In late Roman times, Solomon's knots, formed by a pair of imbricated loops, were the favored object of this fascination. Although they were often used to purely decorative effect, Professor Kitzinger has recently called attention to the presence of such devices on certain Roman and early Christian buildings at Ostia, Antioch, and Bethlehem, in locations particularly invested with sacred overtones.[43] In such a special context, they most probably served an apotropaic function. The interlace knots on carved slabs and mosaic pavements in Romanesque churches also tend to be congregated around those parts of the structure most charged with supernatural overtones—the threshold and the zone around the main altar in the choir, both within and without. Solomon's knots occasionally in the twelfth century still vie for the same role, but after the ninth century, in quantitative terms at least, interlace constructions were preferred to them. We have in regard to the use of interlace knots on the door proper a far more outspoken example than the work at Chamalières in the bronze valves of S. Clemente in Casauria, which exhibit a variety of starry and knotted devices over the larger part of their surface. (Fig. 43)[44]

The series of square panels with depictions of animals in the lower tier of the crosses have in common with the ornamental constructions above the same insistence on variety in the choice of motif and self-contained detachment in its presentation. Although their eroded state makes a stylistic assessment subject to caution, they display qualities that set them apart from the carving of the Puy doors. The animals are invariably shown in profile, with limbs and wings splayed out to assume the full visibility of each part. Contours are soft, giving a bland and uncertain account of the anatomical construction. The setting is left heraldically undefined. These qualities, allied to the layered technique of the carving, are recalled in carved metopes with animal and fantastic subjects often intermingled on the walls of Romanesque buildings with purely ornamental panels, and products of the same industry of decorative sculpture.[45] A series of such metopes mounted along the cornice of the tower of Saint-Hilaire at Poitiers includes a very comparable *saggitarius* directing his weapon at a fabulous bird (Fig. 55).[46] Hunting centaurs are found on decorative panels at Saint-Paul-Trois-Châteaux, at Ventouse (Charente),[47] and in an exceptionally monumental rendering, on a pair of reliefs associated with Saint-Sernin de Toulouse.[48] A panel of unknown provenance in the Musée Crozatier in Le Puy shows an animal much like the caprine quadruped along the inner edge of the left valve at Chamalières (Fig. 53).[49]

The popular juxtaposition of centaur and goat or stag which straddles the dividing line between the two valves at Chamalières owes much to the contiguity of these subjects as signs of the zodiac, though it is charged as well with a many-sided symbolism.[50] Zodiacal metopes are included among the friezes of the churches of Saint-Martin at L'Ile Barbe, Sainte-Foy-lès-Lyon and the tower of Saint-Restitut farther south.[51] Although the motif is frequently seen in isolation, or, as in the three Rhodanian churches, combined with other subjects, the zodiacal reference is at least vestigially maintained at Chamalières, since centaur and capricorn occupy the lowest position in a circle which might be drawn around a personification of *terra* or *annus* marked here by the presence of the cross. This is the domain traversed by the sun at the lowest point of its annual cycle during the months of November and December. The commentators relate the lowly position of the centaur to his sensual and demonic nature, as faintly irradiated by the Lord's grace as by the distant rays of the sun.[52] The neighboring images along the outer edges of the crosses, unburdened by these didactic and moralizing implications, depart from strict conformity with zodiacal imagery. The dragonlike creature on the right side would not make an unacceptable *scorpio* (October) were it on Capricorn's left, but the damaged quadruped seen there now bears no relation to Aquarius (January).

M. J. Hubert, who has pioneered in calling attention to patterns of diffusion of the decorative metopes, speculated that they were more or less mass-produced in the quarry at some distance from the building site. This would account for the apparently random sequence of subjects which characterizes their assembly, an aspect that seems to have left its mark at Chamalières.[53] Other authors have been inclined to regard these panels as Carolingian work reemployed on a haphazard basis in Romanesque buildings.[54] Neither of these assumptions is well founded. With some rare exceptions, this sculpture is coeval with the structures on which it is found, monuments datable from the mid-eleventh century onward.[55] Most of it must have been made *in situ,* though the shipment of stones ready-made from the quarry, sometimes over long distances is of course well documented. But the anthology spirit which presides in these collections of zoomorphic and fantastic imagery is not due to mechanical causes and must rather be considered as a purposeful element in this category of expressive endeavor. Along the zone of the cornice, it is still largely conditioned by the clear separation of the panels from each other by corbels, recalling the classical alternation of metope and triglyph. But a kindred license persists in the looser arrangements along the walls as well as in such well-contrived ensembles in the area of the socle at Saint-Gilles or in Antelami's baptistery at Parma–sculpture of a stylistically different order, though bound in theme to the same exotic world, pliant and inexhaustibly bountiful, yet in a socially atomized state, and therefore incapable of entering into combinations based on right number, predictable identity, and hierarchical order.

Although an avowedly heraldic stance is maintained in the subjects depicted below the cross panels, the design here assumes another texture. The oblong shape of the scenes has at the outset a less neutral, more representational quality than the square format in which the animals and geometric ornaments around the crosses are inscribed. To this greater representational effect also contribute the framing of each panel by a continuous border, and the rendering not of an isolated subject, but of an action, removed as it might be from ordinary experience. The depictions of warriors in combat in the two panels on the right valve have a quality often possessed by medieval images, serving in some instances as illustrations of very specific subjects or ideas, and elsewhere as vehicles of very broad metaphoric significance (Figs. 35 and 36). The motif of the two horsemen locked in combat is fairly diffused throughout Romanesque art. A. Kingsley Porter compiled an extensive list of such representations, showing them to have been particularly popular in Spain.[56] In central France, examples appear on capitals at Saint-Julien de Brioude (Fig. 56) and Conques, and on a relief from a private house in Cluny.[57] The composition mimes the symmetrical stance of confronted animals in the ornamental repertory of early medieval art like those seen in the corresponding scene on the opposite valve. The subject itself, however, does not belong to the history of ornament in an integral way, and must be seen rather as a reductive transcription of battle scenes in a grander pictorial vein as they appear on Roman sarcophagi, or at a lesser distance in time, on the Bayeux Tapestry.

The drawing in the upper margin of the Beatus Page in the Albani Psalter is one of the rare depictions of the theme in this reduced version to be accompanied by an explanatory text. The image is to be understood here as a figure of the spiritual combat which must be perpetually waged against the forces of darkness.[58] The relationship of the image to this gloss is on first impression rather tenuous. The antagonists are not differentiated as positive and negative personalities, as they are in the more conventional versions of the *Bellum spirituale* represented by the Psychomachia of Prudentius and its offshoots. Neither is the ultimate triumph of one over the other envisaged. Both warriors are shown run through by their opponents' broken lances, but carrying on the fight with drawn swords: hand-to-hand combat would seem to be the unavoidable next stage of the struggle. Finally, according to the text, the Christian soldier is to arm himself with fortitude and wisdom, not with the weapons of war. The gloss probably comes closest to the main thrust of the representation in the assurance that though struck by the sword, lance, or arrow, the Lord's warrior, armed by faith, will not be defeated. The absence of much closer ties between word and image confirms the unavoidable suspicion that we are here dealing with an original but rather makeshift appropriation of a current motif, not really designed for the purpose to which the writer put it.

A second depiction of fighting horsemen with an even more precise topical designation is the well-known combat of Roland and Ferragut on a capital of the "Palace of the Dukes of Granada" at Estella (Navarre).[59] Not only are the protagonists here identified by inscriptions, but the interpretation of the struggle adheres quite faithfully, as has been pointed out, to the account given in the literary tradition. The moment of the story illustrated by the sculptor is that when Roland strikes his victorious blow against the dreaded infidel champion, piercing his body in its only vulnerable place. The fight thus differs in an essential aspect from the stalemated combats which the St. Albans miniature and the scene at Chamalières both exemplify. It seems therefore doubtful that the numerous representations of this kind can in the absence of other evidence be rightly construed as reflecting the epic struggle of the Roland saga, as has recently been done.[60] Such contests, like the combat of David and Goliath, their biblical archetype, require a clear resolution in favor of the hero. The even-handed presentation, on the contrary, brings out the timeless dimension of the subject, and forcibly diminishes its anecdotal purview. Any interpretation that it is to make a reasonable claim to credibility must therefore rise above the incidental to a more general level of reference.

In the crossed lances of the Chamalières knight, the sculptor illustrates a figure of speech which has entered into our own language and remained in it as a familiar periphrase for the idea of struggle. *Croiser le fer* is a well-known dueling term, while persons engaged in a fight or an argument may be said to cross legs or shins, a figure of wrestling.[61] Romanesque art makes frequent use of this verbal image, both in the context of heroic action and for satirical purposes. Thus the mounted and armored riders with crossed pikes have a jocular echo in the lowborn beard-pullers whose limbs are set in the same interlocking grip. On the tomb of Doña Sancha at Jaca and a relief from a house at Cluny, the motif of paired knights in combat with the lance is combined with a representation of Samson breaking the jaws of the lion.[62] In funerary art, such a choice of subjects perpetuates the evocation of heroic virtue on ancient sarcophagi, where the labors of Hercules, the Hunts of Meleager, and the mythical battles between Romans and Barbarians were designed to portend the entry of the deceased into the realm of immortality. The twelfth-century renaissance impulses, powerful and many-sided as they may be, seem to us only imperfectly to account for the reemergence of such themes and their integration into the fabric of Christian symbolism. Of equal interest is the appearance, in the course of the eleventh century of knighthood as a distinct class within the threefold stratification of society recognized in ecclesiastical pronouncements as divinely ordered.[63] Erdmann, in a classic study, has shown, too, how through the impulse of the reform movement, this military caste received a religious vocation. Fighting in the service of the faith became a noble ideal, which did not enter into contradiction with the evangelical spirit of meekness and peace, and Pope Urban II's call at Clermont in 1095 offered knighthood a practical outlet for its implementation.[64] The Chamalières sources, like those of many churches, record donations made on the eve of departure for the Holy Land. Bishop Adhemar of Le Puy, the Crusade's most capable leader, struck his contemporaries as a conspicuous embodiment of knightly virtue. The chronicler of St. Peter of Le Puy characterizes him as "*gracilem per equitandum*" [65] and the author of the anonymous chronicle of the First Crusade pictures him carrying the Holy Lance into battle.[66] In the somewhat later Song of Antioch, the portrait is of dazzling brilliance. Adhemar "wore a helmet of gold set with gems, spurs of gold on his feet, and a bow at his left stirrup, shield at his neck, stole over his arms and a lance with a pennon decorated with two dragons. As he spurred his horse the steed jumped thirty feet into combat, and the bishop with noble mien engaged and defeated the Turks." [67] Such a man would have found the Chamalières image a worthy memorial of his ideals.

Knightly prowess is again conspicuous in the scene of a rider fighting a many-headed monster which appears below (Figs. 35 and 36). From the lore of Antiquity, the Middle Ages inherited the story of Hercules slaying the Hydra, along with a variable nomenclature of the beast. The number of heads is not always clearly specified nor indeed specifiable since it was the creature's outstanding trait that as a single head was cut off, two or three grew back. The story of Odysseus and Scylla apparently illustrated in a ninth-century wall painting in the westwork at Corvey, involves another many-headed monster of composite anatomy.[68] In the Judeo-Christian tradition, it is Leviathan which incarnates the beast.[69] Part crocodile, fish, or reptile, it is represented with three menacing maws in the Rule of St. Benedict from Zwiefalten illustrating its capture (Job, 40,20ff.).[70] A marble decorative panel at Saint-Philibert de Tournus inscribed LEVIATON shows it in dragonlike fashion, with a curling tail and a pair of wings, projecting as at Chamalières, like fins from the sides of the fore-quarters (Fig. 57).[71] The seven-headed beast of Revelations is its New Testament incarnation. Revelations also introduces into Scripture the motif of the struggle of the heavenly host against the dragon.[72] The hagiographical literature was to be the chief repository of this theme, popularized through the story of St. George. Here, we meet as well another component of the scene at Chamalières, the motif of the hero on horseback, perhaps already foreshadowed in certain Coptic representations of Horus in combat with a crocodile.[73] In Gallo-Roman France, the theme is best known through the still mysterious cult images of the *cavalier anguipède,* in which a horseman defeats a fish-tailed monster.[74]

Some constants manifest themselves in this most diffuse tissue of related themes. The association of the beast with death is already explicit in the myth of the hydra, guardian of the marshes of Lerna at the entrance of the underworld. The beast can be overcome only by superhuman intervention or by the heroic deed of the Lord's chosen. Its malignant power is evidenced by the multiple and multiplying heads, which make it invincible to more conventional attack. According to the Jewish tradition, Leviathan will be eaten at the Messianic feast. Its final destruction is thus the end of death itself. Conversely, the hero demonstrates his superhuman attributes by overpowering a terrifying monster. To the exhibition of sheer physical prowess which the hero or archangel possesses *sui generis* by virtue of his divine origin the early Middle Ages were inclined to add the qualification of high social standing denoted by the possession and effective handling of a horse.

The theme of the mounted rider sallying forth with a shield and lance occupies an important place in the figurative repertory of art in the period of the Invasions. In a certain number of finds, the rider is shown in struggle with a serpent. Whether these are images of Christian saints or heroes of Germanic mythology is not, in many cases, ascertainable. Expert opinion stresses their derivation from Coptic, or more generally, Late Antique sources, and they are held to have had an apotropaic function.[75] In these and older versions of the theme in early Christian art the rider is generally poised above the serpent, and the triumphal conclusion more forcefully expressed than the perils of the struggle. The stele of Hornhausen gives us a paradigmatic formulation: above, the mounted warrior striding forth with unruffled assurance; below, a neatly coiled serpent, impotent in defeat.[76] In the roughly contemporaneous Christian amulets, the hero—or Christ Himself—wields his magic power through the attribute of the cross staff, which takes the place of the lance. The appearance of the cross as the arbiter of the issue completes the long evolution of the theme as we encounter it in its subsequent manifestations.

At Chamalières, as most frequently in Romanesque fighting groups, the protagonists face each other or are locked in a combat of doubtful outcome. The beast, far from cringing before the might of the hero, seems appallingly large and unimpressed. It is a *topos* of hagiographic writing that its size exceeds that of conventional animals and that the anatomy is of a composite sort, combining their most fearsome attributes. The description of the *tarasque,* which, according to a text datable around 1200, once terrorized the inhabitants of the lower Rhône Valley until it was tamed by St. Martha, offers a good example of such a zoological marvel. Longer than a horse and larger than an ox, half-mammal and half-fish, the beast had a lion's head with horns, and sharp swordlike teeth, the three pair of feet, nails of a bear, and a serpent's tail.[77] In the face of such monsters, the worthiest champion might well prove insufficient, but the period seems to have been fond of sending against them poorly equipped or scarcely credible adversaries, as Martha herself, laying the emphasis on man's vulnerability and dependence on supernatural assistance to tip the balance in his favor.

Riders in combat with a demonic beast have a fairly sustained association with the iconography of church portals. The tympanum which stood over the entrance of the South Cloister at Bawit, datable in the sixth century, offered an early example.[78] In the ninth century, Einhard's reliquary in the form of a triumphal arch presents two key elements of the Chamalières scheme: a cross mounted on a base which includes mounted warriors defeating serpents, the latter installed as symmetrical guardian figures within the arch opening.[79] Reliefs with warriors spearing rampant beasts flank the entrance of the gatehouse at St. Victor in Xanten,[80] and we may wonder whether the much-discussed series of riders trampling Barbarians which decorate the façades of churches in western France and Spain should not be seen as an independent extension of the same usage.[81] In the sphere of Byzantine art, a pair of warrior saints on horseback, identifiable as George and Demetrius, appear as guardian figures along the base of the wooden doors of the monastery church of Snagov (Walachia) in Bucharest,[82] while confronted pairs of winged cavaliers are seen on the earlier valves of St. Nicholas at Ochrida.[83]

On the left half of the Chamalières doors, only the upper of the two oblong panels still shows a distinguishable image. It consists of a pair of striding quadrupeds, possibly horses, in a confronted stance, their snouts virtually touching. One of the carved metopes on the tower of Saint-Germain d'Auxerre furnishes the approximate outline of the design (Fig. 54). We have once again a symmetrical configuration, maintaining, as in the images of combat of the right valve, a certain representational fiction, which is conveyed by the relative informality of the animal's characterization. Although their relaxed gait is apt to convey a bucolic rather than an agonistic impression of the action, the comparative material admits an interpretation along the first or the second of these lines with equal merit. The nature of the imagery on the right valve makes it in fact more likely that a combat was intended, evenly balanced and stalemated like the horsemen on the opposite side. If this assumption is correct, it would lead us to a further conjecture concerning the lost scene on the left valve, immediately below the latticework grid. It must have been a fourth combat, dissimilar from any of the others, yet following the model of the upper scene, designed as a pendent of the struggle of the horseman and the many-headed monster on the right panel. We would look, therefore, for an asymmetrical grouping of two different animals perhaps a lion and a stag, or other traditional enemies of Romanesque beast combats.[84]

Like the Puy doors, the doors of Chamalières and those related to them embody certain features that were elsewhere integrated into the design of the façade or portal itself. The depiction of the cross above the entrance of a church goes back to early Christian times. A sermon of St. John Chrysostom preached at Antioch probably between 388 and 393 refers to the inscription of the cross on walls and windows of houses as an accepted custom.[85] The supernatural efficacy of the sign on the threshold of the house was based on the Lord's instruction to the Hebrews in Egypt to mark the lintel and jambs of their doorways with the blood of the paschal lamb in order to escape the punishment reserved for their oppressors. Ezechiel's word that the redeemed in the Messianic Kingdom shall bear the sign of the *tau* on their foreheads was also interpreted in commentary to refer to the cross.[86] In the Latin West, the sign of the cross appears above the entrance of the seventh-century church of San Juan de Baños (Burgos),[87] those of the approximately contemporaneous Irish sanctuaries of Clonamery (Kilkenny) and Fore (Westmeath).[88] Until the extraordinary development of portal structure initiated four centuries later, the cross was to remain the major and in most instances the sole overtly symbolic motif in the adornment of the doorway.

In the meantime, the generally unobtrusive display of the magic sign above the church entrance gave way to a pictorially more elaborate treatment. This was effected either by an amplification of the form and size of the cross, or by its incorporation into a comprehensive iconographic scheme including additional subjects of a complementary nature. The first tendency is exemplified in the interlace cross which crowns the gable of the church of Saint-Maur de Glanfeuil, the sole part of a ninth-century structure still standing.[89] The gable crosses of the Romanesque churches of Mehun-sur-Yèvre, Avord (Fig. 58), Jussy-Champagne, Charost, and Vornay in Berry form a coherent group whose interlace construction places them in the same tradition. The Berrichon crosses show the *agnus dei* in a medallion at their center, an unmistakable allusion to the saving sign drawn with the blood of the paschal sacrifice on the houses of the children of Israel in Egypt.[90] In the Rhône Valley, large crosses composed of imbricated red masonry disks appear above the portals of the Manécanterie adjoining the Cathedral of Lyon and the west doorway of Saint-Pierre in Vienne.[91] A group of twelfth-century churches in northern Spain have tympana showing a large isolated cross carved in relief, and polychrome marble encrustation is used to delineate the sign on the doorway of Saint-Pierre de Rhèdes in Narbonnais.[92]

The scheme in which the cross is flanked by ornamental figures or vegetal and zoomorphic motifs has greater interest as comparative iconographic evidence for our group of doors. The monuments which illustrate this type of arrangement are generally of a very modest level of artistic quality and difficult to date according to generally applicable stylistic criteria. Most often, they are rectangular or gabled slabs serving as lintels, with elements laid out in symmetrical fashion on each side of a central cross. The chapel of Saint-Clair in Le Puy offers a convenient example in the region. A Greek cross with flanging arms is seen at the center of the gabled slab. On each side, there are patterned rosettes, which are possible to be construed as the sun and the moon. In the most common formulation, these rosettes are rendered as identical six-petaled flowers or stars, constructed by means of intersecting radii of the full circle. This combination of rosettes with the cross is already found in Late Antiquity on monuments of both Coptic Egypt and Armenia.[93] The examples in

Romanesque Western Europe are widely diffused and no comprehensive inventory of them has thus far been made. A substantial group appears to be concentrated in the area on both sides of the middle and lower Rhine, corresponding to the heartland of the old Carolingian Empire.[94] Others have been signaled in Tuscany,[95] and in the British Isles.[96] In a more elaborate form, trees may flank the central cross, as on the lintel of the parish church at Bierstadt near Wiesbaden, or rampant animals, as at Rüssingen, near Speyer.[97] These accretions to the theme, too, have their footing in a much older realm of early Christian imagery around the Mediterranean world. A fourth- or fifth-century Coptic curtain in Berlin shows the cross within an arch and kneeling animals below.[98] On a sixth-century sarcophagus at Arles, the cross within a *tabula ansata* is flanked by trees and an interlace knot (Fig. 59).[99] It is the now familiar evocation of the cross surrounded by emblematic vegetation, with its arches, its saving signs, its sometimes fabulous fauna in artfully domesticated stances.

The Romanesque versions of this theme take two distinct forms. Following early Christian tradition, they are predominantly visions of paradisiac peace, with its stars, trees, and ceremoniously crouching animals expressing the all-bountiful nature of Creation in a state of perfect harmony. In many instances, the seated Christ, the *agnus dei* or the Constantinian monogram take the place of the central cross while symmetrical birds or quadrupeds defer in submission on either side.[100] The more strife-ridden image, in which the divine presence manifests itself in the midst of epic struggles of uncertain outcome as seen at Chamalières, is more uncommon. It surfaces in still hesitant fashion in an eleventh-century (?) relief at S. Michele in Vittorio (Abruzzi) showing the cross surrounded by Solomon's knots, and below it, an eagle with a hare in its paws: an image of apotheosis rather than of combat, but laden with a measure of pathos foreign to the paradisiac genre.[101] At S. Pedro in Huesca and at Jaca, the substitution of lions in the place of the customary pastoral fauna on each side of the chrismon injects into the old schema a kindred strain of emotion (Fig. 60).[102] The decorative ensemble above the west entrance of Le Mans cathedral comes closer to such an agonistic conception. The crowned figure in bust-length holding a scepter (?) and making a gesture of blessing which appears in a medallion at the center is probably the Pantocrator.[103] At the sides, a centaur aims his bow toward a dragon. Within the large group of tympana centered around the Constantinian monogram in southern France and northern Spain, some additional monuments embodying the same idea can be cited. The tympanum of the church of St. Michael of Uncastillo (Boston Museum of Fine Arts), with its struggle between the archangel and a demon over the possession of a soul is surely one of the most dramatic of these.[104] At Levinhac in Rouergue, the celestial apparition is the pendant of a scene showing a man, probably Jonah, devoured by a monster, another figure of the struggle of the soul against the forces of darkness.[105] The ensemble of subjects of the Chamalières doors, such as it has been reconstructed here, is within this loosely bounded sphere of imagery at once more expansive and coordinated. Eschewing biblical themes in favor of seemingly commonplace quotations from Romanesque ornamental imagery, it binds these together with a perceptible ideographic thread.

The monastery of Chamalières-sur-Loire is situated in a bend of the Loire River some thirty kilometers northeast of Le Puy. It was founded in 937 as a house of nuns on the initiative of the abbey of Monastier-Saint-Chaffre, which had been granted possession of the lands on the site as an allod received ten years earlier by Bishop Gotiscalc of Le Puy from Count Alfred of Auvergne and Velay. Shortly after the original foundation, it was transformed into a Benedictine community of monks dependent or Saint-Chaffre.[106] The church was dedicated to St. Giles. It claimed possession of an important parcel of the body of this saint, brought from his shrine in Provence along with a nail from Christ's cross reputedly given to Saint-Gilles by Charlemagne, which the abbot of the mother house and first prior of Chamalières illicitly appropriated to himself at the same time.[107] Both relics became the object of active cults, which must in good measure have been responsible for the priory's growth. During the later tenth and much of the eleventh century, the pattern of benefactions registered in the cartulary concerns modest domains only and very small sums of money. A period of more active development of the monastery's assets occurred during the rule of Prior Evrardus (1082-98) and that of his successor Jarenton (1096-98), when both the rhythm and the importance of donations assumes far greater importance.[108] Their energy was emulated and perhaps surpassed by Peter III of Beaumont (1162-73), abbot from 1165 onward of Saint-Chaffre as well, under whose rule the cartulary of the abbey was compiled. His is also the largest number of transactions recorded in that document for any single prior.[109] This favorable position was maintained by his immediate successors into the early years of the thirteenth century. Toward 1097, the community consisted of twenty-seven monks.[110] At the height of its prosperity a century later, the number was probably somewhat higher, justifying the reconstruction of the choir accomplished around that time.

The documentary sources are unfortunately entirely silent on the building of the church. The cartulary of Monastier, drawn up at the end of the eleventh century, mentions the existence of a beautiful church at Chamalières in the writer's time, but this does not necessarily refer to the structure now standing.[111] It is one of the more imposing Romanesque edifices in the region, consisting of a short nave of three bays flanked by fairly narrow aisles, a slightly projecting transept and a large choir equipped with radiating chapels (Fig. 37). The barrel vault of the nave is articulated by diaphragm arches reposing on cruciform piers with applied half-columns on all four sides. The aisles are groin-vaulted, and a square tower crowns the crossing. The towers, as well as the first two bays of the nave were constructed anew in the course of a restoration of the edifice by the architect Nodet at the turn of the century, though on the basis of reliable archaeological evidence.[112] The portal of the west façade which had housed the wooden doors up to that time was also renovated as part of these endeavors.[113] But a photograph of the church (Monuments Historiques) in its unrestored state shows that the original design was faithfully copied.

It is generally agreed that the erection of the present building involved two distinct campaigns. Construction was begun with the nave, which was designed to link up with an older choir. Around the middle of the twelfth century, ground was broken for a new sanctuary, resembling the spacious choirs of Saint-Paulien, Saint-Pierre at Blesle, and Saint-Dier in Livradois.[114] The contrast between the older and the newer parts is readily apparent in the lighter fabric, the greater refinement of the masonry and the more complex moluration of the eastern masses. The sculpture of the capitals of the crossing pier juxtaposes the luxuriant forms of Romanesque art with a somewhat hesitant rendering of the more austere vegetation of early Gothic. At the same time the near identity of the design of the window in the first radiating chapel on the southern side of the hemicycle with the windows of the nave and transept, observed by P. Héliot, indicates that the successive stages in the construction followed each other without lengthy interruption.[115] After the completion of the nave, work proceeded eastward with the erection of the perimeter walls of the transept, an intervening straight bay, and the choir. The upper zone of the apsidal enclosure with its arcaded wall faintly touched by early Gothic is a little more advanced in style. The entire building must have stood complete before the end of the century.

The nave has been assigned varying dates within a span of time ranging from the second half of the eleventh through the first half of the twelfth century. What comparative evidence of style can be marshaled toward a more precise determination of date favors the latter end of this spectrum. Along the upper lateral walls of the vessel, the blind arcade which embraces the windows of the clerestory in an alternating sequence of round and tri-lobed arches (Fig. 38) is found also along the outer walls of the nave of Chanteuges, which was probably constructed after 1137, when this house was reformed under the impulse of La Chaise-Dieu.[116] As we have seen, the clerestory zone of the cathedral of Valence, postdating a dedication in 1095, presents the same design. In Le Puy, this type of wall articulation makes its initial appearance along the lateral walls of the two western bays of the cathedral (Fig. 29, lower left) and the stylistically related masonry of the chapel of Saint-Clair.

A critical element in the picture is the relation of the western parts at Chamalières to the church of Monastier-Saint-Chaffre, for in this period, the two houses entertained very close ties with each other. We are also comparatively well informed on the dates of construction of the latter edifice. It was begun under abbot William III (1074-86) with the help of gold and masons sent by Abbot Hugh of Cluny, but on William's death, the structure was only just rising from the ground. Work was completed under his successor who died after the year 1136.[117] The two structures differ in many if not the most important respects, a situation to which the participation of workmen from outside the region may have contributed. Moreover, the building seems to have been altered not long after its completion through the raising of the height of the aisles and the establishment above their vaults of an ample attic space, bringing the lateral walls to a level where it intercepts the path of an unbroken roof line. The choir was entirely reconstructed in the fifteenth century, and the vaults of the nave were replaced at the same time. As the relationship of the two houses would lead us to expect, the nave of Monastier-Saint-Chaffre is not only larger than that of Chamalières, but in almost every regard, of greater elaboration and refinement in both conception and workmanship. Among the elements best suited for comparison are the capitals in the respective interiors. At Chamalières, Corinthian capitals of various design—some of them modern replacements—occupy the zone of the arcade. Zoomorphic combinations predominate in the capitals at the springing of the vaults, in some cases based on the same motifs as those which figure in the nave capitals at Monastier. There is much similarity between the capitals in the two churches devoted to the theme of lions in pairs symmetrically confronted, though the components of the design at Chamalières are more tightly integrated, and the treatment of the creatures and foliage, at once livelier and subjected to a greater degree of ornamental schematization (Figs. 61 and 62). In the two capitals with confronted griffons, the greater buoyancy of the Chamalières version is once again in evidence (Figs. 63 and 64). The volutes and rosettes of the Corinthian form are retained, and the large leaf upon which the confronted beasts rest their raised paws commemorate its foliage. At Monastier, on the other hand, the surface of the block is pared down, and save for the curling vegetal excrescence at the corners, stripped of its traditional decorative features. The rendering of the animals give them a calmer, more monumental aspect. All in all, the Monastier sculptor's inflection of the theme seems more advanced, though surely not decisively so. A certain number of design elements are indeed common to both churches. Voussoirs have the same stepped construction, with round moldings lodged within each angular recess, and a plump, pearly decoration on the outer rim of the arch.

The juxtaposition of the two façades brings greater differences than similarities to the fore, Monastier's showing a much more sculptural articulation of the wall mass, molding profiles in the upper story of considerably greater complexity and a rich polychrome masonry to Chamalières's somber basaltic exterior. These differences, as much a matter of kind than chronological distance, are also apparent in the sculpture around the portals of both churches.

The capitals of the outer walls of the nave at Chamalières, the richly carved decoration of the portal giving access to the third bay along the northern aisle, and the surviving fragments of sculpture from the adjoining cloister were executed by a workshop also active at Retournac, Vorey, and other churches in the narrow valley of the Loire both up and downstream from the priory.[118] Somewhat gross, though full of life, this art grew out of the Gallo-Roman sculpture of the region, good specimens of which were conspicuously available to view in the animal friezes embedded around the choir of Le Puy cathedral (Fig. 87). This is where the workshop likely originated, for the tower and parts of the cathedral cloister show unmistakable evidence of its industry. The sculpture of the west entrance at Monastier occupies a much more isolated position in the art of the region. The carving, even though worn, is much more finely scaled, with a marked relaxation of the schematism in the construction of figures and foliage. The iconography, according to an inscription preserved in fragmentary state, was devoted at least in part to the cardinal virtues, which must have been personified by the four standing figures on the capital of the outer left splaying of the doorway. This theme is variously represented in the doorways of Bourg-Argental and the Hôtel-Dieu of Le Puy, as well as in the portal along the south side of the church of Saint-Pierre in Vienne, all works belonging to a comparatively late phase in the local evolution of Romanesque sculpture.[119] The date of Monastier's completion can thus stand as a rough but fairly secure outer limit for the construction of Chamalières.

NOTES

1. L. Blondel, "Chronique archéologique pour 1948," *Genava,* XXVII, 1149, 29ff., reports a curiously similar practice followed in rural areas in connection with the doors of barns. The two large valves opened only to allow carts filled with hay to enter at harvest time, while a smaller door cut and hinged onto one of them was designed for daily use by the farmer.
2. Mandet, *Histoire du Velay,* VI, 339-41.
3. Normand, "Rapport sur l'église de Chamalières," *Annales Soc. Puy,* XVIII, 1853, 106-115, esp. 110-11. Normand's watercolor copy is in the archives of the Monuments Historiques, No. 5560.
4. N. Thiollier, "Porte en bois sculptée à l'église de Chamalières-sur-Loire," *L'Illustration moderne,* II, 1896, 161-62. *Idem, Architecture religieuse,* 99-100, and *Congrès arch.,* 1904, 68-69.
5. Published in De Baudot and Perrault-Dabot, *Archives de la Commission des Monuments Historiques,* IV, pl. 23 and p. 13. The original is in the Archives des Monuments Historiques, No. 61.Z.418.
6. Published by Thiollier, *Illustration moderne, loc. cit.*
7. I am grateful to Dr. Susanna Jutte of the Yale Forestry School for making this determination on the basis of a small fragment of the wood. The doors measure 4.10 x 2.50 m (161 3/8 x 98 3/8").
8. For an example of Islamic art, see the ceiling of the mosque of Sidi'l-Halwi in Tlemcen, constructed in 1353 (G. Marçais, *Architecture musulmane d'Occident,* 278, 335, and fig. 206). The door at Gannat is illustrated by Viollet-le-Duc, *Dictionnaire,* art. "Menuiserie," VI, 361 and 363, fig. 11. The door at Blassac seems to be unpublished but is cited in Abbé Martin's pamphlet *Lavoûte-Chilhac. Le prieuré, l'église, le pèlerinage, les environs,* Le Puy, s.d., 18. The doors of S. Anastasia in Verona (G. Biadego, *Verona,* Bergamo, 1909, 48) constitute another example of this technique.
9. Escorial, Cod. D.1.2, fol. 19. In France, the earliest example of this cross-joint technique of joinery that I have come across in the literature is the armature of an eleventh-century (?) window at Château-Landon (E. Socard, "Le vitrail carolingien de la chasse de Séry-les-Mézieres," *Bull. mon.,* 74, 1910, 23, who speaks of a "système d'assemblage à mi-bois").
10. L. Bégule, *La Cathèdrale de Lyon,* Lyon, 1880, 214ff. Dr. Loison, "Manécanterie," *Congrès arch.,* XCVIII, 1935, 91ff.
11. See Vallery-Radot, *La limite méridionale,* 295, who cites additional instances of the appearance of this motif at Buellas and Saint-Nizier (Ain).
12. Gounot, *Collections lapidaires,* 195, Nos. C8, 10, 11 and 12.
13. See on this type of imagery in early medieval art the illuminating remarks of M. Schapiro, "The Bowman and the Bird on the Ruthwell Cross and other Works: The Interpretation of Secular Themes in Early Medieval Religious Art," *Art Bulletin,* XLV, 1963, 351-55.
14. *Trésors des églises de France,* 220, No. 403.
15. V. Elbern, "Ein fränkisches Reliquiarfragment in Oviedo, die Engerer Burse in Berlin und Ihr Umkreis," *Madrider Mitteilungen,* II, 1961, 186ff.
16. V. Elbern and H. Reuther, *Der Hildesheimer Domschatz,* Hildesheim, 1969, No. 23, 35-36.
17. M. Sulzberger, "Le symbole de la croix et les monogrammes de Jésus chez les premiers chrétiens," *Byzantion,* 1925, 337-448. H. Leclercq, "Croix et crucifix," *Dictionnaire d'archéologie chrétienne et de liturgie,* III, 2, 3045ff. R. Bauerreiss, *Das 'Lebenszeichen'. Studien zur Frühgeschichte des griechichen Kreuzes und zur Ikonographie des frühen Kirchenportals,* Munich, 1961. E. Dinkler, "Das Kreuz als Siegeszeichen," *Zeitschrift für Theologie und Kirche,* 62, 1965, 1-20, reprinted in the author's *Signum Crucis,* Tübingen, 1967.
18. S. Fuchs, *Die langobardischen Goldblattkreuze aus der Zone südwarts der Alpen,* Berlin, 1938, Cat. Nos. 1 and 2 (Cividale), 30 (Civezzano), 44 and 45 (Fornovo S. Giovanni).
19. N. Müller-Dietrich, *Romanische Skulptur in Lothringen,* Munich and Berlin, 1968, 114ff. The cross worn in the same manner on the breast by the apostle Bartholomew on one of the columns from San Pelayo de Antealtares, Santiago de Compostela (L. Seidel, *The Renaissance of the Twelfth Century.,* ed. S. Scher, Providence, 1969, No. 35), on the other hand, is of the type with flanging arms. The latter was clearly the preferred form, even though no single type prevails. R. Randall, "An Eleventh-century Pectoral Cross," *Journal of the*

Warburg Institute, 1962, 161-62, gives a list of representative examples.

20. As, for example, in the sphere of book illumination, in the Book of St. Chad (Litchfield Cathedral Library, p. 219), or the Book of Kells (Dublin, Trinity College Library Ms. 58, fol. 27v). A substantial list is given by B. Bischoff, "Kreuz und Buch im Frühmittelalter und in den ersten Jahrhunderten der spanischen Reconquista," *Bibliotheca docet. Festgabe für Carl Wehmer,* Amsterdam, 1963, 19-34, reprinted in the author's *Mittelalterliche Studien,* Stuttgart, 1967, II, 284-303, following an earlier discussion of the use of the cross on medieval bindings by K. Christ, "Karolingische Bibliothekseinbände," *Festschrift Georg Leyh,* Leipzig, 1937, 100ff. See also on this type of design M. Werner, "The Four Evangelist Symbols Page in the Book of Durrow," *Gesta,* VIII, 1969, 3ff.
21. V. H. Elbern, "Das Engerer Bursenreliquiar und die Zierkunst des frühen Mittelalters," *Niederdeutsche Beiträge zur Kunstgeschichte,* X, 1971, 74ff., with reference also to the same author's earlier studies related to this theme.
22. In addition to the piece in the Musée de Picardie, Amiens, illustrated here, see the cross found at Verrines-sous-Celles (Deux-Sèvres), published in *Gallia,* XXVII, 1969, fasc. 2, 279; or that of Marchelepot (Somme) signaled by E. Salin, *La civilisation mérovingienne,* Paris, 1959, IV, 374. Additional examples in Marseille are published by Rohault de Fleury, *La Messe,* VIII, pl. DCLXXXI, and Cabrol-Leclercq, *Dictionnaire,* III, 2, 3105. Other material is found in P. Chevreux, "Les croix de plomb dites 'croix d'absolution' de la région vosgienne," *Bull. arch.,* 1905, 391-408. Comparable pieces have been brought to light in various places around the Mediterranean. See on some of these N. Duval, "Luminaire chrétien de Sbeitla (Tunisie) et de Salone (Dalmatie)," *Bulletin de la Société Nationale des Antiquaires de France,* 1962, 52ff.; *idem,* "Nouvelles recherches d'archéologie et d'épigraphie chrétiennes à Sufetula (Byzacène)," *Mélanges de l'Ecole Française de Rome,* LXVIII, 1956, 259, and fig. 3; M. Chehab, "Mosaiques du Liban," *Bulletin du Musée de Beyrouth,* XIV, 1958, 161, and XV, 1959, pl. IV, 2. Rosettes or designs imprinted from coins are used as substitutes for gems on some Longobard gold leaf crosses (Fuchs, *Langobardischen Goldblattkreuze,* No. 40 (Loreto near Bergamo), 62 (Monza), 93 (Novara), and 109 (Toscana).
23. Bayerische Nationalmuseum No. 68/4. Dated V-VIIIth century; *Münchner Jahrbuch der Bildende Kunst,* XX, 1959, 253-54.
24. Werner, *Four Evangelist Symbol Page,* 3ff.
25. Bauerreiss, *Lebenszeichen,* 19ff. J. Flemming, "Kreuz und Pflanzenornament," *Byzantinoslavica,* XXX, 1969, 59-115. Some representative examples of this type of imagery are found on a panel from S. Salvatore in Brescia (G. Panazza and A. Tagliaferri, *Corpus della scultura altomedievale.* III. *La diocesi di Brescia,* Spoleto, 1966, No. 62, 72-73; the panel of S. Pietro at Villanova (R. Kautzsch, "Die langobardische Schmuckkunst in Oberitalien," *Römisches Jahrbuch für Kunstgeschichte,* V, 1941, 38; Panels from Sirmione; Vicenza, Museo Civico, and the sarcophagus of S. Vittore, Ravenna (*idem,* 36-38, and G. Valentini-Zucchini and M. Bucci, *Corpus della scultura paleocristiana, byzantina ed altomedioevale de Ravenna,* II, Rome, 1968, Nos. 65, 60.
26. C. Ihm, *Die Programme der christlichen Apsismalerei vom vierten Jahrhundert bis zur Mitte des achten Jahrhunderts,* Wiesbaden, 1960, 179-81, No. XXXVI.
27. Ihm, *idem,* 165-67, No. XXV. On this work, see most recently E. Dinkler, *Das Apsismosaik von Sant'Apollinare in Classe,* Köln-Opladen, 1964.
28. This vegetal insertion is already seen on several interlace panels of pre-Carolingian date from the region of lower Languedoc. See J. Ward-Perkins, "The Sculpture of Visigothic France," *Archaeologia,* LXXXVII, 1937, 104, note 2, and J. Puig y Cadafalch, *L'art wisigothique et ses survivances,* Paris, 1961, 71.
29. On this sculpture, see most recently the survey of E. Doberer, "Die ornamentale Steinskulptur an der karolingischen Kirchenaustattung," *Karl der Grosse. III. Karolingische Kunst,* Düsseldorf, 1965, 203-33. It should be noted that much of this work, formerly and still occasionally labeled Barbarian or Longobard, is now regarded, following the studies of Ginhart and Von Bogyay, to be a specifically Carolingian industry. On the origin and character of these interlace knot constructions, there are some observations in Puig y Cadafalch, *Art wisigothique,* 69ff and J. Capitan, "L'entrelacs cruciforme," *Comptes rendus de l'Académie des Inscriptions et Belles-Lettres,* 1918, 197-209.
30. P. Dubourg-Noves, "Moirax," *Congrès arch.,* CXXVII, 1969, 295-308, esp. 305. For the Romanesque metopes in general, see Deshoulières, "Les corniches romanes," *Bull. mon.,* 1920, 27-64, with a list of examples on 37-39.

31. R. Crozet, *L'art roman en Saintonge,* Paris, 1971, 119, note 3.
32. G. Nicot, *Basilique de Saint-Julien de Brioude,* Clermont-Ferrand, 1967, 86, but not visible on published photographs of the church.
33. Viollet-le-Duc, *Dictionnaire,* IV, 420ff.; E. Lefèvre-Pontalis, "Croix en pierre des XIe et XIIe siècles dans le nord de la France," *Gazette archéologique,* X, 1885, 222-23; Crozet, *Art roman en Berry,* 155; Müller-Dietrich, *Romanische Skulptur in Lothringen,* 122-23.
34. Crozet, *Art roman en Berry,* 201, and J. Favier, *Berry roman,* Coll. Zodiaque, 1970, 143f., and pl. 62.
35. J.-F. Buholzer, "Notes sur quelques églises romanes du Gard," *Annales du Midi,* April 1962, 128, and pl. opp. p. 132. At Claret (Hérault), an interlace knot appears on an impost in the narthex (E. Bonnet, *Monspelliensia,* II, 1935-40, 31).
36. J. Lauffray, "Remarques sur les mosaiques de l'abbatiale de Sorde pour servir à leur datation et à leur restauration," *Bulletin de la Société de Borda,* 1962, 325-39, and M. Durliat, "Actualité des mosaiques de pavement romanes du sud-ouest de la France et de la Catalogne," *Bull. mon.,* 1971, 265-71.
37. H. Stern, "Les mosaiques de la cathédrale Saint-Jean de Lyon," *Cahiers arch.,* XIV, 1964, 217-32; *idem,* "Mosaiques de pavement pré-romanes et romanes en France," *Cahiers de civilisation médiévale,* V, 1962, 27.
38. Stern, *Mosaiques de pavement,* 25.
39. L. A. S. Butler, "Minor Medieval Monumental Sculpture in the East Midlands," *Archaeological Journal,* CXXI, 1964, 111ff., esp. 117. See also the material discussed in V. E. Elbern, "Die Dreifaltigkeitsminiatur im Book of Durrow," *Wallraf-Richartz Jahrbuch,* 1955, XVII, 7-42.
40. Reproduction in O. Beigbeder, *Lexique des symboles,* Coll. Zodiaque, 1969, fig. 68. B. Brincard, *Cunault. Ses chapiteaux du XIIe siècle,* Paris, 1937, 100.
41. E. Chartraire, *Inventaire du trésor de l'église primatiale et métropolitaine de Sens,* Sens-Paris, 1897, No. 207, 79.
42. P. Wolters, "Faden und Knoten als Amulette," *Archiv für Religionswissenschaft,* VIII, 1905, 1ff.; C. L. Day, *Quipus and Witches Knots,* Lawrence, Kansas, 1967; A. Schulze, "Das Riemenornament," *Mitteilungen der Forschungsinstitut für Kulturmorphologie,* Heft 3, 1928, 37-55.
43. E. Kitzinger, "The Threshold of the Holy Shrine," *Kyriakon. Festschrift Johannes Quasten,* ed. P. Granfield and J. A. Jungmann, Münster, 1970, 639-47.
44. Götz, *Bildprogramme,* with the older bibliography.
45. Attention to these panels was called by H. Focillon, "Recherches récentes sur la sculpture romane en France au XIe siècle," *Bull. mon.,* XCVII, 1938, 54-56, and they are treated more fully by J. Hubert, "L'avant-nef carolingienne de Saint-Germain d'Auxerre," *Cahiers arch.,* V, 1951, 151-62. Anglo-Saxon metopes of the same kind are treated by R. N. Quirk, "Winchester New Minster and its Tenth Century Tower," *Journal of the British Archaeological Association,* XXIV, 1961, esp. 27ff.
46. R. Crozet, "La corniche du clocher de Saint-Hilaire de Poitiers," *Bull. mon.,* 1934, 341-45
47. J. George and A. Guérin-Boutaud, *Les églises romanes du diocèse d'Angoulême,* 62, No. 350.
48. P. Mesplé, *Toulouse. Musée des Augustins. Les sculptures romanes* (Inventaire des Collections publiques françaises), Paris, 1961, Nos. 209-10. D. Scott, "A Restoration of the West Portal Relief Decoration of Saint-Sernin of Toulouse," *Art Bulletin,* 1964, 271-82, and the critical remarks of M. Durliat, "Le portail occidental de Saint-Sernin de Toulouse," *Annales du midi,* 1965, 215-23.
49. Gounot, *Collections lapidaires,* 226, No. DB 11. Here identified as a representation of a dog.
50. J. Bayet, "Le symbolisme du cerf et du centaure à la Porte Rouge de Notre-Dame de Paris," *Revue archéologique,* XLIV, 1954, 21-68. The subject is also touched upon by J. Adhémar, *Influences antiques dans l'art du moyen âge français,* London, 1939, 179ff., and V.-H. Debidour, *Le bestiaire sculpté du moyen âge,* Grenoble, 1961, *passim.*
51. M. Cottinet-Bouquet, "Frises romanes provenant de l'Ile-Barbe-lès-Lyon," *Actes du 89e Congrès National des Sociétés Savantes,* Lyon, 1964, Section d'archéologie, 329-41. For the panels of Ste.-Foy-lès-Lyon, see F. Thiollier, "Vestiges de l'art roman en Lyonnais," *Bull. arch.,* 1892, 396-403. For Saint-Restitut, E. Bonnet, "Les bas-reliefs de la tour de Saint-Restitut," *Congrès arch.,* II, 1909, 251-74. Some of the panels on the north side of the tower of Saint-Benoît-sur-Loire have been identified as parts of another zodiac (E. Michel, *Monuments religieux, civils et militaires du Gâtinais,* Paris-Orléans, 1879, 147, and pl. LXXVII), but this must remain doubtful.
52. Macrobius, *Saturnalia,* I, 21, 26, and Honorius Augustodunensis, *De imagine mundi,* II, 100 (Pat. lat. 172, 143), as cited by Bayet, *Symbolisme du cerf et du centaure,* 42, note 1.

53. J. Hubert, "L'avant-nef carolingienne de Saint-Germain d'Auxerre," *Cahiers arch.*, V., 1951, 158.
54. J. Hubert, *L'art pre-roman*, Paris, 1938, 164-65; M. Aubert, "Saint-Benoît-sur-Loire," *Congrès arch.*, XCIII, 1930, 599.
55. Dr. Marilyn Low Schmidt has made a thorough study of this problem in her unpublished Yale dissertation, "The Church of Selles-sur-Cher," 1972.
56. A. K. Porter, *Spanish Romanesque Sculpture*, Florence-Paris, 1928, I, 66-67, who regards this motif as of Spanish origin. See further R. Crozet, "Le chasseur et le combattant dans la sculpture romane en Saintonge," *Mélanges offerts à Rita Lejeune*, Gembloux, 1969, 669-77, and G. Priem, "Les cavaliers combattants dans la sculpture romane," *Recueil de publications de la Société havraise d'études diverses*, 1958-59, 13-24.
57. R. Lejeune and J. Stiennon, *The Legend of Roland*, London, 1971.
58. O. Paecht, C. R. Dodwell, and F. Wormald, *The St. Albans Psalter*, London, 1960, 149-50.
59. Lejeune and Stiennon, *Legend of Roland*, 92.
60. *Idem*, 72-75, 85-91 (among other examples). It is also difficult to follow these authors in the identification of horn-blowing personages like that found on a medallion at Cluny as referring to the Roland legend (86-87). For criticism along the same lines, see I. Short, "Le pape Calixte II, Charlemagne et les fresques de Santa Maria in Cosmedin," *Cahiers de civilisation médiévale*, XIII, 1970, 229-38.
61. F. Godefroy, *Dictionnaire de l'ancienne langue française*, Paris, 1938, II, art. "Croissir," 380. A. Tobler and E. Lommatzsch, *Altfranzösisches Wörterbuch*, Berlin, 1936, II, 1081-83.
62. The parallel between these two works was pointed out by Porter, *Spanish Romanesque Sculpture*, 97.
63. The division of society into three classes-priests, knights, and serfs–is recognized by Adalbero, *Carmen ad Rotbertum regem francorum*, Pat. lat. 141, 781-82. On this question, see also G. Duby, "L'image du prince en France au début du XIe siècle," *Cahiers d'histoire*, XVII, 1972 (Etudes médiévales en mémoire de Jean Demian), 211-16, and *idem*, "Les origines de la chevalerie," *Ordinamenti militari in Occidento nell'alto medioevo*, Settimane di Studio . . . , Spoleto, 1968, 739-61.
64. K. Erdmann, *Die Enstehung des Kreuzzugsgedankens*, Stuttgart, 1965.
65. DeVic and Vaissete, *Histoire du Languedoc*, V, 23.
66. *Histoire anonyme de la première croisade*, ed. and trans. L. Bréhier, Paris, 1924, 152.
67. *La chanson d'Antioche*, ed. P. Paris, Paris, 1848, II, 197, cited by J. H. and L. Hill, *Contemporary Accounts*, 36.
68. H. Claussen, "Karolingische Wandmalerei im Westwerk zu Korvei," *Westfälische Zeitschrift*, 1963, 475-77, and M. Vieillard-Troiekouroff, "Sirènes-poissons carolingiennes," *Cahiers arch.*, 1969, 61ff.
69. C. H. Gordon, "Leviathan: Symbol of Evil," *Biblical Motifs: Origins and Transformations*, ed. A. Altmann, Cambridge, 1966, 1ff., and J. Gutmann, "Leviathan, Behemoth, and Ziz. Jewish Messianic Symbols in Art," *Hebrew Union College Annual*, XXXIX, 1968, 219-30.
70. Stuttgart, Württemb. Landesbibl. Cod. 415, fol. 87v. K. Loeffler, *Schwäbische Buchmalerei in romanischer Zeit*, Augsburg, 1928, 56-57.
71. Vallery-Radot, *Saint-Philibert de Tournus*, Paris, 1955, 219. The relief is mounted on a wall of the *chauffoir*, along the south side of the narthex. A many-headed monster is seen on one of the ambulatory capitals at Saint-Aignan-sur-Cher, and another on a capital of Saint-Sauveur of Nevers (Musée de la Porte du Croux). There is another creature of this kind, confronted by an archer, among the decorative roundels mounted along the base of the wall of the Parma baptistery.
72. H. Wallace, "Leviathan and the Beast of Revelations," *The Biblical Archaeologist Reader*, ed. G. E. Wright and D. N. Friedman, Chicago, 1961, 290-98.
73. See. P. Paulson, *Drachenkämpfer, Löwenritter und die Heinrichsage*, Cologne-Graz, 1966, esp. 115ff.
74. P.-Fr. Fournier, "Le dieu cavalier à l'anguipède dans la cité des Arvernes," *Revue archéologique du Centre*, I, 1962, 105-27, and F. Benoît, *Les mythes d'outre-tombe, le cavalier à l'anguipède et l'écuyère Epona* (Collection Latomus, 111), Brussels, 1950.
75. Paulson, *Drachenkämpfer*, 116; H. Kuhn, "Die Reiterscheibe der Volkwanderungszeit," *Ipek*, 1938, 95ff. W. Holmqvist, "Zur Herkunft einiger germanischer Figurendarstellungen der Volkwanderungszeit," *idem*, 78-95; the same author's *Kunstprobleme der Merowingerzeit* (Kungl. Witterhets och Antikvitets Akademiens Handlingar, 47), Stockholm, 1939, 110ff. H. Menzel, "Ein Christlicher Amulett mit Reiterdarstellung," *Jahrbuch der Röm.-German. Zentralmuseum*, 1955, 253ff.
76. W. Schultz, "Eine Nachlese zu den Bildsteinen

von Hornhausen," *Jahreschrift für Mitteldeutsche Vorgeschichte,* 40, 1956, 211-29; Holmquist, *Kunstprobleme,* 120.

77. L. Dumont, *Le tarasque. Essai d'un fait local d'un point de vue ethnographique,* Paris, 1951, and R. Salomon, "Aftermath to Opicinus de Canistris," *Journal of the Warburg Institute,* 1962, 137ff.
78. Thorp, *Carved Decorations of the North and South Church,* 38-39.
79. B. de Montesquiou-Fezensac, "L'arc de triomphe d'Einhardus," *Cahiers arch.,* IV, 1949, 79ff., and *idem,* "L'arc de triomphe d'Eginhard," *Karolingische und ottonische Kunst. Werden, Wesen, Wirkung,* Wiesbaden, 1957, 43ff.
80. R. Wesenberg, *Frühe mittelalterliche Bildwerke,* Düsseldorf, 1972, 75. These reliefs were destroyed in World War II.
81. R. Crozet, "Le thème du cavalier victorieux dans l'art roman de France et d'Espagne," *Principe de Viana,* 1971, 125-43. The apotropaic significance of fighting groups on doorways is also discussed by A. Grabar, "Deux portails sculptés paléochrétiens d'Egypte et d'Asie mineure et les portails romans," *Cahiers arch.,* XIX, 1970, 23ff.
82. K. Wessel, *Die Holztür des Klosters Znagov,* Munich, 1966.
83. L. Bréhier, *La sculpture et les arts mineurs byzantins,* Paris, 1936, 81, pl. XLIII.
84. On the subject of Romanesque animal combats, see R. Bernheimer, *Romanische Tierplastik und die Ursprunge ihrer Motive,* Munich, 1931, 108ff.
85. Kitzinger, *Threshold of the Holy Shrine,* 640. Bauerreiss, *Lebenszeichen,* Examples have been signaled in various sites around the Mediterranean. See J. B. Ward-Perkins and R. Goodchild, "The Christian Antiquities of Tripolitania," *Archaeologia,* 1953, 1ff., pls. Xc, XIVa, and fig. 20. M. de Vogüé, *La Syrie centrale,* Paris, 1865-77, I, Pls. 10, 20, 31-32, 45-46; II, 99, 114. M. Gough, *The Early Christians,* London, 1961, fig. 26.
86. J. Daniélou, *Le symboles chrétiens primitifs,* Paris, 1961, 143-52, and E. Dinkler, "Jesu Wort von Kreuztragen" *Signum crucis,* 77ff.
87. P. de Pallol, *Early Medieval Art in Spain,* New York, 1966, 467, Nos. 2-3.
88. F. Henry, *Irish Art in the Early Christian Period,* Ithaca, N.Y., 1965, 85. On the subject most recently, A. Grabar, *Deux portails paléochrétiens,* 25, note 30.
89. Ch. Urseau, "La croix de l'abbaye de Saint-Maur," *Bull. arch.,* 1898, 136-41.
90. Crozet, *Art roman en Berry,* 153-54 and 200-201.
91. J. Vallery-Radot, *La limite méridionale,* 302. The formally related cross on the tower of St.-Martin d'Ainay in Lyon belongs to the restoration of the church in 1858. One might add, however, the interlace cross formerly seen on the Romanesque façade of the now destroyed church on the island of Lérins (H. Moris, "L'abbaye de Lérins, son histoire. . . ," *Annales de la Société des lettres, sciences et arts des Alpes-Maritimes,* XXI, 1909, 277-316, and esp. 312. In Burgundy, tympana with crosses of the *potencé* type are found at Versailleux (Ain), La Bénissons-Dieu, Saint-Germain-des-Bois, and Semur-en-Brionnais (Vallery-Radot, *La limite méridionale,* 294-95). In Auvergne, a large cross may be found on the transept gable, as at Ebreuil and the south transepts of Saint-Nectaire and Orcival. Le Puy cathedral adheres to this latter group, assuming the cross now seen on the gable of south transept antecedes the nineteenth-century reconstruction of this part of the structure.
92. J. Nougaret and A. Burgos, *Un prieuré. Saint-Pierre de Rhèdes,* Montpellier, 1967, 13f., and M. Thibout, Saint-Pierre de Rhèdes," *Congrès arch.,* CVIII, 1950, 261-70. Another, with a pair of Orans figures flanking the cross, is at Roubignac (Bonnet, *Monspelliensia,* II, 1935-40, 11). A portal from the same region with a cross incised at the center of the tympanum is in the Detroit Institute of Arts (Cahn, *Gesta,* X/2, 1971, 71, No. 1). A number of other examples, carved in relief, are found in northern Spain: Santa Maria de Mored (J. Ramón y Fernandez, "Jornadas románicas por tierras de Lugo," *Archivo español de Arte,* XV, 1943, 239ff., and fig. 5); Arturesco and Pazos de Arentiero (M. Chamoso Lamas, "Ejemplares arquitectónicos de románico popular en Galicia," *idem,* XIV, 1940-41, 333ff, figs. 7 and 12); Santa Maria de Razamonde, San Pedro de Trasalba and Santa Maria de Fea (J. Ramón y Fernandez Oxea, "Un grupo de iglesias románicas gallegas," *idem,* XXIV, 1951, 141-53.
93. O. Wulff, *Altchristliche und Mittelalterliche Bildwerke,* (Königliche Museen zu Berlin. Beschreibung der Bildwerke der Christlichen Epochen), Berlin, 1909-11, 84-85, Nos. 255-56). J. Strzygowski, *Der Baukunst der Armenier und Europa,* Vienna, 1918, I, 412f., figs. 442f. Cabrol-Leclercq, *Dictionnaire,* III, 2, 3276; M. Gómez-Moreno, *Ars Hispaniae,* Madrid, 1951, III, 25. In Le Puy, the underside of the fragmentary PISO SENATUR ARTEFEX lintel exhibited a design of the same type (Gounot, *Collections lapidaires,* 111, No. AA).

94. A number of examples are listed and discussed by Bauerreiss, *Lebenszeichen, passim,* who first drew attention to their interest as a type and possible implications for the development of portal decoration in Romanesque times. Additional monuments of the same character have been published by F. Volbach, "Ein mittelalterliche Turstürz aus Ingelheim," *Mitteilungen des oberhessischen Geschichtsverein,* 44, 1960, 15-19; L. Devliegher, "Een romaanse latei mit haringe in het Gruuthusmuseum te Brugge," *Bulletin de la Commission royale des monuments et des sites,* XV, 1964, 49-52; R. Will, "Recherches iconographiques sur la sculpture romane en Alsace. Les représentations du paradis," *Cahiers techniques de l'art,* 1948, I, 29-68; E. Hagemann, "Zur Ikonographie des Ronnenberger 'Bonifatius-Portal,' " *Niederdeutsche Beiträge zur Kunstgeschichte,* XI, 1972, 24-46.
95. Lintels of Canonica di Cedda, Canonica di Casaglia and Pieve di Sant'Agnese (I. Moretti and R. Stopani, *Chiese romaniche in Valdelsa,* Florence, 1968, 149f., and 198-99).
96. E. Keyser, *A List of Norman Tympana and Lintels,* London, 1927, XXXI ff and figs. 8-25.
97. Volbach, *Ein mittelalterliche Turstürz,* 17-18.
98. H. Swoboda, "Ein altchristliche Vorhang," *Römische Quartalschrift,* IV, 1892, 95-118.
99. J. B. Ward-Perkins, "The Sculpture of Visigothic France," *Archaeologia,* LXXXVII, 104, who mentions other sarcophagi with the same device. Puig y Cadafalch, *Art wisigothique,* 71-72.
100. A. Séné, "Quelques remarques sur les tympans à chrisme en Aragon et en Navarre," *Mélanges Crozet,* I, 365-81; L. Torres Balbàs, "La escultura romanica y el chrismon de los tympanos de las iglesias de la region pirenaica," *Archivo español de arte y arqueologia,* 1926, 287-91; P. Mesplé, "Les chrismes du Departement du Gers," *Mémoires de la Société archéologique du Midi de la France,* XXXV, 1970, 71-90; E. Lacoste, "Les chrismes des églises béarnaises," *Bulletin de la Société des sciences, lettres et arts de Pau,* 1970, 53-81.
101. O. Lehmann-Brockhaus, "Die Kanzeln der Abruzzen," *Römisches Jahrbuch für Kunstwissenschaft,* VI, 1942-44, 265-66. On this theme, see L. Werhann-Stauch, "Aquila-Resurrectio," *Zeitschrift für Kunstwissenschaft,* 1967, 105-27.
102. G. Gailllard, "Notes sur les tympans aragonais," *Bulletin hispanique,* XXX, 1928, 193-203, reprinted in his *Etudes d'art roman,* Paris, 1972, 231-39.
103. G. Fleury, *La cathédrale du Mans* (Petites monographies des grands édifices), Paris, s.d., 78-79, and most recently, F. Salet, "La cathédrale du Mans," *Congrès arch.,* 1961, 34-36.
104. F. Abbad Ríos, *Zaragoza monumental* (Catalogo monumental de España), Madrid, 1957, I, 722-23, and most recently, Cahn, *Gesta,* IX/2, 1970, 73ff.
105. G. Gaillard, *Rouergue roman,* Coll. Zodiaque, 1963, 230, fig. 119.
106. R. Pontvianne, *Le prieuré conventuel de Chamalières-sur-Loire,* Le Puy, 1904. The cartulary of the abbey was first published by H. Fraisse, *Cartularium conventum Sti. Aegidii Camaleriarum ordinis Sti. Benedicti,* Le Puy, 1871, and in a better edition, now standard, by A. Chassaing, *Cartulaire de Chamalières-sur-Loire en Velay . . . ,* Paris, 1895. Some of the documents are also included in the cartulary of Monastier-Saint-Chaffre (ed., U. Chevallier, Paris, 1884).
107. Pontvianne, *Prieuré conventuel,* 16ff. Chassaing, *Cartulaire,* No. 2. The *Liber Sancti Jacobi* alludes to this event and rails against the claims of Chamalières to the body of the saint, which according to the author, could not have left Saint-Gilles (*Guide du pélerin,* ed. Vieillard, 46-47).
108. Pontvianne, *Prieuré conventuel,* 36ff.
109. Pontvianne, *idem,* 51ff.
110. Chassaing, *Cartulaire,* 4, No. 5.
111. Chevallier, *Cartulaire,* 57-58: ". . . locum Camalariae . . . tunc quidem parvum oratorium in honore beatae semper Virginis Mariae, nunc vero per divinam gratiam nobile monasterium effectum. . . ." R. Suaudeau, "Etude sur les choeurs à chapelles rayonnantes dépourvus de déambulatoire," *Revue d'Auvergne,* LII, 1938, 189, maintains that the church was constructed by Prior Jarenton between 1096 and 1098, but this has no foundation in the sources. For the architecture of the church, see N. Thiollier, "Chamalières-sur-Loire," *Congrès arch.,* 1904, 65-69, and *idem, Architecture religieuse,* 94-103.
112. The documents bearing on the restorations of the church are found in the Archives Departementales de la Haute-Loire, No. 49.0.XII. Other papers are found in the Archives des Monuments Historiques in Paris.
113. A letter by Nodet dated November 25, 1898, speaks of the work of the Monuments Historiques "qui fournit les fonds nécessaires à la consolidation de la porte d'entrée et à la mise à l'abri des superbes vantaux qui la fermait." An earlier letter by M. Petitgrand, dated November 1892, urges that the doors be removed and preserved in a better place. At the same time, he observes that "Il

sera nécessaire de restaurer les seuils, piedroits, ébrasements, l'arc et l'archivolte de la baie ainsi que les parements latéraux, toutes ces parties étant dans le plus mauvais état." A *devis* for these restorations is dated November 16, 1892.

114. P. Héliot, "Problèmes d'architecture dans le centre de la France et l'Aquitaine, à propos du choeur de la priorale à Chamalières-sur-Loire et la nef de Saint-Cerneuf à Billom," *Bulletin de la Société Nationale des Antiquaires de France,* 1962, 179-97. The choir was earlier dealt with by M. de Fayolle, "Les églises de Saint-Paulien et de Chamalières-sur-Loire avaient-elle un déambulatoire," *Bull. mon.,* 1906, 106-12, and Suaudeau, *Etude sur les choeurs à chapelles rayonnantes, loc. cit.*
115. Héliot, *Problèmes d'architecture,* 181-82.
116. Thiollier, *Architecture religieuse,* 101. A document dated 1137 quoted by this author after *Gallia Christ.,* II, 84 seems to confirm the rebuilding at this time: "Ego Raimundus quondam Cantojolensis abbas videns temporibus meis Cantojolense monasterium ad tantam destructionem pervenisse, ut spoliato sanctuario et castellificata ecclesia, nullus ibi serviens Deo reperitur."
117. Thiollier, *Architecture religieuse,* 119, and *idem, Congrès arch.,* 1904, 84-90. Chevallier, *Cartulaire,* 46-47. Mallay, "Le Monastier," ed. Thiollier, *Mém. et Procès-Verbaux,* XI, 1899-1901, 220-29. Exh. Cat. *L'église du Monastier-Saint-Chaffre. Mille ans d'histoire,* Le Puy, Musée Crozatier, 1962.
118. For Retournac, see Thiollier, *Architecture religieuse,* 133-35. The portal at Vorey, all that remains of the church, is now set up in the public garden of the city of Le Puy. It is published in Thiollier, *idem,* 173.

VI Blesle

THE DOORS OF THE CHURCH of Saint-Pierre at Blesle have been less well publicized than the other monuments in our group. Until 1904, they stood in the south transept portal, presently the major entrance of the structure (Fig. 70). As part of a superficial restoration of the church conducted at that time, they were then replaced by a set of modern valves and separately mounted against the lateral walls in the dark, porchlike entry way beyond the portal (Figs. 66 and 67). Passed over in silence in a well-documented nineteenth-century history of the abbey, they were first brought to general attention by N. Thiollier in 1905.[1] This otherwise most conscientious student of medieval monuments of the region records here only a very general impression of the appearance of the doors, possibly based on the inadequate drawing by the architect A. Ventre which accompanies his remarks, rather than personal observation. The carving was then already in its present much worn condition as is indicated by a still older photograph made when the doors were still in place,[2] and only a close examination would have revealed additional details. It is more than likely that more elements of the design would come to light even now if such an examination were conducted under modern laboratory conditions. But following the publication of Thiollier, who recognized the connection of the work with the doors of Le Puy, Lavoûte-Chilhac, and Chamalières, there has been no further investigation or attempt to correct and complete his description.

The monastery of Blesle was a Benedictine nunnery founded before 885 or 886 by Ermengarde, the spouse of Bernard II Plantevelue, Count of Poitiers. According to a letter sent in 1095 to Pope Urban II by the then ruling abbess Florentia, which relates the history of the foundation, Ermengarde placed the convent under the direct jurisdiction of the See of Peter.[3] The new house received in return a black marble altar which the pope himself had consecrated. This elegantly proportioned slab served as the high altar of the church and was subsequently placed against the end wall of the north transept, where it can still be seen. The material possessions of the monastery were relatively modest. A bull of Pope Lucius dated in 1185 enumerates fourteen priories and dependent churches.[4] During the fourteenth century, the community consisted of about forty nuns, and this number was probably never exceeded. The abbess was invested with the feudal lordship of the town of Blesle. In the late eleventh century, and increasingly thereafter, these privileges were coveted by the lords of Mercoeur, installed in the burg, and nominally at least, vassals of the abbey. Following Florentia's example, the twelfth-century abbesses addressed themselves to successive popes in order to have their rights confirmed and be freed of both secular and ecclesiastical interference. Two agreements made with royal approval in 1227 and 1241 finally enabled the contending parties to compromise their differences, recognizing the monastery's legal claims but conceding the effective power of the Mercoeurs. This period of turbulence coincided with an intense building activity which imprinted onto the town much of its present character. The church of St. Peter first and foremost, a Romanesque house and what remains of the castle of the Mercoeurs are still highly impressive witnesses of this activity.[5]

The sources are entirely silent on the construction of the church, though its fabric reveals this to have been the result of several campaigns spanning a period extending in time from the early stages of Romanesque to the advent of Gothic art.[6] The structure consists of a large choir of three rectangular bays terminated in the east by an apsidal hemicycle and flanked on the southern side by an aisle of two bays itself closed by semicircular chapels on its eastern and southern extremities (Fig. 65). On its western side, this sanctuary space is delimited by an elongated but narrowly proportioned transept. The short nave, originally flanked by aisles, was transformed toward the end of the fifteenth century into a *choeur des dames.* Its wooden floor lies well above pavement level, and the entire western mass is imbricated into the residence of the abbess, reconstructed in 1783, which now serves as Blesle's town hall. The ground plan of the church reveals at a glance the grandiose conception of the whole, and, at the same time, the accidented course which its building history must have taken.

The older parts of the church now standing are found in the perimeter walls of the north transept. The masonry here consists of roughly cut blocks set in thick mortarbeds and patched out with rubble. A capital of Corinthian derivation lodged in the eastern wall of the transept and showing on its exposed face a graphically delineated interlace knot plainly belongs to the type illustrated at Figeac, Aurillac, and, further north, in one specimen at Saint-Léger in Ebreuil. The style of this sculpture points to a date in the second half of the eleventh century.[7] The capital rests on a partially exposed pier or colonnette and sustains a red standstone arch which has been walled in. The arch and its support in all likelihood mark the location of an apsidal chapel formerly opening onto the transept. Traces of a similar chapel are visible in the masonry of the eastern face of the south transept wall, though this area was even more radically altered in later reconstruction. It is quite possible, as has been suggested, that this archaic masonry continued westward and constitutes the substructure of the present nave. Nothing of this, however, is now visible.

The end wall and upper part of the north transept belong to a second phase of construction. The masonry here is composed of yellowish limestone blocks fairly carefully dressed. There is a large window in the upper zone of the end-wall whose round-arched outline exhibits a luxuriant decoration of rosettes and striding quadrupeds arranged on a pair of concentric voussoirs.[8] The assertive and muscular style of this sculpture is in sharp contrast with the surface-bound refinement of the capital embedded in the eastern wall. Within the broader evolution of Romanesque stone carving, this work would have to be placed after the critical developments in Languedoc and Burgundy in the decade immediately preceding and following the year 1100. Bréhier's guess that the enlargement of the transept, connected with a first plan for the construction of the choir, might have followed the bull of Callixtus II in 1119 confirming the privileges of the monastery, represents in the absence of more definite testimony from the sources a likely date for the beginning of this campaign.[9]

This phase of construction continued eastward with the building of the aisles and the chapels flanking the choir. On the north side, the emplacement of the aisle is marked by the chapel of St. Catherine, occupying a single bay in the angle where the transept arm and choir meet. On the south side, two full bays terminated by apsidal chapels remain. That these antedate the construction of the choir proper is proven by the position of the window displaced close to the eastern extremity of the choir bay at the point of junction in order to accede to daylight. On the exterior, the windows lighting these chapels show a heavy moluration whose flattened profile leaves the layered thickness of the wall undisguised. The capitals resting on the squatly proportioned colonnettes placed in the embrasures are unfortunately very worn, but recognizably more archaic than those flanking the windows in the choir. The disposition of these apsidal chapels is one of the more puzzling features of the design. The suggestion that they are the remnants of a much older chapel with a trefoil sanctuary, which was amputated of its northern apse when the choir was erected, must be considered doubtful.[10] I am inclined, rather, to believe that the aisle and chapels already had their apparently truncated form from the beginning and that they were intended to connect with a choir of somewhat narrower dimensions in a scheme such as that which may be seen in the church of Riotort, northeast of Le Puy.[11]

The choir in its present form was erected in a third campaign of construction. It is a vessel of exceptionally large dimensions, without interior supports, and as such, comparable to the choir of Chamalières and Saint-Paulien nearby in the region, which were remodeled along similar lines in the same period.[12] Unfortunately depreciated by a thorough nineteenth-century repainting of every available surface, this space is articulated by compound piers with applied half-columns rising, like the giant arcade between the supports, uninterrupted to nearly the full height of the wall. In its general effect the architecture is closer to the aisleless and similarly vaulted buildings of Languedoc and Provence like Saint-Pons-de-Thomières than to typical monuments in Auvergne.[13]

The semicircular apse lit by five substantial round-arched windows, whose complex and finely scaled moldings give a good account of the stylistic distance which separated this stage in the construction of the church from the preceding one (Fig. 69). The sculpture of the moldings and the embrasure capitals both within and without is distinguished for its diminutive and sometimes convulsively animated forms, rendered with an attention to the texture of surfaces that might seem chased rather than carved. The subjects are largely freed from the block and may grip the torus molding with their feet. The imagery itself, notable for its fantasy and diversity, stands outside the repertory principally compiled from motifs in provincial Roman sculpture particular to the better known Auvergnat Romanesque churches and generally taken as representatives of that school: Saint-Nectaire, Orcival, Issoire, Mozat, and Notre-Dame du Port in Clermont-Ferrand. As Bréhier has pointed out, however, the sculpture of the Blesle choir is not entirely an isolated phenomenon. It is particularly allied to the capitals of the cloister of Lavaudieu and to the workshop responsible for the decoration of the exterior of the choir of Saint-Julien in Brioude.[14] Neither of these monuments is firmly datable. For Brioude, the old but not yet superseded analysis by E. Lefèvre-Pontalis assigns to the eastern parts of the church a date toward the end of the twelfth century.[15] The Blesle choir with its sculpture, which Focillon took as one of the illustrations of the "Baroque" phase of Romanesque sculpture, must have seen the light of day roughly in the same period.[16]

Subsequent to the completion of the choir, the pier supports of the crossing and south transept were remodeled. In the capitals on the lower zone of these piers as well as several fine heads serving as corbels along the inner western wall of the south transept, the influence of northern French early Gothic models vies with the residual hold of local traditions.[17] At this time, a monumental portal was erected at the southern extremity of the transept arm (Fig. 70). Lodged between two heavy buttresses, this portal was assembled in horizontal courses of limestone alternating in a richly coloristic effect with blocks of a darker basaltic material. It has a stepped design of three concentric archivolts. Above the first three courses of stone, these divide into parallel moldings roughly shaped like enlarged bead-and-reel ornament. Large and deeply undercut five-petaled flowers, carved in the limestone courses only, spill out of the hollows between each of the three paired moldings. The arched space at the center is now filled with masonry of a later date. The profile of the molding around the inner doorway, above which the arms of the monastery are carved in relief, indicates that this alteration, made for the purpose of accommodating the Romanesque wooden doors, must have been carried out in the course of the second half of the fifteenth century.[18]

In the original parts of the Blesle doorway, the small-scaled treatment of the ornament and the absence of assertive volumes lying within its path creates the effect of a sequence of parallel framing elements outlining the arch in an uninterrupted sequence from base to base. No tympanum was foreseen.[19] The style of the portal is recognizably that of the luxuriant late Romanesque of lower Auvergne and Velay best represented by the *Porche du For* of Le Puy cathedral.[20] The tubular treatment of bead-and-reel ornament is found here in the even more stiffened form of a colonnette on the splay of the porch joined to the east wall of the transept. The use of flowers laid out in rows around the windows and doorway moldings was initiated in Burgundy around the beginning of the twelfth century. In the doorway of the west façade at Saint-Paul-Trois-Châteaux some decades later, the gullies between the moldings are made deeper and the flowers correspondingly more assertive. Such bands of open flowers decorate the portal of the church of Mailhat in Auvergne, the archivolt of the portal sheltered by the *Porche du For,* as well as the arch of the *Porte Dorée* within the west porch of Le Puy cathedral.[21] Elsewhere at Blesle, another example occurs on the double arcaded window of a Romanesque private house.[22] As for the earlier stages of construction, an approximate date only can be assigned to the erection of the portal and related work carried out in the southern arm of the transept. Although the portal sculpture is stylistically more advanced than the choir capitals, the gap in time which must have separated the two enterprises cannot have been very great. For the *Porche du For* from whence the newer impulses must have come, a date at the end of the twelfth or in the early years of the thirteenth century is generally proposed.[23] Such a date is also the earliest which could be attributed to the Blesle transept portal.

The nave of the church, constructed last, is in its present state less accessible to thorough examination than the rest of the structure. The very pure high Gothic crocket capitals surmounting the western crossing piers indicate that the work proceeded well into the middle of the thirteenth century. As has been suggested, the builders probably used as a foundation walls of an earlier nave linked with the remains of the eleventh-century transept,[24] but the exposed masonry in the upper walls of barely two bays makes unprofitable all speculation concerning the possible incorporation of parts of the older fabric into the Gothic structure. The large windows in the two bays are of post-medieval date, as are the constructions which now occupy the site of the aisles. The design and appearance of the west façade in the original plan are also uncertain. A plan of the monastery made in 1778 before the construction of the new residence of the abbess shows the nave closed off by a flat wall pierced by a door located off center and nearer the south aisle (Fig. 65). This entrance, however, along with another opening near the eastern end of the northern flank of the nave, appear on the plan as passages projected by the architect of the abbess's residence rather than as a part of the original fabric. The end of the nave now houses an organ, behind which, these passages, subsequently constructed, can be seen. Only a close archaeological survey and soundings on this part of the site, which cannot now be undertaken, might make possible a solution of this problem.

The complicated unfolding of successive campaigns of construction also leaves unanswered a question of more immediate concern: With what phase of the building history should the wooden doors be associated? It is apparent that the early Renaissance threshold in which the doors were set until their removal within the church was specifically tailored to their measurements. Thus it can safely be concluded that they were installed within the south transept portal only then, a conclusion buttressed by their comparatively small dimensions in relation to the size of the archway of the early thirteenth century. To be sure, given the rugged Auvergnat climate, it is unlikely that the late Romanesque archway can ever have been open to the elements to its full width and height. A narrower entranceway must have been initially present, either where it is now, or possibly set somewhat further back and thus framed within a kind of open porch. Some of the blocks used in the building of the late medieval partition wall within the present portal could well stem from such an older screen arrangement. But we also lack all information about the appearance of the south transept end-wall before the erection of the late Romanesque portal. Since the fabric of the south transept belongs in its essence to a building campaign of the first half of the twelfth century, there is a reasonable likelihood that the existing portal replaced an older doorway in the same location. The comparative dates obtained for the door of Le Puy and Chamalières would offer support for the possibility that the valves at Blesle were made for this doorway.[25]

Before the suppression of the monastery in 1793, the nuns, who bore the title of canon, resided in houses still standing around the square (now Place Saint-Pierre) west of the church and in the area to the east and northeast of the choir.[26] From the west, they could reach the south transept entrance through a passageway which leads under the old fifteenth-century *maison abbatiale* leaning against the southwest corner of the nave. Access to the church from the houses behind the choir was more circuitous since the only available passage led along the northern flank of the monastery complex into the courtyard opposite the north transept. It was nevertheless possible to avoid a long march around the entire church by using a small entrance formerly located at the junction of the west wall of the north transept arm and the nave, which is clearly marked on the plan of 1778.

In addition to the portal on the south transept, it is safe to assume that there must initially have been a doorway in the west, which must thus be regarded as another possible location of the wooden doors before their displacement. The archaeological and historical record is unfortunately most meagerly supplied with evidence concerning its existence and institutional function. The transformation of the nave into a nun's choir is said to have taken place toward the end of the fifteenth century. Toward the year 1335, however, the still standing church of Saint-Martin was erected not far from Saint-Pierre in order to serve the parish.[27] It is tempting to make a connection between these events and to assume that the nave of St. Peter was freed already at this time for its subsequent employ. With the transferral of the parishioners a western entrance to the nave would have lost a good deal of its reason for being, and it could be closed off to make the nave suitable as a second sanctuary. But the lavish decoration applied to the south transept portal would indicate to us that as early as the late twelfth century, this entrance had become the preferred means of access to the church.

The wooden doors of Blesle have come down to us in badly eroded condition (Figs. 66 and 67). Below a line roughly represented by the lower edge of the two panels with the cross, virtually no traces of the original carving remain. It was possible, however, to ascertain that the interlace border along the edges continues along a predictable path to the bottom (Fig. 68). Just above this point, on the left side, the design ends in a kind of leafy form, indicating that although some wood has been lost along the bottom of the door, the present external dimensions of the work are probably not far from its measurements in the original state. But at an unknown time, perhaps coincidental with the occasion when the doors were installed in their early Renaissance setting, extensive repairs were made in areas within the borders. In both valves, all of the wood exposed to view below the first two horizontal boards under the panels with the cross was replaced. The original planks, though quite worn, are distinguishable from later insets by the carefully rounded contour of the edges along the longer sides, which is fully comparable to the treatment of the carved boards at Lavoûte-Chilhac. The newer planks have straight, untooled edges. The surfaces of the two valves are not in identical condition. On the right panel, the bare wood, which is pine,[28] is exposed throughout, save for some deposits of grime along the upper and outer edges. The left side is by contrast covered with a heavy deposit of dirt, gradually thinning out below the transversal arm of the cross. This uneven pattern of preservation would seem to have been caused by the unequal exposure of the panels to daylight and air currents since they have been hung separately along the facing lateral walls within the portal. The traces of vermilion, blue, and green which Thiollier reported seeing in 1905 are no longer in evidence.

The armature of the doors is composed of planks half-joined along their longer edges; four boards make up the left valve, five somewhat narrower ones the right (Text fig. 6). The left valve is also wider than the other owing to the addition along its inner edge of the batten, only partially preserved, which formed the median line between the two halves of the design. A half-join profile along its edge made possible a flat and interlocking closing of the doors. Except for this central strip, all of the carving, including that of the outer borders, was carried out on separate panels nailed to the backing planks. In addition, the two boards laid horizontally beneath the cross panels are secured to each other by loose cross-tongues inserted in the wood and probably designed to minimize warping. The quality of the assembly is of the same high order as at Chamalières, though there is a much more copious use of nails. Desiring first and foremost to avoid interfering with the substance of the design, the artisan was not equally successful in subjecting their placement to a consistent pattern, thereby reducing the disruptive effect of their presence.

Each valve is dominated by a Greek cross surrounded by panels decorated with designs executed in low relief carving (Fig. 68). The treatment of the edges of the cross and the contiguous sides of the panels with a cable molding takes a form identical with Chamalières. Only the proportions of the cross are somewhat plumper, and lobed protrusions seem to have been dispensed with. The two facing panels above the transversal arms of the crosses are devoted to the group of Saggitarius and

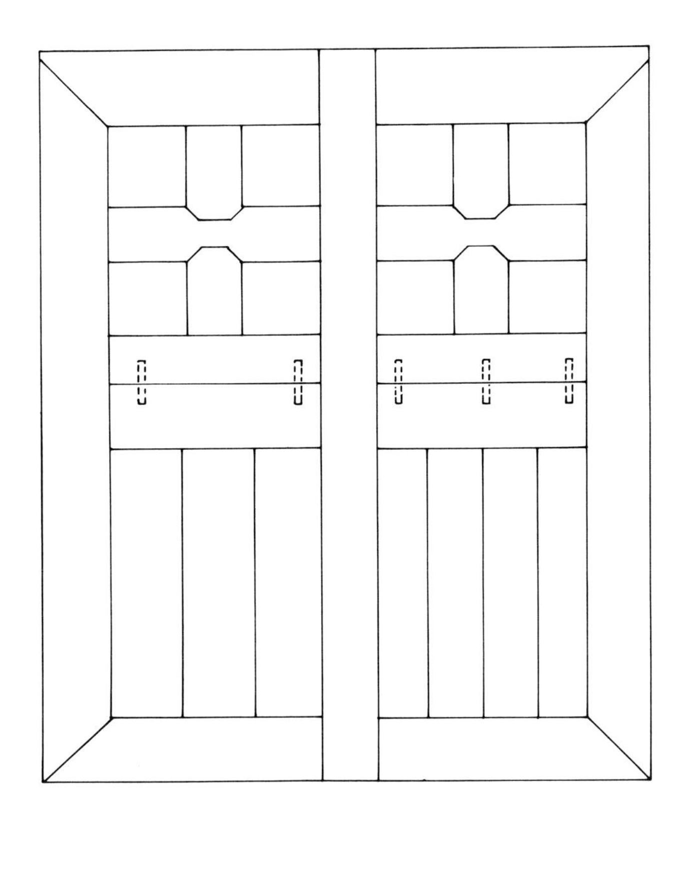

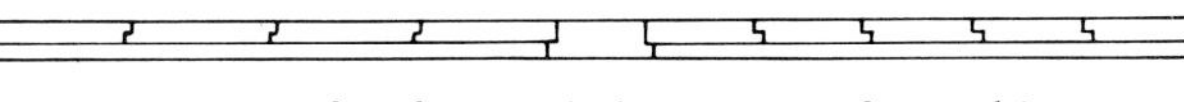

6. Wooden doors, Blesle. Schema of assembly

Capricorn (Figs. 72 and 73). The outer and lower panels around the crosses are filled with three distinct designs, each twice employed and symmetrically disposed: an interlace knot with a single interlocking circle, the same motif imbricated within a pair of circles, and a rosette composed of seven small interlocking circles. All three designs, represented singly rather than in pairs, appear also in the cross panels at Chamalières. The arrangement at Blesle must strike us as an economical, though probably also as an impoverished version of the schema realized in the doors of the former church. Below the crosses, some original wood remains, but all traces of decoration which it might have borne has been lost. It is thus no longer possible to say how much more of the Chamalières program might have been held over in the lower sections of the doors.

However this may be, the decoration of the framing elements sounds an entirely different note. The batten shows a meandering tendril with curling tri-lobed leaves, a very common device of architectural ornamentation (Fig. 72). The design along the border consists of a pair of parallel bands interlocking at regular intervals to form interlace knots shaped like the number eight. Such frames are found in works of Carolingian art heavily indebted to the Hiberno-Saxon tradition, such as the late eighth-century Montpellier Psalter,[29] one of the panels of the Genoels-Elderen ivory in Brussels,[30] the Codex Millenarius,[30] and later in manuscripts of other schools on ninth-century illumination of the Continent.[32] During the eleventh and early twelfth centuries, they are an aspect of the strongly insular and Franco-Saxon coloration of miniature painting in central and southern France.[33] The knot formation in these antecedents of the Blesle design is generally more elaborate than the eight-shaped figure found on the door. The simpler form is found in the framework of the Canon Tables of the so-called Deffech Gospels, Limousin work of the first quarter of the twelfth century which matches the structure of the Blesle border on every point.[34] Yet at Blesle, the roughly rectangular space between the interlace knots was not, as usually elsewhere, left blank, but filled with figurative compositions. Traces of these were noted in the Ventre sketch published by Thiollier, but it is possible, as we shall see, to go much further toward the identification and reconstitution of the original design. The late twelfth-century portal of the church of S. Fede at Cavagnolo (Piedmont) presents another example of the otherwise altogether rare use of this type of interlace border with figurative motifs inserted in the open spaces (Fig. 71).[35]

The disposition of the border provided six markedly vertical spaces along each of the sides and four oblong ones at the top (Fig. 68). The change in directions in the upper corners is managed through the placement of the knot at an oblique angle. The border seems to have terminated in a leafy excrescence near the bottom, though evidence of this was found on the left side only. While the identification of the scenes in the open spaces within the border is open to discussion on secondary points, enough remains to leave no doubt that we are dealing with a cycle of the Labors of the Months. The sequence beginning with January in the fourth space on the left side, unfolds upward and around to the corresponding place along the right border. The two spaces nearest the bottom on both sides are unaccounted for in this scheme and may well have been devoid of any illustration. The contrasting quality of the spaces also taxed the sculptor's ingenuity to the limit. Along the sides, the scenes had to be cramped within narrow confines. Along the upper edge, on the other hand, the figures are casually spread out, if pinched for room top and bottom. Two of the four scenes, in addition, have been fleshed out through supplementary figures, alien to the traditional iconography.

The months are personified as follows:

1. *January* (left valve, fourth space). Lost.
2. *February* (Left valve, third space). Seated figure warming himself by a fire.
3. *March* (Left valve, second space). Lost.
4. *April* (Left valve, first space). The composition shows two figures facing each other. The first, on somewhat higher ground, holds an unidentifiable object, perhaps a plant. The second directs a half upraised arm toward him in a gesture of prayer or acknowledgment. The subject appears to be identical with that illustrating the month of April on a capital of the cloister of Tarragona, which Webster tentatively describes as the taking of the knight's vow.[36] Another possible interpretation would connect the scene at Blesle with the ancient feast of the Rosalia, which forms the basis of the illustration of the month of May on the portal of San Marco in Venice.[37] Here, we see a young man crowned by two young ladies, who hold a wreath of roses over his head. These rites have an extension in the customs associated with the arrival of Spring and the celebration of Love in native folklore. It is reported that in Haute-Loire, on the Sunday after Easter or at the beginning of May, a collection of eggs and other foodstuffs is made for the preparation a banquet in order to invoke the favor of nature and of the love goddess. Flowers are offered in exchange. Young girls, or sometimes couples, are crowned with white roses and offered floral scepters.[38]
5. *May* (Left valve, upper border, left space) (Figs. 68 and 74). The scene shows a lance-wielding figure galloping on horseback. A smaller animal preceding the horse while looking back is probably not the hunter's quarry, but a prancing dog accompanying him on the chase.[39] May is frequently personified as a warrior, or through the attribute of a falcon, as a hunter.
6. *June* (Left valve, upper border, right space) (Figs. 68 and 75). A figure holding a lamb on his shoulders in the manner of the Good Shepherd appears on the left side. On the right, a second figure manipulating a long-handled scythe. Mowing with a scythe is the most common subject chosen for the month of June. The sheepbearer, included in order to fill the leftover space, is rare among the Labors of the Months. An example, however, occurs as part of the bucolic scene representing May in the calendrical cycle of the eleventh-century copy of the Marvels of the East in the British Museum.[40] It is taken as an illustration for the month of April in the cycle of San Marco, at Trogir, and in the mosaic pavement of Otranto.[41]

Hay is now harvested in Auvergne from the feast of Saint-Jean (June 25) until the end of July.[42] Animal husbandry is an important element in the agricultural economy of the region since a good deal of its mountainous terrain is unsuitable for cultivation. Much of the high plateau country west of Blesle is thus used as grazing land. Because of the persistence of snow through much of the spring, however, the flock is not led out-of-doors until the middle of May.[43] All this may help to explain in some measure the inclusion of the sheepbearer among the monthly labors at this time and place.

7. *July* (Right valve, upper edge, left space) (Figs. 68 and 76). The scene once again shows two separate activities. On the left, a figure whose head is shielded from the sun by a hat, bends, in the act of reaping, over two sheaves of grain. This is the occupation which generally typifies this month. A second figure, apparently a woman holding or nursing a child, is seated on the ground at the right side. I know of no other instance of this choice of subject in the labors of the months.
8. *August* (Right valve, upper edge, right space). Threshing. Three men, a pair on the left side, a single one on the right, wield flails which they bring down on a sheaf of grain at the center of the composition. Threshing is the characteristic activity for August, particularly in the French cycles[44] of the labors, but fluctuates elsewhere in accordance with seasonal custom.
9. *September* (Right valve, first space along the side). Gathering grapes (?). The scene apparently shows two figures flanking a vat (?). The foliage seen above their heads must be the vine, but is unclear whether they are to be construed as harvesting the fruit or pouring wine into the vat.
10. *October* (Right valve, second space). Harvesting acorns and feeding pigs. A single figure, wearing a hood or pointed bonnet, strikes a tree with a pole. The silhouette in the foreground seems to be that of a single or a pair of hogs. The subject is fairly common for the month of October, and predominates especially in the French cycles.[45]
11. *November* (Right valve, third space). Lost. Webster notes that the western French cycles show a preference in the illustration of this month for the feeding of oxen.[46]
12. *December* (Right valve, fourth space). Lost.

The choice of a cycle of the Labors of the Months as a subject for illustration on the doors is entirely exceptional, if we set aside the four seasonal images identified by A. Goldschmidt on the bronze doors of Augsburg cathedral.[47] The idea no doubt derives from representations of the Labors around the portal opening itself, as exemplified in churches of western France, Burgundy, and northern Italy, though, paradoxically, not in central France.[48] Indeed the disposition of the subjects to embrace the upper contour of the valves mimes the outline of an arch, which the leftover border beneath the months of January and December furnishes with a kind of *soubassement.* The sequence of the Labors around the pair of large crosses also places the work within that pattern of exegetical reflection which emphasizes the cosmological dimensions of the sign through the analogy of the sun set at the center of the celestial sphere.[49] This is a line of interpretation which has left its mark on other monuments of Romanesque art, though in these, the cycle of the months is impersonated by the signs of the zodiac rather than the Labors. A cross with the apocalyptic letters Alpha and Omega is thus inserted in the middle of the zodiacal frieze along the upper northern aisle wall at Saint-Maurice in Vienne.[50] The sign of the zodiac within roundels mounted around the apse of Saint-Paul at Issoire might be seen as taking the choir of the church in its entirety as the focal point of their yearly revolution.[51]

NOTES

1. L. de Saint-Poncy, "Notice historique sur Blesle et l'abbaye de Saint-Pierre-de-Blesle," *Annales Soc. Puy,* XXIX, 1868, 385-529. N. Thiollier, "La porte romane en bois sculpté de l'église de Blesle (Haute-Loire)," *Bull. mon.,* 108-13, and *idem, Architecture religieuse,* 102-3.
2. Mon. Hist. Cliché Durand No. 11954, made around the year 1888. The doors are 2.62 m high and 2.10 m wide (103 1/8 x 82 5/8″).
3. G. Segret, "La fondation de l'abbaye de Blesle," *Almanach de Brioude,* 1921, 87-106. L. Bréhier, "Blesle," *Dictionnaire d'histoire et de géographie écclesiastique,* IX, 187ff.
4. G. Segret, "Les biens et revenus de l'abbaye de Blesle," *Almanach de Brioude,* 1929, 129ff and A. Chassaing, *Spicilegium Brivatense,* Paris, 1886, 19.
5. A useful and readable account of the history of the abbey and the town has been published by J. Pothier, *Blesle. Notes d'histoire et d'architecture,* Brioude, 1970.
6. L. Bréhier, "Les chapiteaux du chevet de Saint-Pierre de Blesle," *Almanach de Brioude,* 1929, 97-121, still constitutes a basic study. See also the same author's "L'art roman dans la région de Brioude," *idem,* XXVII, 1946, 7-41, *passim.,* and most recently, the 4th revised edition of B. Craplet, *Auvergne romane,* Collection Zodiaque, 1972, in which, 285ff., a chapter on the church has been added.
7. On the sculpture of this type, see M. Schapiro, "A Relief in Rodez and the Beginnings of Romanesque Sculpture in Southern France," *Studies in Western Art* (Acts of the Twentieth Congress of the History of Art), Princeton, 1963, I, 40-66, and Cahn, *Gesta,* X, 2, 1971, 73-74. Bréhier, *Art roman dans la région de Brioude,* 16, dates this part of the church "au plus tard au début du XIe siècle," which seems too early.
8. Reproduction in Craplet, *Auvergne romane,* 121.
9. Pothier, *Blesle,* 69. The author credits Bréhier with the substance of her remarks on the architecture of the church, though I have not been able to find an expression of this particular opinion in the latter's publications.
10. *Idem,* 70, and Bréhier, *Art roman dans la région de Brioude,* 16. This seems to contradict the latter's

earlier and better founded view (*Chapiteaux du chevet de Saint-Pierre-de-Blesle,* 103) that the erection of the chapels was followed by an interruption "plus ou moins longue," preceding the construction of the choir on a new plan, leading the author to deny that a trefoil scheme was ever contemplated or carried out.

11. For this structure, see Thiollier, *Architecture religieuse,* 135ff.
12. Heliot, *Problèmes d'architecture,* 186f.
13. M. Durliat, "Saint-Pons-de-Thomières," *Congrès arch.,* CVIII, 1951, 271ff. This type of structure, where a single vessel is covered by pointed barrel vault with applied transversal ribs is discussed by L. Torres Balbás, "Iglesias románicas españolas con bóvedas de cañón en las naves laterales de eje normal al del templo," *Archivo español de arte,* VII, 1931, 1-21, and A. Anglès, "Les églises à berceaux transversaux dans le Rouergue," *Bull. mon.,* 1910, 10-35.
14. Bréhier, *Chapiteaux,* 118.
15. Lefèvre-Pontalis, *Congrès arch.,* 1904, 553.
16. H. Focillon, *Art d'Occident,* Paris, 1938, 125, note 1.
17. Rather similar in style is a corbel head at Aulnat, Puy-de-Dôme (reproduction in L. Bréhier, *L'art chrétien,* Paris, 1928, 205).
18. For comparable arches, see the windows of the Maison de l'Homme des Bois at Thiers (A. Ojerdias, "Les vieux logis de Thiers," *Congrès arch.,* LXXXVII, 1924, 338-39, and several houses in Blesle itself (Pothier, *Blesle,* figs. 33, 34, and 40).
19. Hamann, *Abteikirche,* 14f., considers in passing the question of Romanesque portals without tympana. Bréhier, *Art roman dans la région de Brioude,* 29-30, lists as examples in the area in addition to Blesle the portals of the churches of Mailhat and Chassignoles.
20. Thiollier, *Architecture religieuse,* 45-47.
21. For Mailhat, see Gybal, *L'Auvergne. berceau de l'art roman,* Clermont-Ferrand, 1957, 205-9.
22. L. Bréhier and G. Segret, "Une maison d'époque romane à Blesle," *Revue d'Auvergne,* XLI, 1925, 33-55, who give additional examples of this kind of moluration in Auvergne.
23. Thiollier, *Architecture religieuse,* 45: "Nous ne le croyons pas antérieur à la fin du XIIe siècle."
24. Pothier, *Blesle,* 70.
25. Bréhier, followed by Pothier, *Blesle,* 69, argue that the decorated window of the upper north transept end-wall once functioned as one of the portals of the church. This seems to me doubtful.
26. J. Pothier, "Vieilles maisons abbatiales," *Almanach de Brioude,* 1967, 165-77.
27. Pothier, *Blesle,* 38.
28. Dr. Susanna Jutte of the Yale Forestry School made a determination of the wood on the basis of a small sample.
29. V. Leroquais, *Les Psautiers manuscrits latins des bibliothèques publiques de France,* Mâcon, 1940-41, I, 273-77.
30. Goldschmidt, *Elfenbeinskulpturen,* I, 9, No. 2, pl. II.
31. W. Neumüller and K. Holter, *Der Codex Millenarius,* Linz, 1959, 78ff. and 112-113.
32. Cologne, Dombibl. Ms. 14 (Franco-Saxon Gospels), fol. 104v; Cambrai, Bibl. Mun. Ms. 327 (Gospels), fol. 67; Hague, Ms. A.A. 260 (Gospels of Egmond), fol. 161v. Paris, Bibl. Nat. Lat. 11959, fols. 17 and 17v (Gospels of Saint-Maur-des-Fossés)
33. See on this the remarks of G. Micheli, *L'enluminure du haut Moyen âge et les influences irlandaises,* Brussels, 1939, 168ff.
34. Bibl. Nat. lat. 252. Gaborit-Chopin, *La décoration des manuscrits à Saint-Martial de Limoges,* 179.
35. L. Mallé, *Le arti figurativi in Piemonte,* Turin s.d., pp. 57f., and R. Jullian, *L'eveil de la sculpture italienne,* 106. It should be noted that many of the initials in the so-called Second Saint-Martial Bible (Bibl. Nat. lat. 8) incorporate in their structure interlace constructions with open zones in which diminutive beasts are seen.
36. J. C. Webster, *The Labors of the Months in Antique and Medieval Art,* Princeton, 1938, 86.
37. H. Stern, "Poésies et représentations carolingiennes et byzantines des mois," *Revue archéologique,* 1955, 251ff.
38. A. van Gennep, *Le folklore de l'Auvergne et du Velay,* Paris, 1942, 123ff., and the same author's *Manuel du folklore français contemporain,* I, 4, 1949, 1421ff. P. Charrié, *Le folklore du Haut-Vivarais,* Paris, 1968, 93ff.
39. This motif has a long history, some examples being found in Greek Archaic art: Ch. Picard, "Sur un motif accessoire des chars en course," *Revue archéologique,* XLIII, 1954, 220-24.
40. Brit. Mus. Cotton Tib. B.V. Webster, *Labors,* pl. XIX, fig. 34a.
41. O. Demus, *The Church of San Marco in Venice,* 154. J. Richer, "Les sculptures des mois à Trogir et à Ferrare," *Bull. mon.,* CXXIII, 1965, 25-35, and A. Venturi, E. Pais, and P. Molmenti, *La Dalmazia monumentale,* Milan, 1917, 69, pls. XXV-XXVII. Sheepbearers are an occasional motif in Auvergnat Romanesque sculpture, as noted by Bréhier, "Les traits originaux de l'iconographie dans la sculpture romane de l'Auvergne," *Medieval Essays in*

Memory of A. Kingsley Porter, ed. W. Koehler, Cambridge, 1939, II, 326, and *idem,* "Les traces de l'ancien art chrétien dans l'art roman auvergnat," *Cahiers arch.,* I, 1945, 74-75. An example on a capital at Lanobre (Cantal) is signaled by B. Porcher, "Bestiaire roman auvergnat," *Revue de la Haute-Auvergne,* XLI, 1968, pl. opp. p. 337.

42. See L. Chaumeil, "Travaux et jours d'un paysan auvergnat," *Annales de géographie,* XLVIII, 1939, 138ff.

43. Chaumeil, *Travaux et jours,* 153f. It is possible to reconstruct the older pattern of agricultural activities through the reports of travelers such as Legrand d'Aussy, *Voyage fait en 1787 et 1788 dans la ci-devant haute et basse Auvergne . . . ,* Paris, 1794-95. This has been done by A. Poitrineau, *La vie rurale en Basse-Auvergne au XVIIIe siècle (1726-1789),* Paris, 1965.

44. Webster, *Labors,* 71. O. Koseleff, *Die Monatsdarstellungen der französischen Plastik des 12. Jahrhunderts,* Diss., Marburg, 1934.

45. Webster, *Labors,* 71-72. According to Chaumeil, *Travaux et jours,* 156, the care of pigs is now entrusted to the woman of the house.

46. *Idem,* 70.

47. A. Goldschmidt, *Die deutschen Bronzetüren des frühen Mittelalters. I. Die frühmittelalterlichen Bronzetüren,* Marburg, 1926, 30ff. Götz, *Bildprogramme,* 267.

48. Koseleff, on the strength of Chaudruc de Crazannes, "Coup d'oeuil historique et architectonique sur l'église de l'ancienne abbaye bénédictine de Figeac," *Revue archéologique,* 1859, 139, mentions the possible existence of six Labors on the porch of the church of St. Sauveur in that town. But Webster, *Labors,* 79, indicates that too little remains of this sculpture to reach any clear conclusion on the matter.

Interesting for its location half way between central and western France is the destroyed church of Notre-Dame de la Règle in Limoges, which is also said to have had a portal decorated with Labors of the Months (Abbé Texier, "Mémoires sur l'étude de l'art limousin," *Bulletin de la Société archéologique et historique du Limousin,* I, 1846, 15. However, the reliefs still preserved from this monument do not show any trace of such subjects (*Musée Municipal de Limoges. Collection archéologique,* Limoges, 1969, Nos. 162-73, 78ff.

The portals of the churches of Mauriac and Ydes in Cantal, southwest of Blesle, have archivolts with zodiacal signs.

49. J. Daniélou, "Les douze apôtres et le zodiaque," *Les symboles chrétiens primitifs,* Paris, 1961, 131-42.

50. L. Bégule, *L'église Saint-Maurice, ancienne cathédrale de Vienne,* Paris, 1914, 130f. The sign occurs between the Scales and Scorpio.

51. Ch. Terrasse, "L'église d'Issoire," *Congrès arch.,* LXXXVI, 1924, 22-23.

VII Lavoûte-Chilhac

THE MONASTERY OF Lavoûte-Chilhac was founded by St. Odilo of Cluny and dedicated by Bishop Stephen of Clermont-Ferrand on September 14 of the year 1024 or 1025. The event is mentioned in Jotsaldus's biography of the saint and formally recorded in an unusually detailed charter.[1] The inscription in leonine verse on the wooden door of the church commemorates it also: HIC TIBI REX REGUM HOC CONDIDIT ODILO TEMPLUM/ AGMINIBUS SUPERIS QVEM MISCUIT ARBITER ORBIS (Figs. 77 and 79). The church is located on a rocky escarpment in a meander of the Allier River, which surrounds it on three sides (Fig. 80). The land was Odilo's own, being situated near the ancestral seat of the powerful Mercoeur clan to which he belonged. The monastery and the church were quite probably designed to serve as a burial place or pantheon for the Mercoeurs. Jotsaldus states explicitly that Odilo constructed the church "toward the end of his life," and the foundation charter speaks of his wish that the monastic community offer prayers for him and his brethren.[2] In 1053, Bishop Stephen II of Le Puy, Odilo's nephew, was buried at Lavoûte, as was Bishop Peter II, another Mercoeur, twenty years later.[3] The monastery was placed by Odilo under the protection of the Holy See and subordinated to the authority of Cluny. In a Bull dated 1109, Paschal II authorized abbot Hugh of Cluny and his successors to retain the monastery, as well as Odilo's two other Auvergnat foundations, Ris and Sauxillanges, under his personal control.[4] The visitations made on behalf of the mother house show that Lavoûte housed about twenty-five monks and this number remained more or less constant until the middle of the fifteenth century. It was thus about equal in size to such houses as Marcigny and Charlieu in Burgundy and Saint-Saturnin-du-Port in Auvergne, and hierarchically equated with them on the list of Cluniac priories.[5]

With the possible exception of a section of rough rubble masonry imbricated in the south lateral wall of the present church, Odilo's original construction has entirely vanished. The now-standing structure was begun around 1460 under Prior Barthélemy de la Farge and completed by his successor Dom Moussy. Their arms, together with those of the reforming abbot of Cluny and bishop of Le Puy Jean de Bourbon, appear on one of the keystones of the nave.[6] The splendid, and in scale, truly palatial conventual buildings which cradle in their midst the much more modest late Gothic church, were added in 1747.[7]

Pending archaeological exploration, the design of Odilo's church must necessarily remain a total mystery. In view of the size of the monastic community and the exiguous nature of the terrain, however, it is unlikely to have been larger than the existing structure, which is an aisleless edifice of six bays terminated in the east by a polygonal apse and measuring approximately 45 m. in length and 23 m. in width. The church was dedicated to the Holy Cross. Through the efforts of its founder, it was at the outset provided with an imposing collection of relics, which was carefully inventoried by a contemporary chronicler.[8] Archbishop Poppo of Trier, patriarch of Aquilea, sent a finely carved ivory reliquary containing parcels of the bodies of various saints, and the empress Cunegunde obliged the abbot with a sizable fragment of the True Cross for which a golden and jeweled reliquary was made.[9] The dedication of the church and the nature of this precious relic would seem to be announced in the iconographic program of the door.

The Romanesque wooden door, preserved in the sacristy of the church, was until 1893 installed in the now walled-up Gothic portal, situated in the second bay along the south side of the present church (Fig. 78). The earliest record of its existence known to me is found in A. Duchesne's *Additamenta* to the *Bibliotheca Cluniacensis* (1614), when it was already in that location.[10] This is also where nineteenth-century authors, beginning with Aymard,[11] and followed by Gailhabaud [12] and Viollet-le-Duc, all discovered it.[13] The doorway is surmounted by the arms of the monastic community and was intended to give the monks a separate access to the church from their living quarters nearby. Duchesne describes its situation as facing the cloister, which vanished in the eighteenth-century constructions. The door has been extended along the right side and possibly trimmed top and bottom in order to adapt it to the size and contour of the Gothic setting (Fig. 79). That it has been preserved at all was almost certainly due to the inscription naming Odilo as the founder of the church which was incorporated in its design. It is generally assumed that the work was made for the entrance of the eleventh-century church, and on the analogy of the other doors of the group, likely to be the remaining half of an initial pair of valves.

A number of representations of the door of varying accuracy were made in the nineteenth century. The earliest, due to Normand and published in Aymard's description, is the least reliable.[14] Its only claim to our attention is that it represents the border along the right edge of the door in a slightly more complete state, though it is more than doubtful that the draftsman saw it this way. The engraving made for Gailhabaud's history of architecture is, by contrast, of excellent quality and reliability (Fig. 77). Comparison with the door in its present state shows that little change has occurred in its appearance since that time. The only loss of note is a narrow strip of wood including the strip of cable molding adjoining the right side of the lower arm of the cross, which has now been patched up. Some additional nails are also visible, especially along the left edge and the bottom. They are distinguishable from the original nails by their flatter and rounder heads. The watercolor copy of Petitgrand made in 1889 records these changes faithfully.[15]

The state of preservation in which the work has come down raises some problems that are difficult to elucidate in their entirety. As presently constituted, the framework of the door consists of six planks joined along their longer sides (Text fig. 7). Although the rear cannot be inspected since the panel is now permanently mounted against a wall, an examination of the left side discloses that three planks spaced at roughly regular intervals furnish horizontal bracing. All parts of the design visible on the outer surface are executed on separate boards nailed to this armature. Since the other doors in our group all consist of two valves, it is likely, though this cannot be conclusively proven, that a second panel, similar in format and design to the existing one, was initially extant. The surviving panel would have been the left half of this ensemble: rings, on which the doors swung open and shut, are present on this side. At Chamalières and Blesle, the left valve terminates at the right edge of the cross panel, while the wider right valve carries the batten. It seems very probable that the doors of Lavoûte adhered to the same scheme and the strip of wood now mounted along the right side was added when the panel was adapted to its late Gothic architectural setting. The alteration is of course plainly revealed by the extreme heterogeneity of the elements fastened along the right edge. It is also indicated by the coincidence between the terminal edges of the backing plank and the decorative material mounted onto it. In the body of the door, the boards along the surface lie across the joints of the framework underneath.

The original core of the work is formed by the cross with the surrounding four

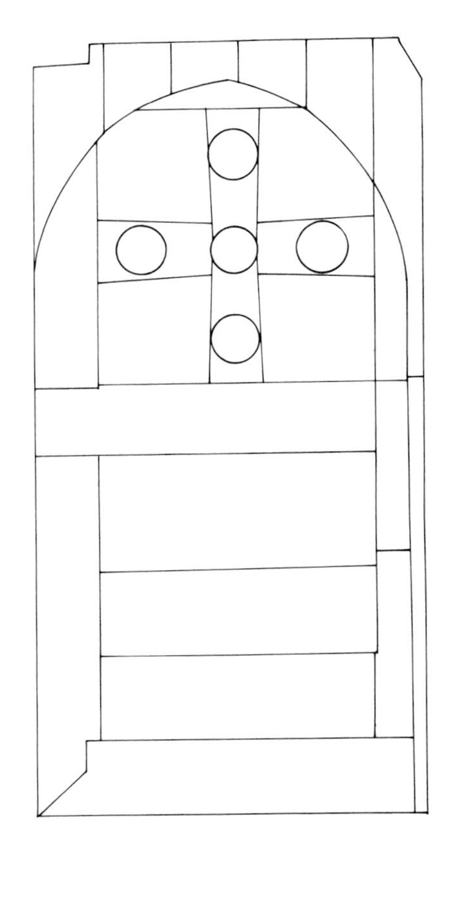

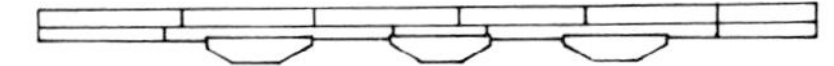

7. Wooden door, Lavoûte-Chilhac. Schema of assembly

panels (Figs. 77 and 79). The cross has flanging rather than rectilinear arms as at Blesle and Chamalières. It is outlined by the familiar cable molding, though in single rather than double form. The horizontal sections of this border are carved directly on the arms of the cross; the vertical ones are hewn along the edges of the four panels. Within this patterned border, the arms of the cross are additionally framed by a narrow strip of wood on which nails set in a row are mounted. The central part of the cross arms does not lie uniformly level with the surface of the doors but descends at a slight taper from the outer extremities toward the middle. It is this slight recession which gradually discloses the raised band along the sides as well as four interlace knots carved in the spaces between the four lobes on the arms and mounted at their intersection in the center. The turned lobes have a more flattened, less bulbous quality than those at Chamalières. At the top, they show cupped hollows, and they are set in recesses rather than nailed to the surface of the cross.

The trapezoidal panels which fill the spaces around the cross are, save for the cable molding along the vertical edge contiguous to the cross, devoid of carving. However, the polychromy has left traces upon them in the form of dark silhouettes standing forth against a surrounding whitish ground. On the lower left side, the shape of what was probably a horseman wielding a spear can be distinguished. The head of a horse and torso of a rider, remnants of a second and opposing cavalier, appear in the panel on the right. In the upper right field, the silhouette of an unidentifiable quadruped is faintly, but clearly, outlined. Its pendant on the left side, no doubt another animal, hunting centaur or kindred subject, has totally disappeard. The panels are set in place by means of a pair of diagonally intersecting rows of nails, positioned at regular intervals and without regard for the contour of the painted design.

The collective effect of these measures lends to the cross a heightened importance within the composition. All of the relief elements are concentrated on it rather than dispersed over the entire surface of the design. Relief not only serves to set it apart but enhances its material substance, conferring upon it the qualities of a tangible object. Although the predominance of the cross was formerly challenged more forcefully by the polychromed designs around it, the regular and four times repeated pattern of nails superimposed on them must have robbed them of some of their expressive force. The shift to a Greek or processional type with flanging arms also sharpens the allusive focus of the miraculous sign, since at the possible cost of slightly greater complexity in the process of joinery, the form now transcends the dimensions of the pictorial and refers the observer to a category of real works within the corpus of medieval crosses. The processional form is common among the Longobard gold leaf crosses[16] and in Visigothic Spain. The two surviving arms of a jeweled processional cross in the Guarrazar Treasure or a smaller hanging cross found at Torredonjimeno (Jaen) can be cited as examples from the latter cultural sphere.[17] The Cross of Desiderius at Brescia [18] and two of the monumental Oviedo crosses show arms attached to a central roundel designed to house a relic, but otherwise faithfully perpetuate the same shape.[19] The standard or cross staff carried by Christ or St. Peter in certain depictions of early Christian art often exhibit what appear to be smaller crosses of this kind.[20] Ultimately, the form is derived from the chrismon or labarum cross associated with Constantine's triumph on the Milvian Bridge, in which the flanging arms convey the effect of luminous rays, while their equal length is determined by the circle of light which surrounds the vision. The words MMI VICTORIA, all that is preserved of an inscription which appeared over the cross at Lavoûte, makes this triumphal symbolism explicit.

It is obviously tempting in this light to see in the cross on the door some reflection of the cross reliquary made in connection with Cunegunde's gift to Odilo, kept in the treasury of the church. Henry II and his spouse made a number of donations of crosses to churches of the Empire, without committing his goldsmiths to any single, consistent type.[21] The cross which, according to a fairly reliable tradition, he gave to the Cathedral of Basel on its dedication in 1019, comes close to the design at Lavoûte.[22] It is a jeweled and totally aniconic work whose arms, flanging at the extremities only, are punctuated by large roundels upon which crystal cabochons are mounted. The work stands isolated within the imperial tradition, and must have been based upon a model of pre-Carolingian origin similar to the unfortunately much restored Cross of Agnellus in Ravenna.[23] But the relic does not seem to have reached its destination in this form. The anonymous chronicler of Lavoûte clearly states that the receptacle, whose outward shape is not revealed, was made on his instructions, though "possibly not as well as might have been suitable." [24] The object was still seen at Lavoûte in 1710 by the traveling cleric Jacques Boyer,[25] but disappeared some time thereafter, presumably in the chaotic aftermath of the French Revolution.

However this question might be resolved, there is no doubt that the cross type represented on the Lavoûte door was by Romanesque times no longer in active currency. But the nearly complete eclipse of goldsmithwork monuments embodying this form was accompanied by a certain persistence of the design in a representational context. In Spain, the memory of the hallowed emblem was kept alive in the frontispiece illustrations of the copies of Beatus's Commentary on the Apocalypse.[26] Portal decoration in its more compressed utterances shows the Greek cross in isolation, often mounted on an abbreviated staff as a reminiscence of its original function as a standard.[27] Among the archaic lintels where the cross stands in the midst of paradisiac animals and vegetation, it is this type which predominates. It is seen on the pedimented lintel above the entrance of the octagonal chapel of Saint-Clair in Le Puy[28] and at Saint-Victor-sur-Loire, some distance to the north, where the Greek cross is inscribed in a circle flanked by Alpha and Omega.[29]

To the initial conception of the door also belongs the interlace border on its left side. Its design is similar to the border of the doors of the chapel of St. Martin of Le Puy cathedral, though the interweaving ductus is somewhat thicker and the resulting pattern more dense. The border is interrupted in its path by the outline imposed by the late Gothic portal. It is also incomplete at the bottom, though there appears to be a departure from regularity in the design just above the point where it meets the modern inset at the lower left corner, indicating that either a termination or a shift in direction was near. Along the right side of the door, another small section of interlace border can be seen. Cut down to half of its initial width and poorly preserved, it must represent part of the pattern on its horizontal course, marked, as in Le Puy, by a sequence of triple-peaked formations. We thus have here a fragment either from the upper or lower segments of the border, or possibly, from the corresponding parts of the hypothetical right valve.

The inscriptions contiguous to the upper and lower side of the cross panel are the most atypical features of the door when compared to the valves of Blesle and Chamalières. The lower plank on which the Odilo inscription is carved cuts across the interlace border, though the joint was carefully made and the design suffers no interruption. The operation would probably have been entirely hidden by the polychromy, which according to a nineteenth-century observer, had a bluish cast in this area.[30] The inscription also does not fit very well in the available space. On the left side, it impinges slightly onto the inner edge of the border. A certain crowding is apparent along the right side, and the final letters of the first two lines are in fact partly cut off. The artisan unaccountably made his task more difficult by carving forms of a predominantly vertical orientation against the horizontal grain of the wood. This may help to account for the rather squat proportion of the letters, as well as their variable width and height.

The panel at the top of the cross now constitutes little more than the summit of the late Gothic arch whose outline is superimposed on the door. Above the word VICTORIA, the remains of a second line of text are visible, and the space left in the denuded area above the outline of the arch is sufficient for still another line. The character of the epigraphy is identical to that of the Odilo inscription, Thus it might be suspected that the inscription in a complete state was identical in length with the panegyric of Odilo below the cross. A panel of such dimensions could accurately be fitted in the space between the top of the cross and the upper edge of the door. Yet the presence of an inscription in this location is as unexpected and even more jarring than the verses in commemoration of Odilo below the cross. Although we can now no longer determine whether the upper panel was similarly lodged into the fabric of the border on the left side, it takes the place which we should expect to have been reserved for the continuation of the interlace strip across the top. Taken collectively, these factors are bound to raise the strong possibility that both inscriptions were added to the door as part of a change in plan or afterthought. Since the width of the existing interlace border on the side is about equal to the space filled by the Victoria inscription, the substitution would not have posed major practical difficulties. Below the cross, the artisan had to replace a decorative panel no wider than the outer extremities of its horizontal arms. But finding it difficult to accommodate the inscription in its entirely within this space, he gave to the substitute plank the full width of the door, thereby gaining some small, but welcome room along the inner edge of the border. The change in design cannot have occurred long after the completion of the work. The character of the epigraphy would rule out anything but a Romanesque date, and as we have noted, the Odilo inscription was observed *in situ* as early as the beginning of the seventeenth century. The alteration may quite plausibly have taken place before the door was ever initially installed, in the course of manufacture itself, following special requirements formulated by the patron.

The three planks with ornamental designs below the Odilo inscription are even less harmoniously fitted within the fabric of the work. These planks are of darker and more close-grained wood than that employed in the other parts of the door. Unequal in height, their shape also departs considerably from true square, something which is not characteristic of the joinery around them and in the other doors of the group. In all three panels, the design is complete along the left side. But along the right edge, only the frieze of Pseudo-Cufic ornament in the middle panel comes to a full stop, though not, in fact, at the very edge of the plank. In the other two boards, the path of the ornament is interrupted rather than concluded, as if these panels had been trimmed, having initially had somewhat longer dimensions. The joints along the abutting sides of the boards are given stress by means of a rounded, molding-like treatment of the edges, though care was taken against excessive emphasis by connecting every rounded contour with a flat opposite number. It may be noted that this procedure was also observed in the assembly of the boards with the Odilo and Victoria inscriptions, which have rounded profiles along their sides contiguous with the cross panel. It apparently figures at Blesle in the joint between the border and the body of the door, but it is avoided in the corresponding location along the lateral sections of the border at Lavoûte and not employed at all at Chamalières or in Le Puy.

The uppermost of the three boards below the Odilo inscription shows two rows of splayed palmette leaves enclosed within a sequence of roundels formed by interlocking bands. Six-pointed rosettes appear in the voids between each group of four circlets. The pattern avoids the implication of endless repetition by means of rounded extensions which anchor each leaf within its circle to the border top and bottom. The narrower middle panel is given over to Pseudo-Cufic ornament, much more remote from readable script than that which appears along the sides of the Infancy doors in Le Puy, thinned out and rather lifeless. The panel in the lowest position is incomplete along the bottom and badly eroded by wear. It shows a double row of large openings in the form of an irregular honeycomb. In each of these spaces, there is a stylized flower formed by intersecting diagonals, with palmette leaves along the four extremities. It is a more nervous and attenuated version of the type of plant seen in the lower section of the right valve at Chamalières, duplicated also in some examples of stone carving at Saint-Romain-le-Puy and l'Ile Barbe.[31] The visual effect produced by the combination of the planks is bound to impress the observer as of a more unsettled kind than that which prevails in the more self-evidently authentic parts in our group of monuments. The insistent horizontal (or near horizontal) subdivisions resulting from the juxtaposition of the wide and flat borders of the boards loom assertively in this sense of discordance. The ornamental designs, though expertly rendered tend to a degree of complexity and variety verging on the prolix. We are bound to suppose on the basis of both material and formal considerations that the door must have necessitated, not too long after its completion, some alteration or repair.

There remains a section of wood carving which it is most difficult to fit into a reconstruction of the work in one of its earlier states. This is the fragment of an inscription on the upper right side of the door. It is the left side of a panel which must once have been much wider, and possibly somewhat higher as well. What is left are the first two or three letters of eight lines of text, as follows:

M
SV
QV
DIT
AN
CRV
MV
VIT

The endings (?) in the fourth and eighth lines—DIT/—VIT—make it most probable that this text was also in verse form, while the letters CRV in the sixth line point to another invocation in honor of the cross as its subject.[32]

The narrow border along the left side is interrupted at the top but continues along the bottom under the last line of text. This border has the same rounded contour as is in evidence along the sides of the Victoria and Odilo inscriptions. Although the letters are somewhat larger, the epigraphical character of this fragment fully matches that of these inscriptions. It is therefore most probable that all three panels were made at the same time. But if, as it is tempting to assume, the fragmentary panel was made for the hypothetical right valve, we have not the slightest clue as to the nature of the design of which it was once a part. Such an assumption could only mean that the alteration of the work was much more substantial than the appearance of the existing panel would tend to indicate, resulting in two valves of asymmetrical format. It would have been a monument without parallels within the existing body of early medieval doors.[33]

The foundation charter indicates that the church at Lavoûte was not yet complete on its dedication in 1025.[34] The doors themselves must have been executed after Odilo's death in 1049 at the earliest, since the inscription refers to him as part of the heavenly choir of the saints.[35] The monument should therefore take a place among the many testimonials of Odilo's posthumous cult, which have been very thoroughly studied by Dom. R.-H. Hesbert.[36] Odilo died at Souvigny and was interred near the body of Mayolus, his predecessor as abbot of Cluny. Miracles were soon reported, and in 1063, Peter Damian, the papal legate, proceeded to a translation and consecrated the new church of the monastery, which became the site of an important pilgrimage. The monks of Lavoûte could ultimately lay claim to no more than the vestments and the crozier of the saint.[37] The liturgical cult of Odilo was introduced into the diocese of Clermont of which Lavoûte was then a part by a figure also named Odilo of Mercoeur, who, as a canon and *praepositus* of Saint-Julien de Brioude, made a donation for this purpose.[38] The date of this foundation is not known, but the donor's name and title are mentioned in a charter dated 1137.[39] The occasion, we may assume, was soon followed by the execution of the doors.

NOTES

1. Jotsaldus, *Vita Odilonis,* Pat. lat. 142, 897. The foundation charter has been published a number of times, most accessibly in A. Bernard and A. Bruel, *Recueil des chartes de l'abbaye de Cluny,* Paris, 1870-1903, III, No. 2788, 811-15, and Chassaing, *Spicilegium Brivatense,* No. 2, 2-5. All modern histories of Cluniac monasticism take note of the event. See J. Hourlier, "Saint Odilon bâtisseur," *Revue Mabillon,* LI, 1961, 303ff.; *idem, Saint Odilon, abbé de Cluny* (Bibliothèque de la Revue d'histoire ecclésiastique, vol. 40), Louvain, 1964, 93, 170-71, and earlier, E. Sackur's classic study, *Die Cluniacenser in ihrer kirchlichen und allgemeingeschichtlichen Wirksamkeit,* Halle, 1894, II, 189, 379. The cartulary of the abbey is lost in its greater part, but some excerpts have been published by P.-F. Fournier, "Cartulaire de Saint-Martin des Aloches. Extrait d'un cartulaire du prieuré de La Voûte-Chilhac," *Revue d'Auvergne,* 65, 1951, 85-98, after Bibl. Nat., Collection de Bourgogne, LXXXIV, No. 526. An unpublished history of the monastery by M. Fournier-Latouraille was not accessible to me.
2. *Vita Odilonis, loc. cit.:* "in ultimis suis."
3. As reported in the chronicle of St. Peter of Le Puy, printed in De Vic and Vaissete, *Histoire du Languedoc,* V, 23.
4. Boudet, *Cartulaire du prieuré de Saint-Flour,* Monaco, 1910, No. XIII, 41-42.
5. A. Duchesne and M. Marrier, *Bibliotheca Cluniacensis,* Brussels-Paris, 1915, 1736-77, 1717. G. de Valous, *Le monachisme clunisien des origines au XVe siècle,* Paris, 1935, II, 177, 183.
6. R. Eymère, *Notes historiques sur Lavoûte-Chilhac,* Le Puy, 1912-13, 33ff. On the career of Jean de Bourbon, see G. de Valous, "La carrière épiscopale de Jean de Bourbon," *Le Moyen Age,* 1928, 282-311,

and *idem, Jean de Bourbon,* Saint-Wandrille, 1949.

7. Eymère, *Notes historiques,* 97ff. J. Evans, *Monastic Architecture in France from the Renaissance to the Revolution,* Cambridge, 1964, 52.
8. P.-F. Fournier, "Histoire anonyme de la fondation du prieuré de Lavoûte-Chilhac par Odilon, Abbé de Cluny," *Bulletin philologique et historique du Comité des travaux historiques et scientifiques,* 1958 (1959), 103-15. The document is datable on internal evidence in the period 1031-53. It was copied at Lavoûte by Dom Fonteneau in the eighteenth century and is found among his papers, housed in the Bibliothèque Municipale of Poitiers.
9. *Idem,* 108-9. Two ivory pyxes datable in the sixth century from Lavoûte were acquired by the Louvre at the beginning of this century (Volbach, *Elfenbeinarbeiten,* 84-85, Nos. 185, 186), but I incline to the view that these are not to be connected with Poppo's reliquary, of which nothing else is known. See also L. Bréhier, "Ivoires chrétiens de la région de Brioude," *Almanach de Brioude,* XX, 1939, 27ff. J. Jacobi, "Erzbischof Poppo von Trier (1016-1047). Ein Beitrag zur geistigen und politischen Situation der Reform," *Archiv für Mittelrheinische Kirchengeschichte,* XIII, 1961, 8-26, makes no mention of this donation, which enables him to maintain that Poppo, favoring Gorze, was ill-disposed toward Cluny.
10. *Bibliotheca Cluniacensis,* Appendix, 74: "Ab Odilone autem conditum, praeter locum hunc, testatur et versus super ecclesiae porta, quae claustrum respicit inscriptus qui talis est: Hoc tibi Rex Regum . . . condidit Odilo templum." This information was also reported in Mabillon's *Elogium* of Odilo (Pat. lat. 152, 1037-38), and further, by J. Branche, *La vie des saincts et et sainctes d'Auvergne et du Velay,* Le Puy, 1652, 123. The door is said here to be that of the church "qui sort au cloitre."
11. A. Aymard, "Eglise du XVe siècle, et porte sculptée du XIe siècle à la Voûte-Chilhac (Haute-Loire)," *Annales Soc. Puy,* XIV, 1849, 190-213. The passages of this article dealing with the doors were also published in *Bull. mon.,* 1851, 139-44.
12. J. Gailhabaud, *L'architecture du Ve au XVIIe siècle,* Paris, 1870, II, 31ff., pl. 22.
13. Viollet-le-Duc, *Dictionnaire raisonné,* VI, 361-62.
14. Aymard, *Eglise du XVe siècle,* 190.
15. Published in De Baudot and Perrault-Dabot, *Archives de la Commission des Monuments Historiques,* IV, 13, pl. 20.
16. S. Fuchs, *Langobardischen Goldblattkreuze,* Cat. Nos. 2, 20, etc. . . .
17. H. Schlunk, *Ars Hispaniae,* II, Madrid, 1947, 317, and P. de Pallol, *Hispanic Art of the Visigothic Period,* New York, s.d. 213-15, pls. 109, 118, and 120.
18. V. H. Elbern, "Liturgisches Gerät in edlen Materialen zur Zeit Karls des Grossen," *Karl der Grosse. III. Karolingische Kunst,* Düsseldorf, 1963, 122, with the older bibliography.
19. H. Schlunk, "The Crosses of Oviedo," *Art Bulletin,* XXXII, 1950, 91ff.
20. R. Bauerreiss, "Zur Ikonographie des sogennanten 'Grieschichen Kreuzes'," *Byzantinische Forschungen,* III, 1968, 56-72, with reference to the older bibliography. The theory developed here by Bauerreiss that this type of the cross has its source in the cross staff or the smaller "hand crosses" does not seem acceptable since the Greek cross is by no means the only variety taken up in the illustration of these objects. Some definitely appear to be crosses of the Latin type.
21. P. E. Schramm and F. Mütherich, *Denkmäler der deutschen Könige und Kaiser,* Munich, 1962, 28-29. The monuments in question are the crosses of Bamberg cathedral, lost, but known through a seventeenth-century engraving (No. 119); the Cross of St. Michael in Bamberg, also known through an old print (No. 120); the Portatile of Henry II in the Schatzkammer of the Munich Residenz (No. 134); and the Basel cross in Berlin-Dahlem (No. 139). Odilo himself composed a sermon and prayer in honor of the Holy Cross (Pat. lat. 142, 1031ff. and 1037-38).
22. *Denkmäler,* No. 139.
23. M. Mazzotti, "La croce argenti del vescovo Agnello del Museo Arcivescovile di Ravenna," *Corsi di Cultura sull' arte Ravennate e Bizantina,* 1960, fasc. II, 259-70.
24. P.-F. Fournier, *Histoire anonyme,* 108: "Sed sciendum imprimis quod, excepto illam quam dominus abbas (Odilo) partem detulerat, imperatrix augusta Chuonigondis, quondam conjunx magni Heinrici, imperatoris, misit eodem in loco, ob sui memoriam et sui senioris, maximam partem salutiferae et venerandae Crucis, quam, etsi non ut decuit, tamen auro et lapidibus praetiosis adornare studuimus, prout posse nostrum habuit."
25. J. Boyer, "Journal de Voyage," ed. A. Vernière, *Mémoires de l'Académie de Clermont-Ferrand,* XXVI, 1884, 83.
26. W. Neuss, *Die Apokalypse des hl. Johannes in der*

altspanischen und altchristlichen Bibelillustration, Münster, 1931, I, 113f., and B. Bischoff, *Frühmittelalterliche Studien,* II, 297ff.

27. Bauerreiss, *Lebenszeichen,* 1ff., and above, Chapter V, note 17.
28. Thiollier, *Architecture religieuse,* 72.
29. L. Bernard, "Saint-Victor-sur-Loire," *Bulletin de la Diana,* XLV, 1970, 145-48.
30. Aymard, *Eglise du XVe siècle,* 207.
31. For the first mentioned site, see O. Beigbeder, *Forez-Velay roman* (Coll. Zodiaque), 1962, pl. 69. For the L'Ile-Barbe material, Thiollier, "Vestiges d'art roman en Lyonnais," *Bull. arch.,* 1892, 398ff.
32. A substantial collection of invocations to the cross is found in B. Bischoff, "Ursprung und Geschichte eines Kreuzsegens," *Volk und Volkstum. Jahrbuch für Volkskunde,* I, 1936, 225-31, reprinted in amplified form in *Mittelalterliche Studien,* II, 275-84.
33. J. Evans, *Cluniac Art of the Romanesque Period,* Cambridge, 1950, 17, assumes that the fragmentary panel in a complete state would have been a continuation of the Odilo inscription and filled the lower half of the door, and that the planks with decorative carving now in place in this position "may originally have formed part of an ornamental chest of the thirteenth century." She gives a somewhat faulty reading of the Odilo inscription.
34. This emerges from the text of the foundation charter: "Post peractam vero aliquantum partem aedificii, cum consilio fidelium vicinorum decrevimus in ipso edificio oratorium consecrare a domno Stephano Arvernorum episcopo venerabili" (Chassaing, 3).
35. This is also the interpretation of Evans, *loc.cit.,* based on the tense of the verb *miscuit.*
36. R.-H. Hesbert, "Les témoins manuscrits du culte de Saint Odilon," *A Cluny. Congrès scientifique et cérémonies liturgiques,* Dijon, 1950, 51-120.
37. They are described by Boyer, *Journal de Voyage,* and J. Branche, *La vie des saincts et sainctes d'Auvergne,* Le Puy, 1652, 123-24.
38. *Bibliotheca Cluniacensis,* Notes, col. 69; Mabillon, Pat. lat. 252, 893, and *Acta sanctorum OSB.* VI, 594; Hesbert, *Témoins manuscrits,* 58.
39. Hesbert dates the establishment of this feast day in the diocese of Clermont near the end of the twelfth century. However, the first *praepositus* to bear the name of Odilo that I have been able to discover is the figure who witnessed a charter confirming the attachment of the monastery of Chanteuges to La Chaise-Dieu on March 12, 1137 (A. Chassaing, *Spicilegium Brivatense,* Paris, 1886, 13-14). Chassaing calls this personage "Odilo I de Mercoeur, 16e prévôt de Brioude." Odilo II, the 25th provost, is mentioned in 1275 (*idem,* 144, 149). A. Bruel, "Note sur le tombeau d'Odilon, sire de Mercoeur," *Annales Soc. Puy,* XXXII, 1872-75, 137-48, refers to the donation of the church of *S. Magdalen de Rivara* in Auvergne (now Rivière-L'Evêque, in the diocese of Clermont-Ferrand) to the abbey of St. Laurent d'Oulx in Lombardy, with the consent of Odilo of Mercoeur, dean of Brioude, in 1171. Because of the difference in the titles it is not clear whether this person is the same as that who signed the document of 1137.

VIII Gauzfredus and His Workshop

ALL AUTHORS who have dealt with the doors of Le Puy, Chamalières, Blesle, and Lavoûte-Chilhac have recognized their affinity and presume them to be products of a single workshop.[1] There is much to support this view. The doors form a compact group, distributed in a fairly circumscribed geographical zone and without clear parallels elsewhere. Their date remains uncertain, but such evidence as we possess for Le Puy and Chamalières would lead us to regard these monuments as roughly contemporaneous. At Chamalières, as we have seen, the door is not in harmony with the shape of the portal in which it was installed, nor with the other thresholds of the building. This makes it apparent that the door was not manufactured locally and for the purpose at hand. The distribution of of the four sets of doors also cuts across all lines of institutional affiliation. In Le Puy, the doors were enshrined in a cathedral foundation; at Chamalières, within a priory of a self-standing Benedictine monastery. Lavoûte-Chilhac, an important dependency of Cluny and Blesle, a house of Benedictine nuns, were not situated within the territorial jurisdiction of the bishops of Le Puy, but in the neighboring diocese of Clermont-Ferrand. Layman or cleric, the purveyor of the doors is thus best imagined as a craftsman working on commission at a distance from the building site and independent of the activity of construction.

The extremely uneven state of preservation of the doors, ranging from fair to very poor, may well, on the other hand, lead one to place excessive stress on the common denominator provided by the low relief technique as proof that they were executed in the same time and place. Attention to the method of assembly has shown that the doors signed by Gauzfredus stand apart from the others in the series through their greater simplicity. The joining of the boards and lateral bracing by means of forged iron elements is similar to the technique employed in the construction of more typical Romanesque wooden doors like those of Auzon [2] and Brioude [3] in the region or in Le Puy itself, those of the *Porche du For* and the *Porte St. Jean.* This is also the technique described by Theophilus, who recommends the careful fitting of the planks by means of shaping tools such as were used by coopers and vatmakers, and their joining with the help of cheese glue.[4] Theophilus's instructions concerning the preparation of the surfaces with gypsum and the reddening of doors with a compound made of linseed oil [5] would seem to be echoed in the appearance of the back of Gauzfredus's Passion doors. Writing in a cold and humid northerly climate, Theophilus also envisaged as standard procedure in the making of doors the covering of the wooden panels with leather or cloth.[6] The doors of Auzon, Brioude, and those of the transept entrances of the cathedral follow him in this as well, but for obvious reasons, not the carved panels of our sculptor.

The doors of Chamalières, Blesle, and Lavoûte-Chilhac, by contrast, involve a veneer technique, with the decorative components applied to the backing planks with the help of nails and complicated interlocking joints. The circular elements affixed to the arms of the cross were turned, probably with a pole lathe. A machine of this kind is illustrated in a miniature of the *Bible moralisée,* where a figure is seen turning a ridged bowl much like our lobes (Fig. 83).[7] A collection of turned wooden dishes of this kind is preserved in the Archaeological Museum at Lübeck,[8] and a very fine early example has been uncovered in a Merovingian tomb near Giessen.[9] We must assume that such objects were in fairly common use. The convex moldings along the edges of rectilinear wooden boards are so precisely formed that they must have been executed with molding planes available to the sculptor in a variety of shapes. The oldest planes of this type to have survived do not seem to antedate the eighteenth century, but their earlier existence must be inferred on the basis of the profiled frames of Dugento and Trecento panel paintings.[10] The multiple convex and concave profile given to the edges of the batten at Chamalières is thoroughly worthy of this comparison. The cable molding on the arms of the crosses and the tangent edges around them are also executed with a high degree of exactitude, forming, when they are joined in pairs, an evenly braided effect. They must have been executed with the help of a chisel or gouge possibly armed with a curving blade, since they could not be mechanically produced. These refinements are totally lacking in Gauzfredus's work, in whose execution the use of a simple chisel and mallet alone are in evidence.

The veneer technique employed at Chamalières, Blesle, and Lavoûte had certain advantages which are somewhat obscured by the present condition of the doors. The execution of the carving in the form of separate panels enabled the artisan to take best advantage of the grain of the wood in carrying out the work on each motif. Since, generally speaking, each panel houses a single motif, its outline coincides with and helps to articulate the larger anatomy of the design. Minor shifts due to the shrinking of the wood would take place along these natural frontiers. In Gauzfredus's doors, by contrast, the vertical joint within each half valve cuts indiscriminately across both scenes and inscriptions, and any widening of the gap could only aggravate its ill-effect. On a more practical level, an even-grained panel of small dimensions could be obtained with comparative ease, whereas large planks are apt to be demeaned by knots, which could not be effectively shaped by the chisel. The Puy sculptor encountered this problem more than once.[11] Errors could be rectified more easily since this would necessitate the replacement of only a small section of wood. Against these strong points must be set some drawbacks: the double-layered technique required a further outlay of work and a more sophisticated command of woodwork technique. Neither Theophilus nor the later technical manuals seem to allude to this mode of workmanship.[12] It is perhaps best understood as an extension of the method commonly practiced on a smaller scale in connection with ivory carving or enamels, which might be produced as small and self-contained units, though at the same time as predetermined building blocks to be assembled into larger pictorial ensembles.

Beyond differences of technique, the doors of Gauzfredus and the Chamalières, Blesle, and Lavoûte group also adhere to very different principles of composition. In the Puy doors, the imposition of a regular framework over the entire space imparts to the design and architectural logic based on a clear separation of skeleton from tissue, active structural membering from inert pictorial field. Although this architecture is inscribed on the surface rather than actually worked out in the joinery process, the effect of a paneled construction makes these doors tributary to a long tradition, begun in ancient times, commonly applied in the Byzantine East, in the Muslim world, and in the Latin West, and carried out in bronze and marble as well as in wood.[13] To be sure, the articulating function of the framework skeleton in the doors of Gauzfredus is considerably reduced by the even flatness of the carving and by the contradicting suggestions of the metal bracing. The interlace and Cufic borders also minimize the structural implications in favor of a certain colorism, though ultimately without tipping the balance in this direction.

This approach to the design of doors stands in contrast not only to the Chamalières valves and their relations, but to the far larger number of Romanesque wooden doors, which, like those of Auzon and Brioude, are not carved, but have forged-iron hinges and ornaments applied over their surface. Their pedigree is less lofty and necessarily more obscure. The examples which have been preserved do not antedate the Romanesque period, and with them we often descend to the social level represented by the village church. The splendid doors of Notre-Dame de Paris, however, demonstrate their acceptance in the most elevated reaches. Structural self-assertion also plays a primary role in this type, though it is derived not from a carpentry model, but from ironwork usage. The dominant role is taken by the metal strips, which, as they horizontally brace the wooden door, may unfurl into an elaborate spiraling scrollwork. They constitute a skeletal web which evenly embraces the surface, alternating with blank interstices that may receive a more casual application of forged-iron ornaments. Representations of doors in Romanesque painting and sculpture almost invariably show this type of work in preference to any other, sometimes conveying the artist's particular fascination with locks and complicated hardware.

The doors in the group related to the Chamalières valves depart from this compositional mode in the absence of any definition of such a structuring skeleton. In the place of an even distribution of the subjects, the design has a major focal point in the cross at the top. The rest follows in additive fashion, with a gradual thinning out of the iconographic substance as the eye proceeds downward. The hierarchic stratification of meaning in descending order of importance is tied not to any identifiable older history of door-making. It is a pictorial formula, dependent on the iconographic tradition of theophany images, and evoking the arrangement of apse compositions in which a dado zone of imitation marble paneling or textile hangings shades off into mute decoration a program dominated by the heavenly apparition in the half-dome.

We cannot, of course, rule out the possibility that Gauzfredus's workshop was able to supply its clientele with works of very different type upon demand. The more explicit narrative imagery of the Puy doors was almost certainly better suited to the catechetical requirements imposed on a busy metropolitan cathedral than the visionary and more allusive constructions of the valves furnished to the three monasteries nearby.[14] The work at Chamalières may offer us a useful clue in this direction since it is of a technically hybrid nature, showing a two-tiered, paneled construction side by side with carving carried out, as in Le Puy, into the solid substance of the wooden core. Yet in the final analysis it would seem to us that the combination of technical and compositional factors which distinguish the signed valves in Le Puy from the three doors in the monastic group would argue against the idea that the entire series was the work of the same master or even a single atelier.

Gauzfredus, like so many artists of his time, is and probably must forever remain a name without a known biography. Some authors have sought to identify him with persons bearing his name found in the Le Puy documents, but is obviously too common to permit any clear-cut conclusions.[15] The possibility that he was of Islamic origin or at least of Hispanic extraction is one aspect of his career on which the style of the doors has furnished matter for some speculation. Fikry held that he must have had some firsthand contact with the Muslim world, but leaves the question of origin couched in vague terms.[16] The three monastic doors, on the other hand, struck him as "copies" of Gauzfredus's valves made by artisans native to Velay. Gauzfredus, according to this view, introduced the style to central France, where it was taken up, with uneven results, by local craftsmen. L. Bréhier sought to refute this theory on the grounds that the thematic and technical similarities observable across the entire group of doors would rule out the idea that they could be the work of men of different cultural formation.[17] Accordingly, he concluded that all of the doors must have been made by "Mozarabic" artisans. Neither of these theses seem to me to render the most judicious account of an undeniably uncertain situation. The first is surely mistaken in its assumption that the monastic doors depend in a direct manner on Gauzfredus's panels. The second overstates both the homogeneity of the entire group and the degree of its propinquity to the Islamic tradition. That Gauzfredus or his colleagues might have traveled to Spain or to other territories under Islamic influence certainly lies within the realm of possibility. Contacts between Le Puy and Spain in the eleventh and twelfth centuries were both common and multifarious in nature.[18] But this does not seem to be an article of belief indispensable to an understanding of the art of the doors. Given the diffuse but persistent current of Islamic influence in Velay so well charted by Fikry, our sculptors need not have displaced themselves afar.

Who were the craftsmen who executed these monuments? If Theophilus is to be believed, the arts of joinery and wood carving had not yet emerged at the beginning of the twelfth century into a distinct professional calling. The artisan envisioned by this writer, though primarily a goldsmith, was at the same time a practitioner of woodwork, able to assemble doors, various types of furniture as well as the case for an organ, casting for these and other purposes his own nails. Joinery does not occupy a large place in his treatise. Its practice involved in his time a more rudimentary technology than casting or glass-making, and he does not offer detailed instructions on the procedures which he recommends, seeming to take it for granted that his readers would be able to carry them out as a matter of course.[19] Perhaps the emphasis on metalwork techniques simply reflects the high standing achieved by this art in the region of north Germany where the author's activity was centered. The practice of goldsmithwork and other metallurgical crafts during the twelfth century has left far fewer traces in central France. Nevertheless, the confection of the wrought-iron grilles of the cathedral cloister, the cast-bronze door knockers for the doors of the *Porche du For,* the *Porte St. Jean* and other works of this kind at Brioude and Ebreuil indicates that there were men of Theophilus's broad capacities within the circle of the cathedral builders.[20] If, as we assume, the doors of the *Porte Dorée* leading to the center of the nave were made in conjunction with Gauzfredus's panels, this would be further evidence of a close collaboration, and perhaps actual identity, of wood carver and smith.

In addition to the versatile craftsmen which Theophilus had in mind, the medieval technical vocabulary lists the comprehensive term *carpentarius,* and its romance derivatives or equivalents, applicable to artisans working in wood. In the minds of many writers, this term is one of lexical classification and lacks precise reference to a particular milieu; carpenters are distinguished from stonemasons, goldsmiths, or weavers in accordance with the nature of the materials which they used in their work.[21] The *fabri tignarii* mentioned in Gallo-Roman inscriptions—one of these has been found at Espaly outside Le Puy—belonged to this class of artisans.[22] The illustration of the carpenters' characteristic activities furnished by the texts range from shipbuilding to the construction of timber frames and roofs of houses. There is an emphasis on structural work on a substantial scale, although the exact limits of their professional concerns are difficult to fix on a general plane and must obviously have varied from place to place.[23] The men entrusted with the office of the King's Carpenter in England after the middle of the twelfth century inspected and repaired the royal castles and palaces.[24] Their duties resembled those that would now be carried out by an architect or civil engineer, and their services must therefore have been necessary to any large-scale building or maintenance enterprise. A document datable toward 1215 indicates that the bishop of Chartres invested his carpenter with a fief.[25] In Le Puy itself, the association of carpentry with building remained in force to the end of the Middle Ages, as is shown by the fact that masons and carpenters belonged to a single corporation, whose annual feast day, rightly enough, was celebrated on the day of dedication of the cathedral.[26]

In the course of the twelfth and thirteenth centuries, the carpenter's craft divided into areas of increasing specialization, and door-making became established as a separate profession. Etienne Boileau's *Livre des Métiers* records the statutes of the Paris corporation of *huissiers,* such as they had been established by the King's Carpenter, Master Fulk of the Temple and his predecessors.[27] The *huissiers,* who supplied both doors and windows with their frames, had to pledge themselves to make no joints without the assistance of wooden or metal ties. Their name was derived from the Latin *ostiarus,* a term more commonly associated in both secular and liturgical usage with the guardianship of the threshold, which the emergence of this new class of artisans burdened with an altogether different connotation.[28] The documents concerning the trade corporations in Le Puy are much later in date and they do not show the extraordinary range of professions practiced in the capital. In late twelfth-century Toulouse, a city larger than Le Puy, we hear only of the collective appellations *fustiers* and *marchands de fustes* working in or furnishing wood.[29] Still, within this broad category of craftsmen, there must have been men of narrower specialization whose particular aptitudes have not left their mark in the terminology. The finely carved section of a Gothic window frame from a thirteenth-century house in Blesle, which reverberates with certain echoes of the earlier door sculpture, might have been executed by one of them (Fig. 84).[30]

The process of subdivision of the carpenter's trade into narrower areas of specialization which Boileau's codification enables us to witness may be assumed to have been paralleled in other professions, wherever these were practiced on a certain scale. Goldsmithwork is a case in point. It is well attested in Le Puy in the later Middle Ages, but the oldest documentary references to the practice of the trade in the town do not antedate the middle of the thirteenth century.[31] Such as it can be reconstructed from the sources and a certain number of surviving works, this industry specialized in the production of objects for the cult as well as jewelry for personal apparel. Count Eudes of Nevers in his Testament dated 1266 records among his possessions "douze petiz eniaus (anneaux) du Pui." [32] Le Puy goldsmiths also cut and set gems found in nearby streams and especially in the volcanic stone of the region. Others did enameling and engraved gems. But woodwork, glass or leather work were evidently outside their sphere of competence. Gauzfredus must have belonged to a world much closer still to Theophilus's free-wheeling artisans than to this accomplished class of enterprising professionals.

The reputation of Romanesque wood sculpture and joinery in Auvergne from this earlier era now rests without doubt on the active industry whose particular specialty was the production of cult images of the Virgin Mary seated in Majesty.[33] A series of monumental polychromed images of Christ on the Cross found in churches of Velay, and bust-length figures of local saints represent other facets of this activity.[34] The reliquary statue of the Virgin made for the Cathedral of Clermont-Ferrand, newly dedicated in 946, is the oldest documented work of this type. Its fame was surpassed by the image of the Virgin of Le Puy cathedral, whose existence is apparently mentioned for the first time in our sources in 1095.[35] The well-known relation of the *scholasticus* of Bernard of Angers set down following a journey to Auvergne around 1013 records the author's vivid reaction on his first glimpse of the statue of St. Faith at Conques. We learn from him that the custom of making sculptural images of the Virgin and of the saints for devotional purposes was widespread and well established in central France, but not known in the territories farther north where he exercised his professional activity.[36] Although he was, like later observers, struck by the hypnotic splendor of the precious metals and jewels which bedeck these works, the process of manufacture had of course to begin with a massive core of wood. Many of the polychromed statues to have survived, few if any antedating the twelfth century, may have been only inexpensive substitutes but in the best examples like the Morgan Madonna in the Metropolitan Museum in New York and the statue from Forez in the Louvre, Paris, the exposed wood strikes the viewer as complete and self-sufficient in its own right: side by side with the reliquary container, the *ymaige* makes its appearance.

The carved image of Christ crucified was excluded from ecclesiastical censure reserved for statuary in the early Middle Ages and it did not undergo the complex metamorphosis of effigy into goldsmithwork *majestas.* However, the Auvergnat monuments of this type belong, like the most characteristic among the wooden statues of the Virgin in the region, at a good distance in time from the heroic days of first experiments. The Christ from Lavaudieu, divided between the Louvre and the collection of the Cloisters, has been dated, perhaps too precociously, in the second quarter of the twelfth century.[37] The little-known work at Blesle (Fig. 81), which is somewhat more archaic in appearance, also sets forth a typological nomenclature that is common to the related crosses at Lavoûte-Chilhac, Arlet, Auzon, and Lavoûte-sur-Loire.[38]

A comparison of the carving in these devotional images with our doors is frustrated by an inherent diversity of aims and values, and it is only in the rarest of instances that something like Gauzfredus's idiosyncratic style is recognizable within his branch of sculpture. Not surprisingly perhaps, this is where the carving does not strive to embody the plastic substance of the human figure, but, as in the throne of the Madonna from Ayl in the Trier Episcopal Museum, seeks only to reproduce the arcuated construction of a piece of wooden furniture (Figs. 82 and 85).[39] Nevertheless, this ample and varied body of wood sculpture should make the very existence of the doors seem less exceptional. As has been recently pointed out, the

Auvergnat Madonnas are not made of a single block of wood, but are in fact complex joinery constructions involving a surprisingly large number of separate pieces.[40] This is a feature which sets them apart from those of other regions. Polychromy technique is another area of expertise shared by the cult statuary and the doors. The survival of the monumental crucifixes of Lavoûte-Chilhac and Blesle, and at Blesle, further, of a statue of the Madonna, raises the possibility that images and doors might well have had the same purveyor.

NOTES

1. Thiollier, *Architecture religieuse,* 66, holds that the doors were all made by the same artist or "tout au moins la même école." Fikry, *Art roman du Puy,* 187, speaks of the doors as constituting "un groupe très homogène ou les portes du Puy, les plus belles de la série, sont aussi les plus représentatives." Similar opinions in O. Beigbeder, *Forez-Velay roman,* 267, and Götz, *Bildprogramme,* 283, 288.
2. Reproduction and brief description in A. Gybal, *L'Auvergne, berceau de l'art roman,* Clermont-Ferrand, 1957, 173.
3. The type, of course, is well known throughout western Europe. Examples are collected in H. d'Allemagne, "Les pentures de portes au moyen âge," *Congrès arch.,* LXXIII, 1906, 518-33; G. J. Hollister-Short, "Symbolism in Medieval Wrought Iron Work. I. " *The Connoisseur,* October 1969, 91-97, and January 1970, 25-31; *idem,* "Precursors of the Thirteenth-century Great Hinge," *The Connoisseur,* February 1970, 108-12. I did not have access to the thesis of S. Berthelier, *Le décor des vantaux de porte en France du XIIe au XIVe siècle* (Ecole du Louvre, 1948).
4. *De diversis artibus,* ed. C. R. Dodwell, London-New York, 1961, ch. XVII, 16-17: "De Tabulis altarium et ostiorum et de Glutine casei."
5. *Idem,* ch. XVIII, 18-19: "De rubricandis ostiis et de oleo lini." The practice of reddening the surface is probably reflected in a reference to the doors of Nîmes cathedral (now lost) in a document of 1190: "iuxta januam rubeam Beatae Mariae" (A. Gordon, *La réglementation des métiers en Languedoc au Moyen Age,* Paris-Geneva, 1958, 26-17), and in the Porte Rouge of Notre-Dame de Paris.
6. *Idem,* ch. XVII, 17. In Chapter XXII of the work, Theophilus envisages the decoration of horse saddles, folding chairs and footstools "which are carved and cannot be covered with leather or cloth." These may be covered with ". . . figures or animals or birds and foliage, or whatever you want to draw" and embellished with gold leaf. The manner of execution, which might well be a type of low relief technique, is not made clear.
7. Bibl. Nat. 11560, fol. 84. A. de Laborde, *Etude sur la Bible moralisée illustrée,* Paris, 1911-27, II, pl. 308, illustrated in H. Mercer, *Ancient Carpenter's Tools,* Doylestown, Pa., 1951, 220, fig. 190, who follows L. F. Salzman, *English Industries in the Middle Ages,* Oxford, 1923, 172. The machine is described by Mercer, 218ff., and R. S. Woodbury, *A History of the Lathe to 1850,* Cleveland, 1961, 38ff.
8. Kohlhaussen, *Geschichte des deutschen Kunsthandwerks,* 137-38, fig. 118.
9. *Idem,* and H. Klenk, "Die merowingerzeitlichen Gräberfunde im Räume von Leihgestern/Lang-Gons im oberhessischen Kreis Giessen," *Mitteilungen des oberhessischen Geschichtsvereins,* N.F. XXVIII, 1964, 22ff., 65. It might be of interest to mention for comparative purposes the lobed ornaments which appear on the cypress *arca* executed under Pope Leo III (795-816). Their mode of execution is not clear. P. Lauer, "Le trésor du Sancta Sanctorum," *Monuments Piot,* XV, 1906, 38-39, describes them as "cercles concentriques molurés." See also Leclerq, *Dictionnaire d'archéologie chrétienne et de liturgie,* VIII, 2, 1627-28. Wooden panels with lobed ornaments mechanically executed are found also in Coptic art (E. Pauty, *Catalogue général du Musée arabe du Caire. Les bois sculptés de l'époque ayyoubide,* Cairo, 1931, Nos. 1311, 2236, 2297, etc. . .
10. Mercer, *Ancient Carpenter's Tools,* 123ff. For the Trecento tooled moldings, see M. Cämmerer-George, *Die Rahmung der toskanischen Altarbilder im Trecento,* Strasbourg, 1966.

11. A knot partly obscures the figure of the soldier at the left edge of the scene of the Carrying of the Cross. Another knotlike irregularity partly deforms the capital on the left side of the tri-lobed arch where Herod receives the Magi.
12. The technique has much in common with *intarsia* (or *tarsia),* whose invention Vasari credited to the circle of Brunelleschi and Benedetto da Maiano (Milanesi, *Vite,* I, 202; see also *Vasari on Technique,* ed. G. Baldwin Brown, London, 1907, ch. XVII, 262ff., and the notes on 303). Vasari believed that this wood inlay technique was derived from the design of pavements and painting, but the central French doors perhaps suggest that there were older antecedents in wood work itself. See also on this problem A. Chastel, "Marqueterie et perspective au XVe siècle," *Revue des arts,* III, 1953, 141-54, and C. Finochietti, *Della scultura e tarsia in legno,* Florence, 1873.
13. For doors in Antiquity and their symbolism, see Ch. Picard, "Rhéa-Cybele et le culte des portes sacrées," *Essays in Memory of Karl Lehmann,* Locust Valley, 1964, 259-66, and *idem, Les portes sacrées à images divines* (Etudes thasiennes, VIII), Publications de l'Ecole française d'Athènes, 1962; B. Goldmann, *The Sacred Portal. A Primary Symbol in Ancient Jewish Art,* Detroit, 1966, 104ff. E. Baldwin Smith, *Architectural Symbolism of Imperial Rome and the Middle Ages,* Princeton, 1956, 10ff.
14. On this distinction, see the remarks of J. Hubert, "Le caractère et le but du décor des églises d'après les clercs du Moyen Age," *Moissac et l'Occident au XIe siècle* (Actes du Colloque International de Moissac 3-5, mai 1963), Toulouse, 1964, 47-52, and the ensuing discussion, 52-58.
15. Boudon-Lashermes, *Grand pardon de Notre-Dame,* 33-34, identifies Gauzfredus with a figure of that name who witnessed a Chamalières charter in 1097 (Chassaing, *Cartulaire,* 7, No. 8: "Item . . . Gauzfredus a priore Jarentone pro hac laudatione X. solidos accepit"). Pascal, *Bibliographie du Velay,* 372, cites the entry in A. Bérard's *Dictionnaire biographique des artistes français du XIIe au XVIIe siècle,* Paris, 1872, 318, which states that Gauzfredus ". . . exercait son art au Puy, ou il travaillait en 1320 à la cathédrale." I note that a "Gauzfredus de Fillinis, clericis Aniciensis ecclesiae" made a donation to the cathedral in 1213 (*Tablettes,* VII, 1876-77, 351-53), which was confirmed in 1228 in a charter of Bishop Etienne de Chalançon (*idem,* 363-65). A charter of 1229 cites as a chaplain of the cathedral a man named L. Gaufredi (*Tablettes hist.,* VI, 1875-76, 507).
16. Fikry, *Art roman du Puy,* 179f., 183.
17. Bréhier, *Journal des Savants,* February 1936, 18.
18. C. Rocher, "Les rapports de l'église du Puy avec la ville de Girone en Espagne et le Comté de Bigorre," *Tablettes hist.,* III, 1872-73, Bishop Peter II's presence in Spain was noted by Fikry, *Art roman du Puy,* 283, who supposes that the architect of the cathedral might have accompanied him there. On the question in general, see M. Desfournaux, *Les français en Espagne aux XIe et XIIe siècles,* Paris, 1949. On the other hand, Mâle's report of Muslims coming to Le Puy to offer donations to the Virgin (*L'Espagne arabe et l'art roman,* 64-65) is based on the testimony of Vincent of Beauvais's *Speculum morale* and must belong to the realm of pious legends.
19. The altogether few references in the technical literature of work in wood are cited by B. Bischoff, "Die Überlieferung der technischen Literatur," *Artigianati e tecnica,* Settimane di Studio. . . , Spoleto, 1971, I, 285. They are to be published more fully by the same author in *Anedcota novissima.*
20. For the door knockers of the cathedral, see Thiollier, *Architecture religieuse,* 66-67. Those of Brioude and Ebreuil are reproduced in Craplet *Auvergne romane,* 75-76, 92-93. For the grills of the cathedral and other works of this type in the region, see M.-N. Delaine, "Les grilles romanes en France," *L'information à l'histoire de l'art,* May-June 1971, 122-27.

    It might be noted that Andrea Buvina, who made the wooden doors of Spalato cathedral (1214), is described in a fourteenth-century chronicle as "*magister Andreas Buvina pinctor de Spaleto.*" He is also recorded as having made an image whose nature is not further specified, of St. Christopher (L. Karaman, *Andrija Buvina, vratnice Splitske katedrale,* Zagreb, 1960, p. XIX, and Götz, *Bildprogramme,* 90ff.

    Another kind of dual expertise is represented by Petrus Brunus described as "artifex in opera ligneo et lapideo" in a charter of the Cathedral of Nîmes, dated 1186 (M. Gouron, "Dates des sculptures du portail de l'église de Saint-Gilles," *Bulletin de la Société d'histoire et d'archéologie de Nîmes et du Gard,* 1933-34, 45-50). The artisan is sometimes identified as one of the sculptors of the facade of Saint-Gilles.
21. See for the classification of trades in the early Middle Ages, P. Sternagel, *Die artes mechanicae im Mittelalter* (Münchner Historische Studien, II), Kallmünz, 1966. Rabanus Maurus handles the subject in typical fashion in his *De universo* (Pat.

lat. 111, 565-66), under the heading *De lignariis:* "Lignarius, generaliter ligni opifex appellatur. Carpentarius, speciale nomen est: carpentum facit, sicut navicularius: quia tantum navium fabricator et artifex."

22. DeVic and Vaissete, *Histoire générale du Languedoc,* XV, 2039: "Patronus collegiorum et fabrorum tignariorum." This and similar texts are cited and discussed by A. Gouron, *La réglementation des métiers en Languedoc au Moyen Age,* Geneva-Paris, 1958, 26-27. There is unfortunately as yet no study along linguistic lines of carpentry in the region, such as that which has been done for the French-speaking areas of Switzerland by A. Maissen, *Werkzeuge und Arbeitsmethoden des Holzhandwerks in romanisch Bünden,* Erlenbach, 1943.
23. See the references given by E. Lefèvre-Pontalis, *Répertoire des architectes,* 441ff.; P. Brandt, *Schaffende Arbeit und Bildende Kunst,* Leipzig, 1927, II, 38ff.; F. Hellwag, *Geschichte des deutschen Tischlerhandwerks,* Berlin, 1924, 37ff.
24. J. Harvey, "The King's Chief Carpenters," *Journal of the British Archaeological Association,* 1948, 13-34, and *idem,* "The Medieval Carpenter and his Work as an Architect," *Journal of the Royal Institute of British Architects,* 1938, 33-44.
25. V. Mortet and P. Deschamps, *Recueil de textes relatifs à l'histoire de l'architecture,* Paris, 1929, 220-21.
26. Boudon-Lashermes, *Le vieux Puy,* 228. The oldest reference to a carpenter associated with the cathedral occurs in connection with the foundation of the confraternity of the *chaperons blancs* in 1182. This foundation took place following the vision of a carpenter named either Peter or Durandus, who is said to have received from heaven a painting of the Virgin and Child, along with instructions to work for peace in the kingdom (DeVic and Vaissete, *Histoire du Languedoc,* VI, 106ff., and Bouquet, *Historiens de la France,* XVIII, 219).

    Wood work in Velay is treated by U. Rouchon, *La vie paysanne dans la Haute-Loire,* Le Puy, 1933, 341ff., but without precise indication of the sources. The examples given are also rather late in date.
27. E. Boileau, *Le livre des métiers,* ed. R. de Lespinasse and F. Bonnardot (Histoire générale de Paris. Les métiers et corporations de la Ville de Paris), Paris, 1879, I. 87.
28. Godefroy, *Dictionnaire,* IV, 525, s.v. "huissier." DuCange, *Glossarium,* VI-VII, 77, s.v. "ostiarius."
29. Gouron, *Réglementation des métiers,* 69, note 159.
30. The fragment, now in the little museum installed in the former nave of the church, stems from the house known as the *maison des anglais,* which is a nineteenth-century lithograph (Pothier, *Blesle,* 28) shows as it appeared before destruction.
31. A. Chassaing, "Notes sur l'orfèvrerie du Puy au Moyen Age et de la Renaissance," *Annales Soc. Puy,* XXXI, 1870-71, 41-58. Aymard and Malègue, *Album d'archéologie religieuse,* Le Puy, 1857; U. Rouchon, *Recherches sur les argentiers, orfèvres, lapidaires, émailleurs et graveurs de camées du Puy en Velay (XIIIe-XIX siècles),* Le Puy, 1943. N. Thiollier, "Les oeuvres des orfèvres du Puy," *Congrès arch.,* 1904, 506-41.
32. Chassaing, *Notes sur l'orfèvrerie,* 41-42.
33. Forsyth, *Throne of Wisdom,* 135ff.
34. The Auvergnat crucifixes, with the possible exception of the work from Lavaudieu, divided between the Louvre and the Cloisters (M. Aubert, M. Beaulieu, *Description raisonnée des sculptures du Moyen âge,* . . . Paris, 1954, 45, No. 31, are poorly published. The most accessible reproductions, of excellent quality, are found in *Christs romans* (Coll. Zodiaque), 1963, 70-80. See below, note 38, for the list of known examples. The bust figures are those of St. Chaffre at Monastier-Saint-Chaffre, St. Césaire at Maurs (Cantal), and St. Baudîme at Saint-Nectaire *(Trésors des églises de France,* Nos. 417, 428, and 447). To this list might be added the statue of the seated St. Peter at Bredons (A. Beaufrère, "La statue romane de Saint-Pierre à Bredons," *Revue de la Haute-Auvergne,* XXXIV, 1955, 246-54.
35. See above, p. 61.
36. Bernard of Angers, *Liber miraculorum sancte Fidis,* ed. A. Bouillet, Paris, 1897, 48-50.
37. Aubert and Beaulieu, *Description raisonnée, loc. cit.*
38. To these should be added the crosses of Montsalvy, Valuéjols, and the Cathedral of Saint-Flour, published by P. F. Aleil, "Les grands crucifix de bois en Haute-Auvergne," *Revue de la Haute-Auvergne,* XXXVIII, 1963, 219ff. A monumental cross formerly at Chanteuges is known through documentary reference (A. Casati, "Les recueils de Dom Estiennot concernant la région brivadoise. Le Christ miraculeux de Chanteuges," *Almanach de Brioude,* XVIII, 1937, 128-32).
39. Wesenberg, *Frühe mittelalterliche Bildwerke,* Düsseldorf, 1972, 87ff. A date around 1100 is given in the Exhibition Catalogue *Marienbild in Rheinland und Westfalen,* Essen, Villa Hügel, 1968, No. 6, 59.
40. Forsyth, *Throne of Wisdom,* 17-18.

APPENDIX I Epigraphy

THE DOORS OF Le Puy and of Lavoûte-Chilhac are graced by inscriptions which should be examined in the context of Romanesque epigraphy generally and with particular attention to examples found in Velay. The inscriptions on the Puy doors consist of the *tituli* accompanying the scenes and the text identifying the sculptor and builder on the batten of the Infancy valves; at Lavoûte, the epigraphic matter encompasses the Odilo inscription, the fragmentary verses (?) in honor of the cross, and the parts of text along the upper right side of the panel. These inscriptions are rendered with the letters uniformly in relief against a recessed background. The letters are delineated by strips of wood widening out at the extremities in order to convey, if only in blunted form, the sense of flow and serif structure of Roman capital forms. The necessarily blocky silhouette of letters obtained through this procedure does not lend itself too well to stylistic comparisons with inscriptions incised in stone. It is, however, sometimes matched in renderings of text found in illuminated manuscripts, as, for example, in the *incipit* page of the Life of St. Martial by the Pseudo-Aurelian, a work from the Limousin abbey generally thought to have been executed in the early years of the twelfth century (Fig. 88).[1]

In this ensemble of textual matter, the *tituli* of the Puy doors stand apart through their highly ornate quality. The letters have comparatively elongated proportions and include a fair number of eccentric forms as well as a profusion of ligatures. Owing to the length of the verses in relation to the available space, there is much abbreviation, and a small letter may be lodged in open spaces within or around adjoining ones.

Most of the letters are Roman capitals. Occasionally, a specimen of minuscule is encountered, along with the uncial form of the D, as in VIDENS in the scene of the Magi before Herod (Fig. 20), and U, as in VOBIS, above the Annunciation to the Shepherds (Fig. 7). The artisan delights in varying the form of the same letter. Many variations of the letter A are used. The letter E and C may be either square or rounded in shape. The round strokes in the letters O, D, G, and C have a pointed thickening along their inner contour, a device of graphic rather than lapidary origin, which is seen in a number of instances on the title page of the Limoges page as well as several among the twelfth-century manuscripts from the cathedral: a copy of the Martyrologium of Usuardus [2] and a volume of Burchardus's *Decretum* [3] both in the Bibliothèque Nationale. A copy of Bede's *Historia ecclesiastica* from La Chaise-Dieu, which presents this and some other epigraphic features of the doors, is dated 1093.[4] The Gauzfredus inscription on the Infancy door and the textual matter on the doors of Lavoûte, on the other hand, show much greater sobriety. The proportion of the letters is closer to the square and they are individually spaced out, with a minimum of ligatures and other compound designs. The possibility of such wide variation in the treatment of text in the context of a single work might well be doubted were it not offered here to the eye.

The seventh and eighth step of the final flight of stairs leading to the western entrance of the cathedral are engraved with the verses NI CAVEAS CRIMEN CAVEAS CONTINGERE LIMEN/ NAM REGINA COELI VULT SINE SORDE COLI. It belongs to the restoration carried out by Bishop de Galard between 1778 and 1781, but imitates in part an older inscription which was no longer complete at this time. What was left of it is transcribed in all of the old histories of the cathedral, and two fragments of the original stone showing part of its left side were discovered in the course of the nineteenth-century restorations (Fig. 86).[5] The design of the letter M with the two oblique members departing not from the very top of the verticals but somewhat further down is also seen in the rendering of the *tituli,* as in the words VIDIMUS or ASTRUM in the scene of the Magi on their journey. The letter A topped by a horizontal stroke is also found throughout the verses of the doors and the elongated proportion of the letter is well matched in them.

An inscription along the base of the chevet of the cathedral, which refers to the presence nearby of a miraculous fountain, displays similarly elongated and thinly drawn letters (Fig. 87).[6] E's are both rounded and square in form, and the A is rendered with a straight stroke at the top, as in the NI CAVEAS inscription, but with either a straight or angular cross-bar, as found on the doors. The O's tend to a mandorlalike angularity at the top and bottom, as they generally do in the work of

Gauzfredus. In the N's, however, the oblique stroke meets the verticals at the level of the serifs, and the conception of the whole is informed by a comparatively classicizing character, perhaps organically vehiculated within the experience of monumental epigraphy in stone.

Several capitals employed in the cathedral complex feature inscriptions. A pair of capitals in the Musée Crozatier removed from the tower and replaced on its third story by copies each shows two cardinal virtues identified by name.[7] The inscription accompanying Justice (IVSTICIA)—the only one fully preserved—has a finely disciplined quality closer in spirit to the various specimens of ancient inscriptions found in the precincts of the cathedral than to the epigraphy of the doors (Fig. 89). The exception is the A with a square top and angular cross-bar, which is one of the variants of this letter employed by Gauzfredus. A third capital found near the angle of the north and eastern arms of the cloister shows Evangelist symbols, with Matthew deploying a scroll marked with the words LIBER GENERACIONI(S). The second word shows the use both of a rounded and a square form of the letter E, a combination that occurs also on the doors, as in the words LEGE of the Massacre of the Innocents or GESTAT PUER in the Presentation in the Temple (Fig. 7). The letter A has a stroke at the top and the angular cross-bar and the G is formed, as on the donors, like a somewhat stilted number 8.

Much closer to the spirit of Gauzfredus's art is the inscription on a relief in the Musée Crozatier showing a pair of lions (?) in the process of devouring a human victim. The provenance of this piece is uncertain, but it is stylistically very close to a group of stone carvings found along the western approaches of the cathedral on the site of the former Maison Galien.[8] The inscription, which has been only partially deciphered, mentions a certain Guglielmus Geraldi, possibly the same person who is mentioned as a grand master of the Hôtel-Dieu in a document witnessed by him in 1150. Like the *tituli* of the cathedral doors, it is marked by an unevenness in weight and coloration. The letters are not uniformly of the same height and they lean at different angles. There are letters imbricated into one another and some departure from strict adherence to Roman capital forms. One of these is the use of the minuscule, seen also at the head of the Odilo inscription at Lavoûte. Another is the type of M, of graphic derivation, constructed like an O with a vertical stroke attached. Gauzfredus does not employ it, but twice makes use of a very similar compound form by joining an O with an R in a ligature.[9]

This is perhaps the most appropriate place to make mention of two identifying inscriptions engraved on tablets which were discovered in 1162 in the course of the translation of the bodies of St. Hilaire and the reputed founder of the church of Le

Puy and apostle of Velay, St. George, located in the church dedicated to the latter's name in the town. These tablets are now lost, and known only through rather summary eighteenth-century engravings. The inscriptions have been assigned varying dates from the ninth to the eleventh century, some authors going further to argue that they are not contemporaneous with one another.[10] The engraving does make the inscription of St. Hilaire appear the more irregular in its epigraphic composition, but both texts exhibit features that must rule out a very early date and point unmistakably to Romanesque times. In both, round and square forms of the letters E and C are used interchangeably, as are several forms of the A. Roman and uncial forms of the letter M are seen in the St. George inscription, while the St. Hilaire panel shows also the compound type described above. The appearance of a minuscule H, of certain ligatures, and the uneven weight and proportion of the letters generally come fairly close to the Guglielmus Geraldi inscription. The tablets are thus likely to have been made not much earlier, and though this is contrary to the assertion of the account of the translation of 1162, one might well entertain the thought that they were executed specifically on that occasion.[11]

Two further epigraphical specimens from the cathedral complex may be cited as a means of marking out the stylistic position of the inscriptions of our group of doors against a broader background. The fresco painting of the Crucifixion in the *Salle des Morts* along the eastern arm of the cloister, dated toward the end of the twelfth century, includes representations of prophets bearing scrolls inscribed with appropriate texts and an inscription around the work declaring the hall in which it is situated to have been built in ninety-nine days. The character of this writing is much more advanced than the epigraphy of the doors, so much so that little basis is left for comparison.[12] Less well preserved are the inscriptions of the Transfiguration and Virgin in Majesty frescoes along the walls of the passageway leading to the western entrance of the cathedral. They are, like the paintings themselves, of calmer and less strenuously picturesque effect than those of the *Salle des Morts* Crucifixion, and at a similar remove from the inscription of the wooden doors.[13]

NOTES

1. Bibl. Nat. lat. 5296A, fol. 1v. Gaborit-Chopin, *Décoration des manuscrits,* 121ff. and 205.
2. Bibl. Nat. lat. 5244. H. Quentin, *Les martyrologes historiques,* Paris, 1908, 227-31. On the manuscripts of Le Puy cathedral, see L. Delisle, *Le cabinet des manuscrits de la Bibliothèque nationale,* Paris, 1868-81, I, 473ff.
3. Bibl. Nat. lat. 3861. I note in the rubrication of this manuscript the occurrence of the letter A with a stroke at the top (fols. 1v and 85), as well as the variant with an angular cross-bar (fol. 19v). The ligature TE (TE) (fol. 111v) takes the form seen in the word EUNTEM above the Ascension of the Passion doors; other ligatures found in the epigraphy of the doors and in the manuscript are NC (NC) and INC (INC) on fol. 49. The imbricated letters CI (CI) and LI (LI) are also common to both works.
4. Bibl. Nat. lat. 5228. I note the ligatures EX (EX) and PL (PL) on fol. 26, as well as the imbricated LI and CI on fol. 99v, following the form indicated in the note above. Other constructions in common with the doors is the ligature Æ for AE and the abbreviation L (fol. 45v) as in the word ANGELUS of the Women at the Tomb.
5. Gounot, *Collections lapidaires,* 178-79, No. BC 6.
6. FONS OPE DIVINA LANGUENTIBUS EST MEDICINA/ SUBVENIENS GRATIS UBI DEFICIT ARS YPOCRATIS.
7. *Idem,* 164-65, No. BB 3 and 4.
8. *Idem,* 214-16, No. DA 5, and earlier, Aymard, *Annales Soc. Puy,* XVII, 1852, 199ff.
9. Another monument which might be adduced for comparison here is the inscription of the stucco tympanum within the north porch of Saint-Julien de Brioude. It is unfortunately badly worn, and we are largely dependent for a description of the salient letter forms employed on the study of P. Deschamps, *Bulletin de la Société Nationale des Antiquaires de France,* 1924, 206-13, made on the basis of cast impressions obtained by this scholar.
10. *Gallia Christ.,* II, 688. There is a considerable literature on the translation and the historical significance of the inscriptions, which is most thoroughly reviewed by A. Fayard, *Saint Hilaire au Puy et l'église Saint-George,* Le Puy, 1968.
11. As the charter of 1162 has it, "Petrus Aniciensis episcopus . . . fecit aperiri . . . vas quod erat post altare sancti Georgii, et inveni ibi membra sanctorum cum duabus tabulis marmoreis in una qua erat scriptum sic: HIC REQUIESCUNT MEMBRA SANCTI AC GLORIOSISSIMI GEORGII EPISCOPI. In altera, HIC REQUIESCUNT MEMBRA SANCTI AC GLORIOSISSIMI HYLARII PICTAVIENSIS EPISCOPI (*Gallia Christ., loc. cit.).*
12. Deschamps and Thibout, *Peinture murale,* 85ff.; Denus, *Romanesque Mural Painting,* 431; Enaud, *Monuments historiques de la France,* 1968, No. 4, 34f.
13. Deschamps and Thibout, 82ff.

APPENDIX II The Lost South Transept Doors of the Cathedral

WHILE THE DOORS OF THE *Porte St. Jean* on the north transept arm of Le Puy cathedral are preserved, if in restored state, those formerly installed in the entrance within the *Porche du For* on the south transept are lost. Several descriptions, however, exist. In the most extended of the studies of the church made by the architect A. Mallay, it is indicated that they were made of wood, covered with canvas, upon which forged-iron ornaments and feline masks were mounted.[1] The two masks now exhibited in the Musée Crozatier are thought to be the pieces in question. A smaller door hinged onto one of the valves and also fitted with metal ornaments was designed for casual use. The most unusual aspect of the doors was a pair of lions which could be seen in the upper part. Merimée states that they were carved "d'un relief assez fort," which must mean that their execution did not adhere to the technique employed in the group of wooden doors with which we have been concerned.[2] The doors presumably disappeared in the course of the restorations of the eastern parts of the cathedral during the third quarter of the nineteenth century and were replaced by those still now in use.

While it is difficult to visualize the effect of the two lions or to cite any comparable work among medieval doors, it is the long-established idea of lions as portal guardians which underlies the scheme. Two rather battered Romanesque stone lions still flank the doorway of the cathedral baptistery nearby in the conventional fashion. However, the placement of the lions in the upper section of the lost valves follows more closely the disposition, not infrequent in northern Italy, of the animals in the zone of the imposts. Gruamon's portal of S. Giovanni Fuorcivitas in Pistoia and the portal of S. Bartolomeo a Pantano of Master Biduinus in the same city may serve as examples of this *parti.*[3] Although it is not known in Auvergne, the pair of confronted lions on the impost on the right side of the portal at Vissac (Haute-Loire) [4] would seem to represent a special form of the same idea. This church cannot be dated earlier than the second half of the thirteenth century, but its sculpture is of a very archaic type. At Chamalières, the portal on the north side of the church leading to the cloister shows along the outer rim of the arch rampant quadrupeds belaboring human victims.[5] Given the shape of the portal within the *Porche du For,* it is possible that the lost doors were rounded at the top and that the position of the lions, echoing its outline, would have been comparable to the scheme illustrated in the latter church.

NOTES

1. Mallay, *Monographie,* 19: "La première (porte), celle de la branche de croix sud est remarquable par les deux lions en bois sculpté de la partie supérieure, par les marteaux en bronze à tête de tigre, par le guichet à croisillon de fer, par les pentures et la toile qui couvrait le bois." In his *devis* of December 10, 1842, submitted by Mallay (Arch. Dept. 3 V 21), there is a brief description, couched in similar terms: "La porte placée sous ce porche présente de curieux détails de sculpture, les deux lions en bois de la porte supérieure et les têtes de tigre en bronze du panneau inférieur sont remarquables pour l'époque. J'ai vérifié un fait assez bizarre. Cette porte était entièrement couverte de toile collée, on en retrouve encore des fragments."
2. Merimée, *Notes d'un voyage en Auvergne,* Paris, 1858 (ed. 1971, 559): "Les portes orientales des transepts ne sont pas moins curieuses que celles des chapelles de l'escalier, mais leur conservation laisse beaucoup à désirer. Elles ont perdu la plus grande partie de leurs ornement et l'on peut guère juger aujourd'hui que quelques-unes de leurs ferrures. Parmi ces dernières il faut noter des têtes de lion ou de tigre d'un charactère original. . . . Deux lions en bois, sculptés d'un relief assez fort, sont encore conservés dans les panneaux supérieurs de la porte du transept sud."

   The doors are also mentioned in Viollet-le-Duc's report of 1848 (Thiollier, *Architecture religieuse,* Appendix II, 190: "Deux fragments d'une porte du XIIe siècle consistant en deux lions de bois du caractère le plus étrange.") and in the notes of Baron de Guilhermy (Bibl. Nat. fr. 6106, fol. 277: "Dans mes notes de 1836, j'indique, sur les vantaux, dans leur partie supérieure, deux léopards grimaçants, sculptés en bois."). In 1861, when De Guilhermy was in Le Puy for the second time, the work had disappeared.
3. Biehl, *Toskanische Plastik,* 49ff., and pls. 55a and b, 56. Other examples could easily be cited.
4. G. Paul. "Vissac, ses seigneurs, son châteaux, son église," *Almanach de Brioude* 1960, 89-100. A pair of Romanesque lions in relief are embedded on each side of the upper zone of the thirteenth-century portal on the north side of Saint-Martin at Brive.
5. Beigbeder, *Forez-Velay roman,* 128-29.

Index

Illustrations

. A procession to Le Puy Cathedral in the late eighteenth century. Detail of a drawing by Meunier, engraved by Née

3. Le Puy Cathedral, Porche du For

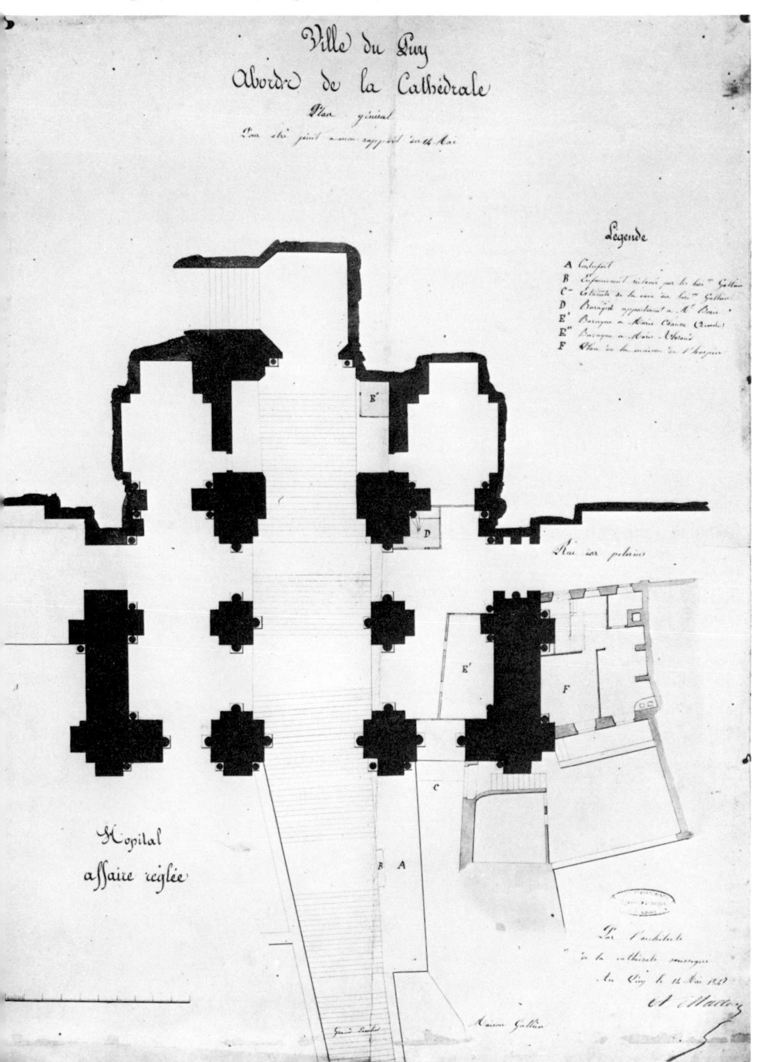

2. Porch and western approach of Le Puy Cathedral. drawing of A. Mallay, 1847

4. Le Puy Cathedral, Chapel of St. Martin

5. Le Puy Cathedral, Chapel of St. Giles, Infancy Doors. Watercolor of M. Petit-grand, 1889

6. Le Puy Cathedral, Chapel of St. Martin, Passion Doors, Watercolor of M. Petitgrand, 1889

7. Infancy Doors, Cast. Paris, Musée des Monuments Français

8. Infancy Doors, state after restoration

9. Passion Doors, state after restoration

10. Paris, Bibl. Nat. lat. 8878 (Apocalypse of Saint-Sever)

11. Ceiling panel from S. Millán, Segovia. After Torres Balbás, *Al-Andalus,* 1935

12. Roof beam from Santa Maria de Tarifa. Cadiz

14. Archangel. Coptic Relief. Brooklyn Museum

13. Interlace fragment from the choir of Le Puy Cathedral

15. Saint-Guilhem-le-Désert, altar

16. Riding Magi, capital from the cloister of Saint-Etienne, Toulouse. Toulouse, Musée des Augustins

17. Le Puy, Infancy Doors, Riding Magi

18. Le Puy, Infancy Doors, Massacre of the Innocents

19. Le Puy, Infancy Doors, Magi before Herod

20. Le Puy, Infancy Doors, Presentation in the Temple

21. Le Puy, Passion Doors, Resurrection of Lazarus

22. Le Puy, Passion Doors, Entry into Jerusalem

23. Le Puy, Passion Doors, Arrest of Christ

24. Le Puy, Passion Doors, Carrying of the Cross, Crucifixion, and Ascension

25. Le Puy, Passion Doors. Three Maries at the Tomb and Descent of the Holy Spirit

26. Le Puy, Passion Doors, Last Supper

27. Le Puy Cathedral, nave interior, bays 4, 5 and 6

28. Le Puy Cathedral, nave interior, bays 1 and 2.

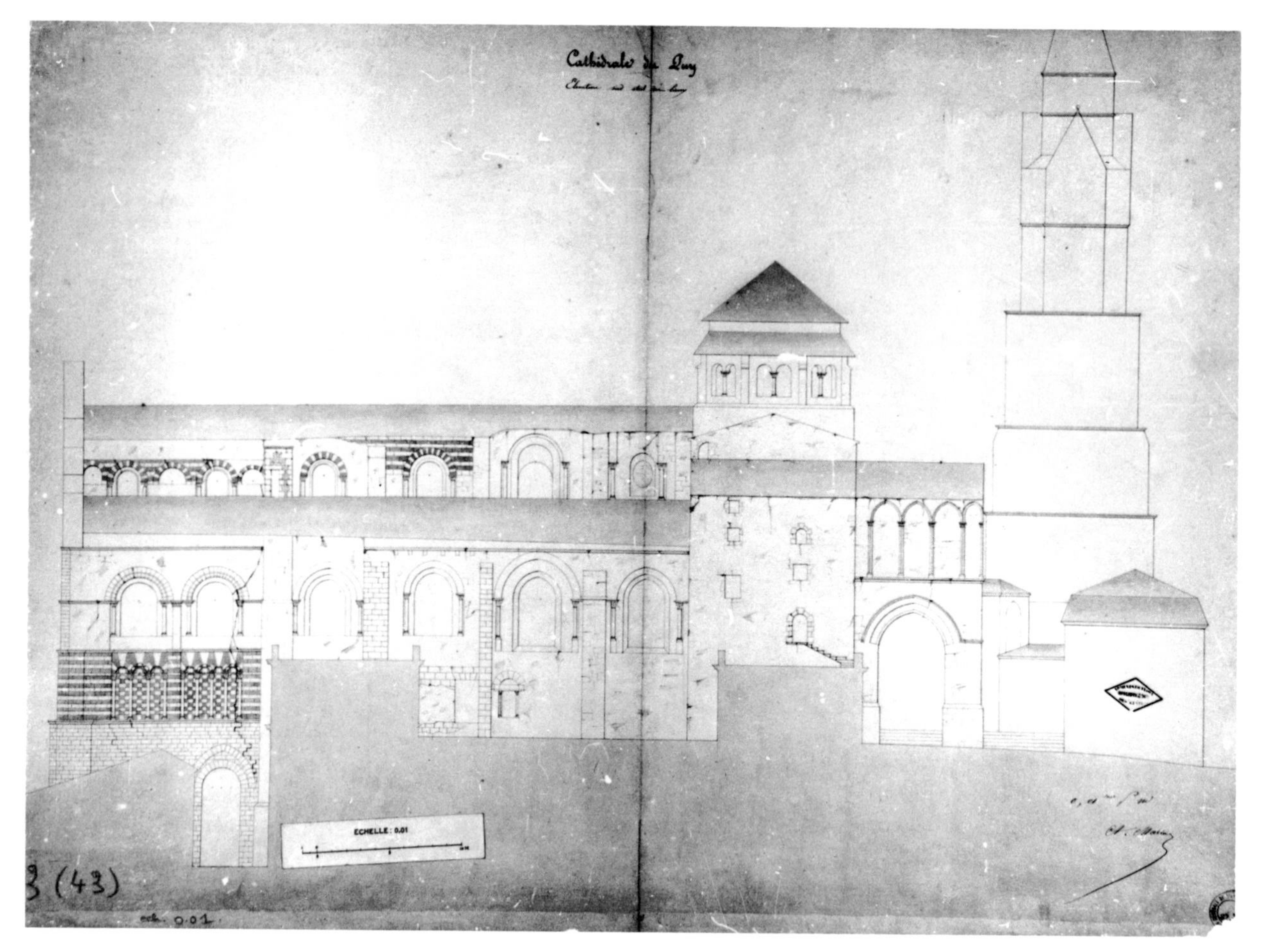

29. Le Puy Cathedral, south lateral elevation. Drawing of A. Mallay

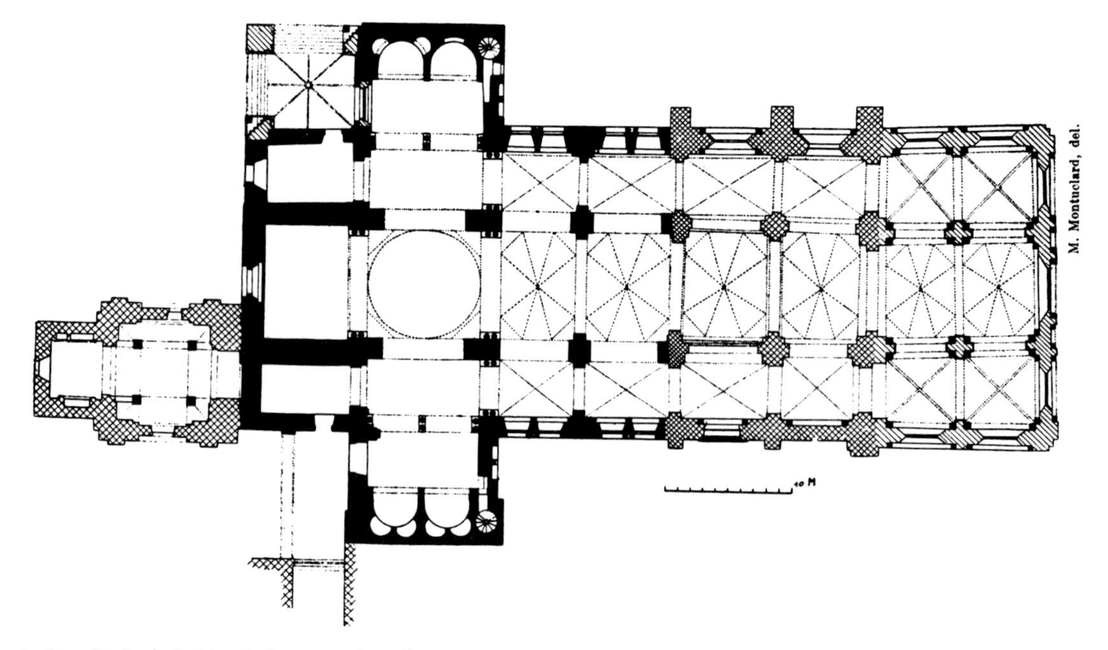

30. Le Puy Cathedral. Plan (after *Congrès arch.*, 1904). Le Puy Cathedral, north lateral elevation. Drawing of A. Mallay

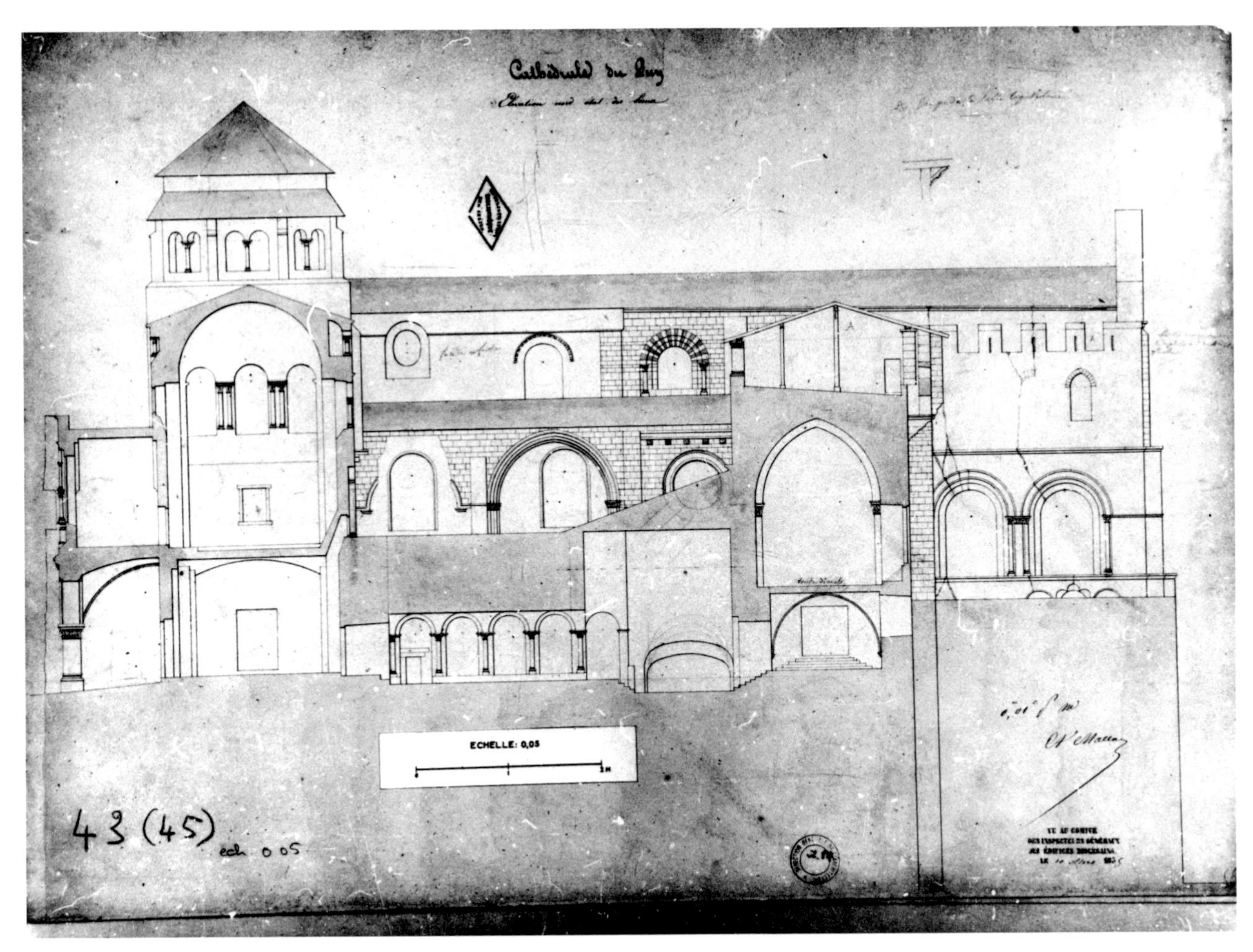

31. Le Puy Cathedral, north lateral elevation. Drawing of A. Mallay

32. Le Puy Cathedral, cloister and north nave wall

33. Le Puy Cathedral, nave capital

34. St. Martin, Polignac, nave capital

35. Chamalières-sur-Loire doors

36. Chamalières-sur-Loire doors, schematic drawing

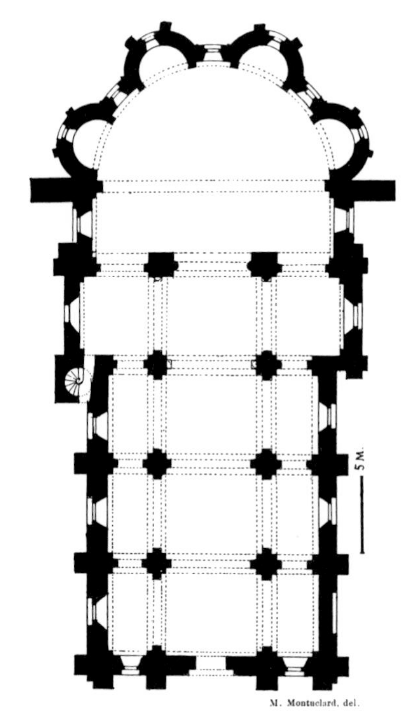

37. Chamalières-sur-Loire. Plan of the church (after *Congrès arch.*, 1904)

38. Chamalières-sur Loire, façade of the church

39. Chamalières-sur-Loire doors, upper part of left valve

40. Chamalières-sur-Loire doors, middle section of left valve

Chamalières-sur-Loire doors, detail of carved and polychromed border, upper left valve

43. S. Clemente in Casauria, bronze doors, detail

42. Chamalières-sur-Loire doors, detail of carved and polychromed border, upper left valve

44. Paris, Bibl. Nat. lat. 3783 (Homiliary), fol. 52

45. Chamalières-sur-Loire doors, detail, lower section of right valve

46. Lead cross with incised circles
Amiens, Musée de Picordic

47. Chamalières-sur-Loire, north lateral portal, jamb capital

48. Cornice section from the cathedral cloister. Le Puy, Musée Crozatier

49. Purse reliquary, Saint-Bonnet-Avalouze

50. Cross, Sens Cathedral Treasury

51. Marignac (Charente-Maritime) apse cornice sculpture.

52. Benet (Vendée), sarcophagus

53. Decorative relief. Le Puy, .

54. Metope frieze, tower, Saint-Germain, A

55. Cornice with metopes, Saint-Hilaire, Poitiers

56. Knights in combat, Brioude, Saint-Julien, nave capital

57. Relief with Leviathan, Saint-Philibert, Tournus (after Vallery-Radot, *Tournus)*

58. Avord (Cher), façade

59. Arles, Les Alyscamps, sarcophagus

60. Tympanum, Cathedral of Jaca

61. Chamalières-sur-Loire, nave capital

62. Monastier Saint-Chaffre, nave capital

63. Chamalières-sur-Loire, nave capital

64. Monastier Saint-Chaffre, nave capital

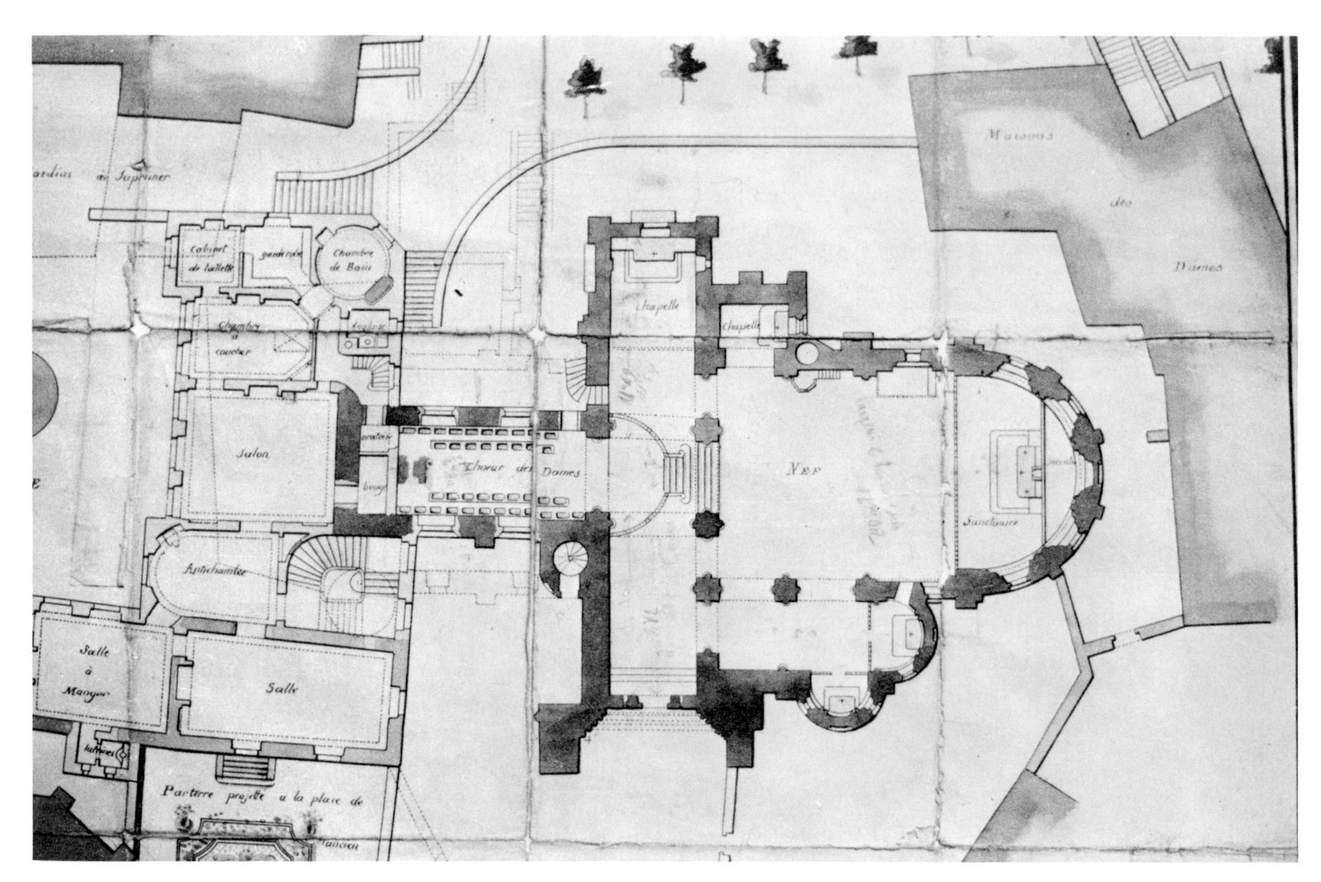

65. Saint-Pierre, Blesle, plan of the church and adjoining structures (1778)

66. Blesle doors, left valve

67. Blesle doors, right valve

68. Blesle, schematic reconstitution of the doors

69. Blesle, choir window

70. Blesle, portal of the church

71. San Fede, Cavagnolo (Piedmont). Portal of the church.

72. Blesle doors, upper right valve, section of batten, border, and panel with Saggitarius

73. Blesle doors, left valve, Capricorn and section of cross

74. Blesle doors, left valve, upper border, hunting scene

75. Blesle doors, left valve, upper border, Good Shepherd and scything figure

76. Blesle doors, right valve, upper border, reaper and nursing woman (?)

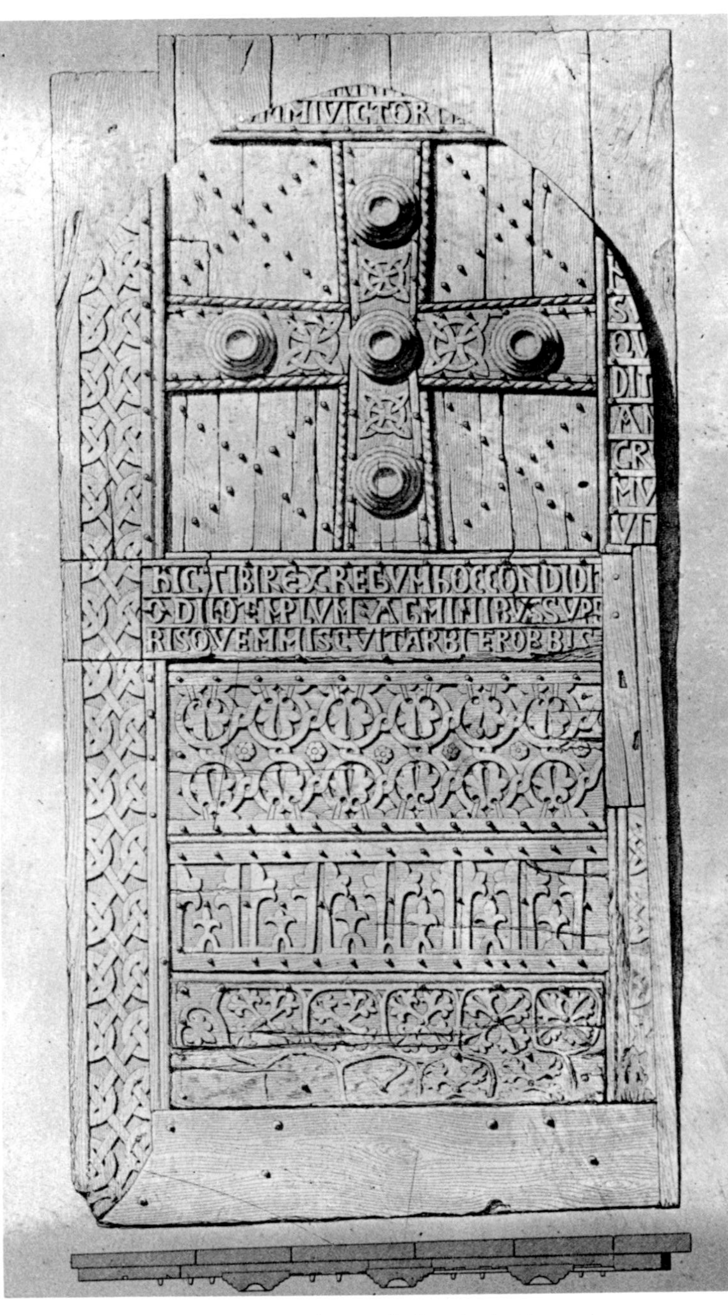

77. Door of Lavoûte-Chilhac (after Gailhabaud, *Architecture*)

78. Lavoûte-Chilhac, former cloister portal

79. Door of Lavoûte-Chilhac

80. Lavoûte-Chilhac, church and monastery, view from the east

81. Crucified Christ. Blesle, Saint-Pierre

82. Madonna of Ayl. Trier, Episcopal Museum

83. Bibl. Nat. lat. 11560 (Bible moralisée), fol. 84 (after Laborde, *Bible Moralisée*).

84. Fragment of a carved window from the *Maison des anglais,* Blesle

85. Shrine of Bishop Ulger. Angers, treasury of the cathedral

86. Section of inscription from the western entrance of Le Puy Cathedral

87. Inscription and animal frieze, choir, Le Puy Cathedral

89. Capital with *Iustitia* from the tower of Le Puy Cathedral

88. Paris, Bibl. Nat. lat. 5296A (Life of Saint-Martial), fol. 1v